JAPANESE LADY IN EUROPE

D0914830

HARUKO ICHIKAWA

JAPANESE
LADY IN EUROPE

by

HARUKO ICHIKAWA

(Mrs. Sanki Ichikawa)

Edited and with an Introduction by

WILLIAM PLOMER

1937

NEW YORK

E. P. DUTTON & COMPANY, INC.

PRINTED IN THE UNITED STATES OF AMERICA, BY THE
NATIONAL PROCESS COMPANY, INC., NEW YORK, N. Y.

CONTENTS

CONTENTS

CONTENTS

TO THE AMERICAN READER

MY grandfather Viscount Shibusawa who devoted the best part of his energies to the furtherance of world peace until he died at the age of ninety-one, was a great friend of the United States. When my grandfather was ninety years old, William H. Taft died. I was at his house on a visit, when a telegram reporting the American statesman's death was delivered to him. Grandpapa grieved for his friend saying, "I first saw him in America when he was the President. And he once came to my house while visiting in Tokyo. When last I met him in 1921, he was the Chief Justice. On my taking leave of him—I was eighty-one years old then—he was kind enough to lead me by the hand down the flight of steps from his front-door and up to my car. He was such a big man that he carried me almost as lightly as a father would carry his boy, and my feet scarcely touched ground. At this sight all burst out into laughter. Even now I can call up his laughing face vividly before my eyes, and that was the last I saw of him. At that time Harding was the President. Harding was also a kind man, and told me that he fully appreciated my trouble and pains in having come a long way from Japan, at an old age, for the solution, among other things, of the anti-Japanese Immigration Law problem.

"Of the Presidents I know Roosevelt was the most talkative, and Wilson was the fewest in words. Vanderlip, Wanamaker, Eliot of Harvard, Jordan the ichthyologist—those good men have all passed away. They were all of them so tall and strong that in shaking hands with them my hand almost seemed to crush in their grasp. Indeed, I hoped they would live to be twice my age and help me to promote the

11

friendship between the two countries . . . " Grandpapa blinked his eyes in his sad recollections.

When I asked him who, of the great men of America, had the finest appearance, he replied, "General Grant." "Dignified, and yet quiet in manners, he was a man of commanding presence," he said. "When he came to Japan in 1879, I invited him to this house. He kept reticent all the time, so that he appeared as if he had come out of his own portrait." "It was a great pity," he would add, "that I could never see Mr. Townsend Harris. So on my first visit to America I at once went and paid a homage to his grave."

To those who only know Viscount Shibusawa's ardent desire for universal peace and his unflagging efforts for its promotion for half-a-century, it might be unbelievable that when he first saw a Westerner in his twentieth year, he composed an ultra-patriotic poem concluding with "The sword at my side is about to unsheathe itself", and even planned the attack and burning of the foreign settlement of Yokohama. This enmity against Westerners was certainly the general trend of the time, but in his case, it was largely due to the fact that born as he was in the year of the Opium War, he read, from his childhood, the records of that event, as written by the Chinese, and from this source alone he derived his knowledge of the Occidentals.

Thus, when he heard of Harris's courage and honesty in his dealings with the Japanese Shogunate, he was much surprised and doubted his ears. But, later, when his Sécretary Heusken was assaulted by *ronins* in Yedo, Harris cared not a bit for his own safety, bearing in mind nothing but the amity between Japan and America, whereas the envoys of other countries thought only of securing themselves from danger. Learning this valour and loftiness of character of the American diplomat, Shibusawa made his great discovery, which first opened his eyes to the broad world, that in countries across the sea as well as in his own, there were people with the real spirit of a *samurai*.

When Grandpapa told us of this story of his youthful days, he used to speak of the American envoy as "Mr. Harris." It sounds to our ears quite as strange as "Mr. Napoleon." But, when Grandpapa said "Mr. Harris," it was proof that the heart of an old man of over ninety was not only full of veneration, but was glowing with a deep sense of gratitude towards the man whose influence greatly served to make his life what it was.

In truth, it is a serious cause of calamity that nations do not understand one another. I, therefore, who told the impressions of my European trip to my countrymen first of all, now turn to tell them to you in the West, hoping to make you realize what sights and scenes of Europe a Japanese woman would admire and what she would knit her brows at. I expect a great deal from you Americans, because I believe that you are the best judge of my frank criticisms of things European, whether they are prejudiced or not. For instance, I said somewhere in my book, that English food is the most insipid in all Europe. Nearly thirty English reviewers quoted this point, with greater or less disapproval. Now, which of us, do you decide, is right—they or myself? There is a saying about travel which I like: "A good traveller treads down the rough earth of the frontiers,"—a saying with which President Wilson once welcomed my grandfather. In my tour of eight months, the heels of my shoes were worn down by the borders of twenty-nine countries.

Treading down the difference in language—a sort of spiritual frontier—I here present to you this travel-diary. I hope that it might contribute a humble share to the dissolution of 'the inscrutability of national character'—a wide gulf between the East and the West, so to speak, which ought to be filled in, bit by bit, from both its shores.

HARUKO ICHIKAWA

Tokyo
May, 1937

JAPANESE LADY IN EUROPE

CHAPTER I

EARLY SPRING IN CHINA

§ 1

In the Yellow Sea

THE *Nanrei Maru*, our cargo boat of 2000 tons, bound for Tientsin, is sailing north skirting the coast of the Korean peninsula. Laden with cotton at Osaka, she has been busy at Moji working with four cranes and has taken her time with packages done up in straw mats, which the cranes took in like so many giraffes seizing gigantic croquettes in their mouths. Above the cargo live 200 rabbits and a number of people. The rabbits are for breeding, fur shawls being now in fashion; I have heard that they will come back to Japan, transformed into fox furs! Won't the people on board also suffer a similar fate, bewitched by Chinese fox-demons? Both are going to be 'fleeced', as it were. The rabbits are indeed poor fellow-passengers with a person who is starting on a foreign tour with a glorious ambition. . . .

Far on the right are bare island mountains of Korea. All the surface of the sea is covered with muddy waves. But there is on the white spumes over the brownish water something which cannot be called simply dirty. The glossy undulations of greyish purple blended with the blue of the sky remind me of Tagore's hair. The grand waves, oh, they are more than curls; they are, so to speak, hairs pointing to heaven in fury. I shall dream to-night of 'a grey Scythian with purple beard and green eyes' dashing on a horse across the desert. As the wind is too strong, I make for our cabin and open the deck-door; an oily smell of warm air from within chokes me, and makes me loath to go in. The chief engineer going up to the bridge says, 'It's a bit stormy. The crazy wind of the blossom season has arrived a little early. But there's no danger at all, because it isn't accompanied by rain. Rest yourself for a while'. On the deck the wind was cracking like a whip. Shall I risk cold staying here, or get seasick below? A cold will continue even after I have landed ... Go and get seasick — mine is not seasickness, for I don't feel sick of the sea, but of the boat. With this strange vanity I go below into the bodily smell of the ship and become seasick, just as I expected. ...

The Chinese mainland has unexpectedly come into view and sprawls all in brown just under my nose. Our boat sails up the serpentine course of the river, which is said to have ninety-nine turns. For some time we see along the river a wide area of salt-fields with here and there windmills used for drawing water from the sea. They are quite peculiar to this locality, the wings being made of canvas and the wheels going round, not lengthwise as in Holland and Japan, but sidewise just like a revolving lantern. From what appears to be a new alluvial formation, with salt-fields and houses where lime is manufactured by burning shells, the scene shifts to a wood of peach trees. When I was a little girl, I was often given a fruit called Tenshin-*momo*, the fruit of a special kind of the peach tree that was cultivated in those days. It had scarlet flesh, and my austere old nurse used to warn me with a shudder not to soil my splash-patterned white summer clothes with its juice. Now that peach plantation makes me feel that Tientsin is close at hand. Soon there come a cluster of houses. Chinamen are standing along the shore with their eyes fixed on our boat, one in every four urinating. And now already we have arrived at Taku, where we were to land.

I was surprised at the customs officers' strict examination on board. They took off the lid of the wash-basin in our cabin. They took out the cardboard cases of books kept in the dining-room, one by one, and examined them carefully to see whether anything besides books might be hidden there. They tapped the walls with wooden mallets to sound the cavities. 'What are they looking for?' I asked the purser. 'Is it opium or morphine?' 'Oh, no, Madam,' replied the purser with a tut. 'It is merely that they have not been oiled sufficiently!'

We took our train for Peiping soon after landing. A waiter fat as Falstaff brought each of us a hot towel and a cup of tea. It was all dark outside, and we found ourselves quite alone in the carriage, but the faint fragrance of the jasmine tea made me sensible of our being in a strange land. That night at eleven-thirty we got to Peiping, where we put up at a Japanese hotel.

§ 2

Three Families

We visited various kinds of families of the upper classes. The first one was living in a large house. It was an Imperial family, and I was told that it was a family of a son of Prince Sh——. The garden was scattered with trees called silver-pines, which have white trunks, with here and there rocks full of holes, characteristic of Chinese gardens. There was

19

also a large stage for plays, which was decaying and accumulating dust. The stage was built separate from the main building of the house, in the style of the dancing-houses of our shrines, and the plank, which was hanging from the ceiling, was now used by pigeons to build their nests on, although it was once used for gods and ghosts in the play coming down from heaven, while the gong music of the gay Chinese play was going on as if to deafen the ears of the audience. Wild morning-glories were entangling everything in the garden — the corridors, whose vermilion varnish was coming off, porous stones, and even the branches of old peony trees. The morning-glories bearing seed on their dead stems seemed as if to remind us of the transition of glory. Among the tiled roofs, nearly falling down, there was one which we could just bear to look at, and a parrot's cage was hanging at the eaves, marking the dwelling-place of the master of the house. The master was still young, with a smooth, round, ivory-coloured face. It was impressed upon me at a glance that he was noble in features, but what he said was nothing but platitudes. Upon his desk he put his brushes and an ink-slab, and as he was a good painter, I was told, he was not living on his art; unfortunately he had to live by his accomplishment. It was rather a painful pleasure to see him blowing off yellow dust almost as thick as half an inch, when he was going to show us an ancient roof tile. Among the rows of paintings and calligraphs, which really showed his good taste, there was placed a cheap organ, about forty-five yen in price, made in Japan. The varnish of the instrument was fresh, and not at all in keeping with its surroundings.

Pointing to the dilapidated tiled roof, he proudly said, 'Those ornamental tiles are not allowed to any people except

Imperial families'. We parted from the master, who was saying this, and going towards the gate across the garden, I saw a pale beauty looking out from a window between shrubs of aronia and lilac. When she tried to hide herself her earrings of jade trembled slightly, and she looked very fragile, like white porcelain, the veins in her forehead also the colour of green jade. She was most probably his concubine.

Next to this we visited a Manchurian nobleman. It was a rather massive house, the keynote of the colours being black and green. The master was a slender, middle-aged gentleman of nearly six feet high and had a long beard. His manners were charming, but he seemed to keep a considerable ambition within himself. The books bound in European style and arranged on the shelves were such sort of books as, for instance, dictionaries and reference books. He had a frame of calligraphy hanging on the wall upon which was written 'Everlasting Bliss', and I was told that it was the writing of the Emperor Hsüan-tung, who gave one copy of this kind of calligraph every year as a New Year's present to each of the Manchurian nobility, and the date, the 13th year of Hsüan-tung, attracted my notice, because this way of naming years according to the name of the Emperor was legally stopped in the first year of the Chinese Republic, i.e. ten years ago.

When we were coming away, he said through our interpreter, 'I am very sorry that we cannot make ourselves understood to each other either in my language or your own, but, even if I knew your language, or you spoke Chinese, a person who gives up his own language is in an unfavourable position, so it would be more convenient if we could both speak Esperanto,' and he burst into laughter, looking much elated.

After this we went to a wealthy family, who came from South China. They were very enlightened and had sent their sons to Japanese universities. The master of the house was an old man of over seventy years with a round, red nose and amorous-looking eyes, and was fat like a prosperous man, while his laugh was light and frank. Looking affable, his inmost feeling was firm, in which he had something in common with the Jews. His wife, who looked a little wizened but clever, came in to welcome us. They showed us all the rooms in their house. Both in the library and their sons' rooms, I could only find books in blue cases. Also in these rooms I found interesting things hanging on the wall. One was a photograph of this old man standing triumphantly upon the famous marble staircase of the Purple Forbidden Castle. Pointing to this picture, I turned to the master with a smile. The master nodded, and said to our interpreter, 'Chow, chow, ching fung . . . that is right, I had that picture taken because I thought that I was fortunate enough to live in very favourable times, able to stand freely in a place where in olden days I could never have even gained access'. I thought he was indeed from the South, and the three families had each its own peculiarity, making a contrast with each other.

§ 3

The Morning Market of Ha-Ta-Men

While I was staying in China, I was greatly fascinated by the people, and, although I was very much fatigued, I was up as early as at half-past five in the morning, eager to go to the market. It was very cold in the streets, and my hands became numbed. The narrow alley in front of our hotel was still very quiet, and such people as rickshawmen stood in the street brushing their teeth. I saw one of them smiling and thought they were very careful about their teeth, in spite of their carelessness about other things, such as lavatories. Then the rickshawman smiled, relaxing his lips full of foam, as he was the one we used to hire from our hotel. The smile was not flattering, but it was a rich smile which, when a man meets a man, comes naturally into the face, caused by the relaxing of the flesh when his mind is entirely satisfied. This young man showed me yesterday one side of the Chinese character. After doing the sights rather thoroughly, when we got out of the rickshaw in front of a temple this rickshawman was going to return without waiting. We called him back, and said, 'We are going to some more places!', but he replied, 'No, I will go back'. I asked, 'Are you tired?', and he replied, 'No'. I said, 'Are you not satisfied with the fare which our hotel fixed?', and he replied, 'Yes'. To the rickshawmen in China, who carry us for twopence an hour, sixpence an hour fixed by the hotel is a very good price. I asked, 'Then why do you want to go back?' He said, 'I have already earned two shillings to-day, which is sufficient for me to spend the rest of the day'. So saying, he took out of his pocket a golden watch as large as a muffin, and looked at it with the satisfaction of displaying it to us, and then went back, walking leisurely. I knew through him, that on one hand they work very hard, bent on profit without sparing any effort, but, on the other hand, they have a way of complacently satisfying themselves with living for the day without thinking of the next, because they have had a miserable experience in the past by being severely taxed on some pretext or another, if they were more or less rich. The same attitude appeared in the Koreans in their inanimateness. But the splendid physique and the smooth flat, care-free faces of the Chinese people, helped by this same stolid and steady attitude, stimulated in my mind an unexpected envious feeling, because they seemed to me like eternal children of the earth. Now, I went out expecting to be steeped in this feeling, but to-day, at the entrance to the alley, I came across the purest kind of eternal children of the earth, who were squatting all round, and made me hesitate. They were a flock of camels, the big, brown, hairy Mongolian camels, who came all the way from the distant mountainous district carrying coal, and now in this place they folded their knees and kept their eyes narrow. Some of them were sitting close to the house so that I could not pass unless I pushed their long faces away, holding them by the nose, under which the protruding lower jaw was slobbering. At first I was not without fear, but I forced through. Even squatting, their faces came near to my face. I thought with a smile that the expression *tête-à-tête* would not do with a camel, and found my face shaking reflected quite small in the brown pupils of its honest eyes. Surprised at this discovery, I peeped into its eyes, but the camel lowered its head, and its soft eyelashes covered its big eyes. Animals seem to hate to be stared at in their eyes, even those continental ones.

The donkeys left behind by the roadside were standing patiently. The morning sunlight was shining on their long ears, making them seem a transparent pink. I set to making a sketch of one with a pink artificial flower on its head, when I had a feeling such as one gets in the summer when a huge cloud spreads and makes the light on the earth fainter, and I looked up and to my surprise saw about a foot above my head the flat, thick faces of coolies surrounding me. Smiling I shook

my head, and they gradually went away, but one among
them slowly pointed to my picture with his long finger, and
then pointed to the donkey, holding up a cage of a bird, as
much as to say, 'Look at this rather than that'. It was a
pleasure to see robust labourers who love little birds. They
do not seem to have homes of their own, without encum-
brance in this world, their bodies being their only fortune —
these coolies hanging their cages, or keeping a bird like a
bullfinch on a T-shaped perch, complacently, not particularly
taking fidgety care of them. I saw such coolies leisurely
standing everywhere in the city, but the stalls which sold
food for them were found in this market, so that I saw them
in abundance especially near here. Most of the cages were of
a round, low shape, and the artistic taste of the little food-pot
was excellent. Such taste seems to be naturally refined
generation after generation. The pot now shown by that
coolie was also lovely, with a design of scattered white plum-
blossoms on a ground of pure blue. 'Hao-hao!' (Very good.)
I knew no other word of praise, but I wrote in a corner of my
sketch-book in Chinese characters, 'pot', 'beautiful', then
the coolie expressed his joy stolidly, at about an inch under
his face-skin, and said something like, 'Chang, Ching, Chong,
Yah', pointing to the north. This was indeed jargon to me,
but I felt a feeling of soothing delight while I was taking the
time of the speed of his fingers slowly stretching out. I
counted one, two, three, four to eight. What a long nail
the little finger had! How dirty it was!

As I was rambling along in such a way, I felt as if the stiffness of my mind was rubbed away, and thought that it was a
good remedy to cure my insular sentiment, which is always
tight and narrow. I did not feel at all uneasy walking among
them, not because I was bold but because the mood of the

people, gentle, and not easily moved, as well as their instinctive cleverness to see through the fact that I was taking a walk without having any money with me, made me feel confident, helped by the good condition of the time in the morning.

Thus mingling among people of great leisure with extremely strong nerves, I thought of various things. If I had been consulted about starting some educational organization in this country to relieve the people from their ignorance, should I have rejoiced with pure delight? This nation who have not yet got their nerves blistered with the stimulating fruit of the tree of knowledge, seem to be likely to inherit the earth and go on for ever, while the Japanese, Italians, and other Latin peoples go neurotic and mad, followed by the English and Danish, who will be a little later in going the same way.

§ 4

A Glance at the Anti-Japanese Movement

The city gates of Peiping were hung with posters with letters each about two feet or three feet square, such as 'Realize the Commonwealth Policy and Crush Japanese Imperialism', 'Boycott Japanese Goods, even if you are killed', 'Drive Away Cunning Merchants and Japanese Goods', 'Abolish Consul Judgment', 'The Equality of Diplomacy', 'Never Forget the Ch—— Disaster', and so forth, and though we arrived at night they at once attracted our notice. If you heard that I rambled about alone under such posters, you might think that I was without nerves, but it was just at the time when the anti-Japanese feeling had abated a little, and there was no danger, when the people were not blindly excited, since the anti-Japanese sentiment was not really deeply rooted in their thought, and the people at large were rather remote from ideas of nationalism. It is obvious that nationally they are faint-coloured, but racially strong and oppressive; therefore, although all Government buildings, including the Military University, have been moved to Nanking from Peiping, and the latter is falling off as a city, and China as a country gives the impression that though it is a vast old country, yet as an old, great nation the people show no sign of decadence. They are permanently young, and show the tenacity and suppleness of a perpetually youthful race.

There is a park called Chung-shan, where in a shrine with an altar exactly in the ancient style, Sun-yat-sen is deified. The altar was used in old days to worship Imperial ancestors, and the inner fences, showing great importance of tradition, have a roof of blue tiles in the east and a roof of white tiles in the west, while the roofs of the south and north fences are tiled in black and white respectively. Between this altar and the sanctuary there was built, with much labour, a thing resembling our *torii* and they hung on it a poster with the words, 'Down with Japan!' I thought this was going too far, as it was a more conspicuous place than in the streets where the people were bent on business. I was confounded for a while, wondering what was the Japanese Embassy doing, but when I saw a family picking herbs under the poster, I was much relieved. The herbs they were gathering were poor dandelions, which they were going to have for supper, and having already plenty of them thrown into their baskets, they were quite indifferent to the altar and Japanese goods. People were unconcerned, whether the word 'Down' having been taken away by somebody during the night, the word 'Japan' was left alone on a gate of the wall like a signboard, and the gate seemed as if to welcome Japan. At the entrance to this park there was quite a new white gate on which a frame with the word 'Victory' was hung. I wondered whether China had recently anywhere gained a victory, but I was told that this was a gate which they were forced by way of apology to the Germans to build at a point where the German Minister had been killed at the time of the Boxer trouble. They took advantage of the confusion at the time of the Great War, and carried the gate off to the present place, so that I could not understand what was meant by the victory, but quite indifferent to such a thing, they hung the frame on the gate. It was rather delightful to see them so thoroughly audacious, but I felt at the same time that since they behaved in this way there would be no end of trouble if one showed too much lenience towards them. Just as Chinese are so thoroughgoing in audacity, so are Japanese in imitating others without scruples. When I came back I saw to my utter surprise an advertisement upon which was written, 'Down with Threadworms!'

We also went up an ancient watch-tower, and on the turret there was a memorial room for national disgraces. They exhibited a panorama of the North China Affair, with small dolls, and a calendar of national-disgrace days was hung. Everything was aimed at Japan, and they hung small posters about, on which were written inscriptions with adjectives of the superlative degree in the Chinese style, but they did not appeal to us at all. Standing on a high tower with the natives who came to visit this place, we ought to have felt uneasy, but actually we did not feel any such thing. On no occasion were we shown any feeling of hatred because we were Japanese.

§ 5

Chinese Plays

In a classical theatre of Peiping, Mei Lan-fang was acting the part of Lady Yang-kuei. As he was a famous actor the theatre was packed to overflowing. At first, a general who looked like a northern barbarian, with his face made up with shading to appear like a villain, snatched away a beautiful girl, pushing off an old woman, and mimicked jumping on a horse with a whip in his hand. The instant he posed himself with the reins as if for driving, the gong that had been going wildly as if to break up the whole theatre, was suddenly held up. The one moment of stillness amid the general noise was very effective. It seemed now that rebels were rising on the border. From the capital three generals drove on, and they went all the way to the border to meet the insurgents. Thus, as several actors mimicked the riding of horses, each using a single whip in his hand, it was quite easy to see which actor was outstanding. During the play there was a scene in which a messenger made a fuss by saying, 'Important news!', which was very much like our comic interludes. Several times actors entered by one end and went out at the other to the sound of noisy cymbals, and they all came to the border where a terrible fight was begun. It was indeed wild and violent. They fought, some with swords, and some with halberds. They brandished the swords round and round above their heads, and when the hilts of the swords came in front, they dexterously caught them and cut at their opponents. Everything was really chaotic. At last, they threw down their weapons to save trouble and grappled with each other, and at the moment they posed the curtain dropped down. Up to this point everything was classical, and it had elements nearer to *no*-plays than to *kabuki*-plays. If you see this superficially you will think that it is quite different from a *no*-play, because it is deafeningly noisy, but in that it has no background or curtain and the figure of an actor entering a house is represented by his mimicry of stepping over the doorstep, while horses and carts are all represented in a similar way, there are many points which can only be understood by those who appreciate the *no*-play, which chiefly depends upon suggestion.

Mei appeared in the next scene, which was lighted and had stage settings and properties, as in an opera, in the European fashion. As in the other scene, property-carriers never walked about on the stage in bulky, padded clothes. It was the Milky Way Festival in the Palace of Long Life. The background consisted of a corridor and perspective lighted scenery. At one end of the stage, a little forward, an incense-burner was placed on a marble table and the orchestra composed of flutes and fiddles was playing quietly and softly. Four court-ladies with lanterns in their hands and four holding offerings appeared, and then Lady Yang appeared. She wore a smart dress of yellow, and a jewelled crown in the shape of a phoenix, which 'quivered as she walked with hair like a cloud, face like a flower', as in a Chinese poem. Mei was indeed a fit person for that role, with his good looks and graceful carriage. The speech which 'she' gave in the scene began like a cat's mewing, 'Miaou, miaou', and ended with a prolonged noise like the siren of a fire-engine. Yet, what was interesting in such a speech was that she always kept her charm and dignity. She had a gold basin brought in, and saw a reflection of stars in it, and looking at herself, she sang. 'Her sparkling eye and merry laughter fascinated every beholder, and among the powder and paint of harem her loveliness reigned supreme', and her actions were indeed graceful. Now the Emperor, with a long beard, appeared in a white robe and a golden crown and the courtiers were all sent away leaving them alone. It was a scene, 'On the Seventh of the Seventh Month in the Palace of Long Life; the night hours have advanced and no human whispering was heard', as a Chinese poem describes it. The Emperor went forward and burned incense, and sang, 'In heaven I wish we become a pair of birds with a single wing', and Yang joined in his song, 'On earth I wish we become a tree with intertwining branches'. It was indeed a splendid love-scene, at which in Japan the gallery might have shouted, 'Bravo!' or 'We've been waiting for this!'

The next scene was in pure Chinese style. An-Lu-shan goes out on an expedition against the enemy in a rebellious frame of mind, and Lady Yang, guessing his intention, sends Kao-Li-shih to him, that in the course of conversation she may give him to understand that she is aware of his rebellious intention. This An had a deep bass voice, and all the generals' faces were made up with shading, so that it was difficult to distinguish their faces from masks, looking rather like Easter-eggs painted in white, red and blue colours, and they so dressed themselves that they looked square and bulky, wearing proudly at the back of their heads, five-colour ornaments, rising like a load of toy paper-windmills on the back of the vendor. The messenger Kao wore a soft green robe with long sleeves, and his face being long and white, he looked weird like a ghost of peppermint jelly. I wondered if all eunuchs used to look like that. The conversation between him and An was amusing, and when Kao guessed the drift of his motive he opened his eyes, mouth and hands all at the same time and shouted 'Hang it!', while Kao laughed helplessly, his body shaking all over — an abominable fellow. The next scene had a beautifully decorated palace placed aslant towards the back, and the Emperor was inside it. In the garden there was a large, raised revolving stage, and Yang danced and danced upon it with many other dancers, among whom some turned somersaults acrobatically. Everything was very gay like a revue, and the music sounded and sounded, almost breaking up the theatre with its shrilling and jangling. The Emperor himself played a hand-drum, in great delight, and drank with the Queen, showing the bottom of the wine-cup to each other. The Queen was beautiful and charming.

Mei Lan-fang is now trying to bring about a great change in Chinese drama, and he seems to be very clever, for he greatly pleased the intelligent audience, who appreciated the scene of the Milky Way Festival, and in the last scene he gave delight to the common audience, who might not have relished such a quiet scene as that of the Milky Way Festival. He seems to be shrewd in every way.

§ 6

Food

There is nothing so cheap, so delicious and so good for the stomach as Chinese food. Chinese cooking is the best in the world, but I was surprised to find in the same restaurant that the same food was entirely different in taste, when we went there by ourselves without giving any notice and ordered from a menu, and when we were accompanied by our Chinese friends. The Chinese are simple in the matter of dress, but very particular about food. We were once invited to dinner by Mr. Fu-Liu, the principal of the Girls' Normal School. We met some professors of Peiping University, among whom were advocates for Romanizing Chinese letters, who asked my husband his opinion of the movement, and also they inquired how many hours we taught in a week at our Imperial University, and so forth. They showed great eagerness in their questions, and I felt from the tone of their inquisitiveness a pleasure as well as a lack of reserve, which is quite common among the Chinese intelligentsia and is often found in Japanese students who are keen to get whatever knowledge they can from other people, so I sympathized with them, because they, as well as we, could not help being in a hurry to learn. In that way, when topics were too much on the side of reasoning and became prosaic, Mr. Hsü, who was a poet and a lover of Shelley, began to talk of drama or other things, and softened the tone of the general talk. He was the type of person who becomes pale when drunk, and after toasting in the Chinese style, he drank one cup after another, showing the bottom of his empty cup. Every dish was delicious. Sheep's stomach was nice, tasting like the skin of a chicken boiled in soup. The cuttle-fish spawn was something like the shape of a cherry-blossom petal, and both in taste and colour it was very much like abalone. For the last course we had porridge of millet sprinkled with red beans and sugar, and for dessert we chewed nutmeg in order to refresh our greasy mouths.

I was very eager to try the things sold on the open-air stalls, and I was told that there was a teashop near the T'ai-i lake where the emperors of old, who had the same mind as myself, went to have some maize dumplings, eaten by the lower classes, so I went there to try them, but I was disappointed to find that everything was in a too much refined taste.

What most charmed me was the Genghis-Khan Pot which I tasted in a restaurant where Mr. S. took us. In the courtyard of the restaurant a coal-fire was burning brightly and an iron grill was fixed over it. We stand around the fire, and put one of our legs high up on the fender, and with long chopsticks we put raw mutton dipped into sauce on to the hot iron grill. With a tempting smell of grilling meat, purple smoke rises. After doing one side we pluck it off from the iron to grill the other side, and we carry it into our mouths. This is the procedure, but the strong-smelling mutton becomes strangely delicious, and one could eat any quantity. Even meat overdone and burnt had its own special flavour. It is the healthy and simple taste of the nomads, although one might not be able to taste the real flavour unless one could drink the strong spirits like fire at the same time.

It had a taste somewhat in common with the boldness of Timour who raged over Europe and Asia like a whirlwind, crossing the deserts and steppes in order to build his great empire. In the evening, after driving a hundred miles and leaving the horses, Genghis-Khan and his staff must have made a camp-fire. The blazing fire of dung-fuel probably made their brown faces still more brightly red, and the scars on the brows of the young men become more conspicuous because of the effect of the wine, while the old

Generals carelessly wipe away the sauce dripping from their silvery beards, and eagerly eat the roast mutton. Then the slices of meat, which were prepared skilfully by old soldiers, who handling lances would easily pierce three or four of the enemy one after the other, are carried on dish after dish, while the fire still burns vigorously. General Mukari's innocent volcanic laughter bursts out into the cold night air. Men full of high spirits never feel cold, but in the Asiatic continent at night the temperature suddenly falls down, and the stars shine like rain. These men, having no such gloomy troublesome things as houses, never feel lonely even in the middle of the desert of a million miles square. Only the sentinels are gazing at the western horizon, towards the country of Horazum their enemy; guide-bonfires are dotted in a row made of piled-up hay of the steppes and burnt by the vanguard troops of General Tubé. The black shadow that approaches like a cannon-ball in the light and shade of the fires may have been a mounted orderly. The range of the bonfires runs towards the east through the burning camp-fire at the headquarters of Timour, and meets the horizon in that direction. The main troops immediately following them march on, and the sign is seen on the sky above them as when a tidal wave is pressing forward in fierce rage.

Just imagining such a scene, as in a cinema-picture, I moved my chop-sticks earnestly. I wished I could have taken all our pale, neurotic young men at home. In the evening, when the cold winter moon is shining bright and clear, and powdered snow is falling ceaselessly, a stand-up dinner of mutton in the open air surrounding the blazing fire would make the roots of our life bigger and stronger.

§ 7

Sightseeing

Every day we did sightseeing, mostly by rickshaw. Even to see signs and notices was a source of great joy to me. 'Steam-car-round-wheel' is 'tyre of a motor-car', 'fire-car' is 'railway-train', and 'turn car' is to 'change train', not to upset it. Chinese, like Finnish and Hungarian, tries to turn every foreign word into native speech-material. Thus a gramophone record is 'sound-register-machine-piece', etc. It is rather amusing to use Chinese words quite at random referring to a dictionary, even without regard to misprints that may be found therein. These words are enough to set a rickshawman moving. On such occasions my joy did not come so much from the thought that I made myself understood in their language, as from the feeling that I moved a big man by a sort of incantation. I felt the same when I gave an order to a conductor in the train in Russian. Young women riding in rickshaws attracted me, women of the intelligentsia, wearing horn-rimmed glasses and reading books. Their faces were dried up by the irritation experienced by persons of poor physique but eager minds, the irritation of those who, at the moment that bandages are suddenly taken off their eyes, feel dazzled with the knowledge which they want to absorb and put into practice. I am the sort of person who can best sympathize with such a state of mind, but even I felt an antipathy to their superior attitude, looking down on the common people. Bobbed hair was not a characteristic of these people, so common was it among the girls of Peiping, and even maidservants, whose ambition in life it is to save money to buy beautiful coffins for themselves, had their heads bobbed around their skulls, which were crammed full of old conventions and super-stitions. Is it also a manifestation of the Chinese character of following others blindly? I wondered what Chinese old women were saying about this custom. Although I saw very little of woman's life in China, what I observed made me think that only a small number of the intelligentsia were what is called advanced, and the level of culture in general was not by any means of a high standard. I did not find in Peiping any strong-looking women of the lower classes engaged in physical labour, as in Hong-Kong. The women whom we saw all looked pale, as if living in the shade, and as if they needed applying court-plaster to their temples, and they appeared not to have the big, strong nerves and health of the common Chinese, which I liked. That the Chinese man's liking for woman is towards the slender waist is known from the lean physique of the girls in the licensed quarters. On the one hand, I was surprised at the strength of Chinese men, considering that these pale, withered women had given birth to those big sedate men, and, on the other hand, I felt dreadful, considering how man was changed by acquired habits of life and that those tottering figures had each a strong father. Especially disgusting was their foot-binding; every time I saw it, I felt anger flaming up in my mind, and I wanted to find some object upon which I could give vent to my feelings. I found in a teacher of the Yenching University the only ideal intellectual beauty who kept the Chinese serene poise. I had been thinking that I would ask this and that when I came in contact with a lady with whom I could make myself understood in a language which I knew, but it was my fault that when I heard this beautiful lady speaking beautiful English, I could not somehow speak as I had wished, because I was ashamed of my broken English before her which I might not have felt if she were an English lady. But we were both speaking a foreign language! Otherwise I thoroughly enjoyed my ten days' sojourn in Peiping. Such strenuous sightseeing as, for instance, coming back at 12.30 at night from the theatre, and starting at five o'clock in the morning for the Great Wall, and arriving back at the station, soon going out for sightseeing again in the city, became a perfectly familiar habit to me. I never felt inconvenienced about the lavatory (anybody who has the experience of travelling in China will admire me when I say that I went out at eight o'clock in the morning and came back at five or six in the evening every day) and without ever being troubled by bugs (in the hotel I had discovered a thing which was just like a buckwheat husk and crushing it it emitted a nasty smell) I left Peiping without mishap.

CHAPTER II

CROSSING RUSSIA

§ I

Into Siberia

THE carriage was quite roomy and comfortable for the week
we were using it, but the hat-rack was about eight feet high
and seemed to say, 'This is no longer a place where a tiny
chit like you can live!' In the meantime, our train started.
In Siberia, writing and sketching are strictly prohibited, but
by locking the door from within, I often wrote my notes.
At stations I saw quite a number of people in Mongolian
style. Let me describe them as closely as I can: they reminded me of pictures of the Mongolian attack upon Japan
in the thirteenth century. They were standing with their
cheek-bones sticking out, in dress like mail, showing much
fancy-stitching around the collar, and on their heads they
had caps with red wool trimmings flying about. The women
have round, prominent foreheads. Outside the windows
there were sand dunes gently undulating and among them
camels were playing under the spring clouds floating quietly
in the sky. With the moving away of the clouds — the dunes
partly shining brightly in the sun and partly shadowed by
the clouds — I could not help looking into the distance and
saying, 'Over there lie the deserts of Gobi!' We crossed the
river Onon. The view of the mountain on the opposite side
with its skirt drooping down in a strong, but long smooth
curve into the meandering river looked foreign.

39

We found ourselves in a forest area, with pines and white birches. Our train ran along the river Hilok, which was still covered with thick ice, marks of sleighs still being visible. While I was taking a stroll on the platform at Hilok station, a freight-train came in, carrying portable houses, tractors, and about twenty tractor locomotives. 'Well! So this is Soviet Russia!' I was saying to myself, as this was the first glimpse I had of it, and I looked, I think, as sober as any adult woman could be, when an old English gentleman came up to me with a handful of tinsel-wrapped chocolates, as if coaxing me to be a good girl.

At each station, crowds stand and stare at our train. A German with whom we have become acquainted in the train told me that the Soviets abolished the Sabbath and substituted a plan whereby each class of workers is allowed one day in five as a holiday. Therefore each day one-fifth of the townspeople have a holiday. In this way, the factories are saved from the loss due to the cooling down of their boilers, but the drawback is that the family do not have a day for social recreation, and, accordingly, the number of idle people who stand and stare at passing trains has increased. They look very puffed up, yet very gloomy, in leather wraps which have become stiff with perspiration and body fat. They impressed me as being useful men and women, showing their bulkiness, necessary for the founding of a new world order with their strong, big marrow of life. They do not give me the same feeling that the lower classes in China give us, whom we would like to leave as they are without changing them. When we see Russians, we hope that education will spread among them as quickly as possible.

At three in the afternoon we go to the dining-car. It is

the time for *abyede*. As this word is translated dinner,
some people were afraid that it would be expensive and went
to the dining-car in the morning, when they were surprised
to find that one egg cost a shilling. The bread was black
rye-bread and rather sour. Butter was not available, yet
the dinner cost two and a half roubles. The taste was not
so bad as to make us frown, but the smell peculiar to all
things Russian — the smell of rotten leather, or duck — was
very strong, and made us hesitate to enter. About four
o'clock we came to the beach of Lake Baikal and the train
ran along the shore. From the right-hand window a lake
covered with snow could be seen, and an enormous silver
disk seemed to be turning from left to right as the train
went past. It shone brightly like the face of a moon that
had come into the innocent imagination of ancient people,
who had never been disturbed by such an instrument as a
telescope. As the day advanced towards evening, the faint
purple became gradually darker, and then the lurid day
turned into night. The subtle, sublime beauty allured one's
mind into exquisite rapture, such as comes from superb
music. On the lake-shore under my eyes, the crests of ice,
pushed forth and broken up by the swelling power of the
ice, were standing in disorder, and between them the traces
of sledges were seen on the face of the lake like so many
traces of slugs, and following them we could see here and
there a small shed, like a black dot, for fishing through the
ice, but most of the traces faded out in the gathering darkness. All the scene is evanescent. Only now and then horse-
drawn sledges cross the ice. A man, heavily-bearded and
swollen in furs, is driving a sledge standing up. He waves
his whole arm and calls to us. We lean out of the window
and wave our handkerchiefs in response. Until half-past

eight it is not considered night, and so the glimmering light of the snow is our only light. It is one of those evenings when one feels at peace with all men.

§ 2

Across the Wilderness of Snow

The snow has been falling incessantly since morning, and the wide desert and wood continue endlessly. Directly our train enters a station, we run down from the car without losing a minute. When it is a small station without any platform, the train stops only seven or eight minutes for watering, so we take exercise by walking on the rails, but when it is a large station, we look for things to buy. Every station has a row of stands which indicate the prosperity of former days, but which are now nearly all shut up. At one station an old woman sells four complete pieces of tough fowl and very primitive sausages. At another, a small boy with a very dismal face sells iced cranberries. We buy twenty-five copecks' worth of them, but before we get in the train, the iced fruit makes me feel as if a knife were cutting my fingers through the newspaper wrapping. I also bought fifty kopeks' worth of cream cheese, pickled cucumber, etc. All these things are sold by peasants; taken from their own scanty provisions, so that unless we go flying up to them to buy almost before the train stops, they will go away. After shopping we take exercise. To our German friend's call of 'left, right, left, right', we walk with long strides on the frozen platform, exhaling and leaving our white breath behind us. Passing before a picture of Lenin at the platform entrance, we walk towards the engine of the train. The engine carries a big pile of white-birch logs in preparation for the crossing of the desert. As I feel unsafe in getting too far away from the train, I turn on my heels and go to the freight-carriages in the rear part of the train, but there are rows of butter vats destined for export, and they prove obstacles in my path. I was told before that every product is being sold by Russia to other countries to make possible the purchase of more machinery to carry out the Five-Year Plan, and we are actually brought face to face with the real situation when we don't eat butter for a whole week, tasting only sour brown bread. Every night I make it a rule to count the number of tractors we have encountered during the day — often as many as thirty in the morning, forty in the afternoon; thus we are made conscious of the dead earnestness of the Soviet Government **and** of the strong endurance of the Russian peasants, whose intense vitality enables them to bear the unwonted strain very well indeed.

The first waiting-room I looked into — it was the one at Tulun — was indeed sickening. There were big men in ragged leathern clothes and tattered wool caps lying on the paved floor, wearing muddy boots. Suffocating smells! All was grey and dilapidated, but not to be dismissed as merely jejune. At the jingling of the bell to start, we flew into the train and saw again snow and only snow; we were rushing into a chaotic world of greyish-white. I set to work making a meal. We had with us a kettle of the hot water provided at Kansk station. With a pan and solid alcohol I boiled four eggs which had cost me one rouble and twenty copecks. I was putting my hand on the kettle to keep it from shaking too much, when my husband looked over to me and said, 'Ten more tractors have just passed'. We used to have our breakfast like this, but after we came into Siberia, where the hours were named according to Moscow time, there arose a difference of seven or eight hours, and we could not determine when we should have our lunch. It is indeed a good preliminary training for one who goes to Europe, where punctuality reigns supreme, to become aware of the fundamental truth that time is, after all, only made by man. Only my husband, our German friend, and myself, attended dinner from to-day on. All the other first-class passengers now shrank from it, behaving as if they had finished, by dining only once, their work as reporters, who merely want materials enough to give Siberian meals a bad reputation. They never appeared again. If you read Japanese accounts of travelling through Europe, you will often find complaints about the food in Siberia. I can understand the writer very well, if he says that the food does not suit him, but what often irritates me is a tone that suggests that it is a personal affront to offer such a grand person as he is such wretched food. He ought to think it worth his travelling to taste in the coarse flavour of the fish the boundless flow of the Amur river, which he might never have seen in his life. At about the time when the saloon is nearly filled with passengers, the waiter sits down at his own table and begins leisurely to eat his own dinner, which from soup to nuts is the same as that served to passengers. After he has finished, he waits on the passengers. At table I usually argue with Mr. P., our German friend. He is so well versed in Japanese as to be able to kill time on the train by reading Doppo's *Fatalism*, a philosophical work in Japanese, yet he is from top to toe instinct with the German spirit, and he thoroughly hates the Soviets. He says, pressing his thumb downward, 'This is the best way to treat students'. After speaking ill of *All Quiet on the Western Front,* saying that the author is a d——d Jew, he asks me whether I found the book interesting. 'Oh, yes,' I replied. 'All the students I taught thought it "boring".' he declared. 'Oh, well, if a stern pedagogue asks them questions with a mark-book in his hand, nobody will tell him honestly what he really thinks,' I answered. He complained of the slipperiness of the frozen platforms, and boasted of his country, saying, 'In Germany every shopkeeper has to sprinkle sawdust in front of his shop to make the walks safe, and if anyone slips and injures himself, he has a right to ask compensation of the shop-owner.' 'How uncomfortable! When I get a stiff shoulder thanks to all these cramping rules,' I retorted to banter him, 'I should want the right to ask a fee for massage from the State, or else I shouldn't like to live in such a country!' 'You are a very naughty person,' he said, simulating anger, but he is very fond of talking, so that I have profited much by my talks and discussions with him. After dinner, he carried coffee for us to our carriage and told us an anecdote of a Zeppelin and a fallen English airship, saying, 'It served the English apes right for trying to imitate men, the poor fools!' He spoke like a first-rate actor, waving his nutcracker in the air. But some of my more serious questions, such as 'Why is White Russia so called?' he would be very careful about answering. Sometimes he would answer me two or three days later, saying, 'I looked into the matter, but I couldn't find out the explanation'. And for such accuracy, I always esteemed him highly. He was indeed, even though a stiff-necked man, good as a companion. We have spent our third day out in nothing but idle talks.

To-day also, we had snow all day long, and the scenery made us as restless as if we had been on an ocean of snow. The first half of the day our train ran through a forest of evergreens and white-birches. The marks on the snow may be either those of foxes or of wolves, but what depresses one with a feeling of intolerable loneliness is not solitude relieved by such 'properties' (to borrow a theatrical term), but rather the wilderness of snow which we traversed during the latter half of the day. We sighted humble villages only at long intervals. The sturdy but dismal huts in the style of our own ancient Japanese 'log-piled' buildings, set in the snow and scattered in small groups, were suggestive of the figures of people living within patiently enduring the long winter. From the low eaves, three poles protrude, indicating that half-buried houses are lying there. Two of the poles are wireless antennae, and on the third is hung a nest-box. I saw in those poles a mind trying to catch the bird of passage, the herald of spring, and to become aware of the resurrection of the earth which has lain stiff and cold for six weary months, and also a desire to believe in the advent of an age of great significance, by catching at the messages of the radio dispelling the mist of ignorance in the dawn of civilization. I saw with a compassionate heart those poles which were lifted like feelers as high as possible in the effort to tug at the sleeves of things going through the air, tangible and intangible, and I imagined that they were the expression of forward-looking minds that expected the world soon to be full of light. The sight of the antennae gives great comfort to travellers. But even such forlorn villages are not easily seen for another hour or two. Even while I gaze at the low grey clouds and falling snow, the earth seems to be swelling up. The air between sky and earth seems to be compressed both from above and from below, and even in such depressing moments the thought makes me feel somewhat at ease, the thought that I am surrounded by waves of music, although intangible, and that the train rushing westward is encountering a rapid succession of electric waves flying eastward, desolate as is the Siberian wilderness of snow.

After a long five hours, we come to a station. The bells have been taken away from the church steeple and have left a cold gap against the grey sky. They were, as it were, the receivers of comforts and teachings from on high. Now instead of the chimes of the bells the voices of enlightenment and the sounds of comfort fly over the earth. I see how cleverly the Soviets have utilized the radio for purposes of propaganda.

On my strolls at the stations, I have passed to and fro before the windows of a third-class carriage, and thus have become acquainted, little by little, with two small girls who are always looking out with their noses flattened against the double panes. I gave them candies and paper storks, and have got into the habit of going to their carriage to play with them. The girls are called Rima and Toma, six and two years old respectively. I once showed them some folding-paper, and made incense-boxes and yeomen for them. Toma was delighted with a helmet made of newspaper. Her elder sister was a very lively girl. I patted her on the head, saying, 'Good girl', and her mother pinched her snub-nose and, laughing, said something like 'Kurunosk'. Rima looked at me with a gesture, as if to say 'That's not true!' and slapped her mother on the hand again and again. I thought the mother's word must have meant 'Snub-nose', so I shook my head and said 'Nyet'. Just about this time, we threw away

our reserve, and became so bold as to tell each other all sorts
of things. 'Did you knit this sweater?' 'Yes, with two
knitting-needles'. At last we spoke even of 'children who
tear stockings soon after they are mended, and are a
nuisance'. Such intimate chats were made entirely by
gestures, in such a way that she had to put down the stocking
which she was mending at the time, and I answered her
likewise, with the paper dropped on my lap. When we
were rather lively, chatting or gesticulating in this manner,
I was suddenly shaken from behind by the shoulders. I
turned round, not a little frightened. A very stout, big
woman, her head covered in wrapping cloth, spoke in
Russian with a very natural attitude, 'Zdravstvooite!
Kakaya...' (Hello, where are you from?...) When she
saw I was making gestures of not understanding, she
stopped for a while, but soon began again in a very loud
voice. I shook my head, and she began to speak slowly.
She didn't seem to realize that there were people other than
deaf-mutes who didn't understand her. I was quite at a loss
and poked Rima's mother, who was laughing with her head
thrown back. She burst out laughing anew, and explained
to the intruder, 'Yaponski...' (She's Japanese...).
The newcomer stared at me with eyes wide open, as Brob-
dingnagians must have gazed at Gulliver, and then suddenly
left. After she went, we all laughed, and a soldier who was
lolling in the upper berth was drawn into our conversation
at this point. He took his hand away from his chin and
gesticulated. He told me that the large woman had entered
the train at Krassnoyarsk and was from the district along
the lower course of the Yenissei River. 'I am going to
Berlin from Tokyo,' I explained. 'I am for Ekaterinburg.'
'Ekaterinburg? Isn't that Sverdlovsk?' This is a name given

to Ekaterinburg in honour of the man who had assassinated the Czar. I should like very much to have seen the expression on my companions' faces, by making a gesture of decapitation and saying 'Czar', but as there were G.P.U.s everywhere in the train, I restrained myself. When I noticed Toma was unusually quiet, I turned round, and found her singing a lullaby and lying beside the paper yeomen over which she had spread her handkerchief. Her mother and I looked at each other and nodded without knowing it, and exchanged a smile which only mothers can appreciate, for it transcends all barriers of country and race. Rima can't stand being neglected. Soon she spoke to me and began to teach me Russian. She told me the name of everything about us, and I put them down in Japanese characters. After that I drew a picture of a dog and the girls said 'Sabaka'. I drew a fish and they said 'Ruiba'. I became charmed by the two sisters, with their curly heads, earnestly trying to tell me in Russian the names of the things I drew. When I drew a pair of long ears, they shouted 'Zayats' (rabbit). While I was drawing a hen, they made a figure of a hen with their fingers and ran about, saying, 'Koko'. When I drew an elephant, they watched silently, with their eyes wide open. I was very happy, playing with those children, but when, after a while, I wanted to say 'Dasvidahnya' (good-bye), they wouldn't let me go. Consulting a dictionary I said 'Zaftra' (to-morrow). They said, 'Uhtro, uhtro' (morning), earnestly begging me to return soon. They were indeed sweet little angels.

Four days have passed, and we are half-way to Moscow.

§ 3

People

The Russian who boarded the train at Irkutsk and whose face is a cross between Beethoven's and Mussolini's, walked along the corridor, and looked like a G.P.U. officer, which made me very uneasy, even though I have my door shut when I am writing. He is the only Russian aboard who speaks German and French, and he promised to send a wire to Mr. K. in Vienna, but got off the train without receiving the telegram fee, so that I feared he would not keep his word. When, however, I saw Mr. K. in Vienna, I was surprised to find that the telegram had actually been delivered to him. I do not know whether the Russian defrayed the cost of the message himself, or how otherwise he managed it, but at any rate it was very kind of him indeed. The G.P.U. officer who took his place at Omsk and travelled to Moscow had an unprepossessing look and wore a black rupashka. Even in the dining-car he had a hunting-cap on and was indeed a disagreeable fellow. The conductor was an old man, dismal yet amiable, and looked just like a bear. He came every morning and evening to make the beds. He was clumsy yet helpful, and satisfied us in everything he did with his hands fat as baseball gloves. He understood not a word of English. The two Americans next door, who were awakened during the night about the arrangement of the compartments, were angry next morning. One of them was in a *crêpe* silk lady's gown with a scarlet silk lining, such as Japanese female impersonators would dress themselves in on the stage; the other was wearing a padded gown which ancient Japanese constables wear on the stage. With both gowns revealing long purple sleeves of pyjamas underneath, the men waved their hands at the conductor and shouted, 'If you do that again, I'll kill you!' But the old man merely smiled, and their words had no effect upon him, so it ended in a roar of laughter. On the following day, at Achinsk station, the conductor brought us five or six girls about fourteen years old, and exhibited them with evident pride, saying 'Anglski', meaning that they knew English. 'Do you understand English?' I asked them. 'Yes, one, two, three'. These are the only English words I ever heard from the lips of Russians. Even customs officers cannot speak so much. Soon the starting bell rang. 'Good morning,' said one of the girls. 'No, that won't do. Yaponski, good-bye, good-bye!' 'Dasvidahnya!'

When we held out our kettle, saying 'Wada' (water), the old conductor stuttered hurriedly, 'Da, da' (yes, yes), but his voice was very sweet, and he was fond of singing. When I found him sitting all alone by a *samovar*, I pointed my finger at him saying, 'Volga', and sang part of the famous boatman's chant. He shook his head and began to teach me another boat-song, 'Volga, Vo-o-olga, something-*kaya*, *doble*-something!...*oliko*'. After this, he tapped my shoulder and said, 'Volga', as if to say, 'Well, have you learned it?' and began to sing in his resonant bass a tune like a grey snaky river winding . . . I thought that its slow rhythm suggested resignation. When we crossed the Irtysh river, he sang it to me again. When I followed him closely, he was pleased, saying, with narrowed eyes, 'Harasho! Harasho!' When we crossed the Volga, the old man was off duty, but he banged open our door and rushed in, in his waistcoat. He made us, who had been looking out of the

51

window, turn towards him, and then he began to sing, 'Volga, Vo-o-olga'. He was merry, forgetting himself. At one time when we were dealing the cards he came up with 'chai' (tea). 'Will you join?' I asked with a gesture. 'Da, da, da,' he nodded. I wanted to tease him, and made a sign with my thumb and finger to indicate money: 'Do you gamble? Will you have your money taken and cry over it?' 'Nyet', was the reply, 'I will take all the money . . .' He made a motion as if to draw money from the table and put it into his pocket, and exclaimed, 'Urah!' throwing his hands up into the air. The word 'Urah!' made me feel a little strange, because I have been used to it since the time of the Russo-Japanese War, when I saw it used in sanguinary descriptions as a war-cry uttered in a charge.

Russians are in some ways very easy to make friends with. While the train stopped at a station for water, a workman was clanking round the wheels and shafts with a hammer to test them. For some unaccountable reason that sound made me feel that I had come very far from home. The bearded man came towards me, bent double, peeping under the carriages. Almost involuntarily I called to him in Japanese, 'I say, thank you for all your care. Look to it well, please!' Then he slowly straightened himself — how tall he was! He put out his hand after wiping oil from it on his trousers. Staring into his eyes, I shook his hands. Looking long after the man as he went clanking away, I felt more confidence than ever in 'travelling like a mute'. Bold as I was, I had to breathe deep and gird up my belt when I stepped into the bustle of the waiting-room at such stations as Taiga and Novo-Sibirisk. It was not because they were unsafe or terrifying, but because of the dark, dismal air, which was thick enough to be called 'palpable'. There was great confusion. Men and women and articles of clothing and furniture, such as big cloth-wrapped bundles, and chairs, with groups of people lolling on the floor, left no available space. And yet the crowd was utterly silent. There were men who seemed to be half rigid, staring vacantly, with aimless glances. The head of an infant could be seen suckling at the breast of a pale-faced mother, whose head and body were wrapped in a large shawl. They didn't look cold in leather, though all in tatters. If they had looked cold, we could have sympathized with them by showing them a manifest desire to warm them, but my sympathy was not so easily to be satisfied, because the touching sight of the situation lay in my heart like a lump of lead, so that the difficulty of adjusting my heart to the desire to give them the joy of life became a dull pain and wounded my heart. I was told that these people were going to be sent by the government to the country districts to establish rural villages. There is nothing strange in their resemblance to people who have lost their dwellings through inundation. They are indeed driven away by the general trend of the country, and like floating grass they do not know whither they are going, torn, as they are, out of their native soil. It is very painful to stand watching their miserable, forsaken figures, which, like rubbish floating in a river, sometimes drift and sometimes are stuck in one place until a force comes to push them on again.

At Tatarskaya station, it was too stuffy, and I ran out from the waiting-room on to the platform, when a down-train pulled into the station. The freight-carriages, in which horses and cattle are carried, were overflowing with people. Children and women were peeping out through the barred windows opened for ventilation. The sentinel

soldiers with fixed bayonets, at every entrance of the
carriages, attracted our attention. In a newspaper I had
bought yesterday, I found again this statement: 'At present,
the property of *kulaks* (rich peasants) is being successfully
confiscated, and shameless *kulaks* will be employed to
cultivate ground in Siberia'. As I looked back at them, I
was pained at the thought that they were *kulaks* now being
deported to Siberia. Side by side with such squalid misery,
the transportation of agricultural implements is even more
vigorously carried on, and at each station, gay, clean paints
of green and red give warmth to the eyes which had been
chilled by snowy skies and snow-covered ground. As the
freight-train, carrying tractors, rapidly crossed our field of
vision, a streak of red was seen against the grey-white sky.
It was like a passing spirit of evil, and was very suggestive.
I hope that the ideas of the Soviet Government and the
progress of their realization will not end like so many red
demons passing for a gay moment across the eternal
grey.

As we drew near Omsk, the number of what seemed to
be newly-built corn silos increased in the villages, and
beyond Omsk, huge wheat barns made of zinc were seen
here and there, raising their modern, efficient towers. It
was tiresome to pass the evenings, because of the poor light,
so I visited Rima to play with her. The children, too, were
very much bored, and were delighted to see me. They
served me peppermint candy, which may have been their
chief treasure. I brought my sugared beans with me, and
the soldier in the upper berth fetched hot water from the
supply at Tiumen. Eating these things we conversed by
means of pictures. These Russians look stolid, but were far
more acute than Englishmen. The senses of the English are

deadened by national pride. Russians understand us better because they are naive and unaffected, just as a dog understands a man's mind. Since I am going to Europe without knowing anything about the customs and the languages, I should like to utilize my childish temperament and sniff and smell the odour of every nationality, as a dog by his nose distinguishes between innocent and suspicious persons. This was my resolution, so I find that I have a great affinity with the Russians. Rima's mother told me by gesture that her children's clothes had all been remade on a sewing-machine from her own, and also that their father was a soldier, which information was communicated by drawing a rugged, bearded face; but when I asked her for the picture as a remembrance, she tore it up, laughing. Rima took out a piece of paper upon which I had drawn a dog and other things yesterday, and made me review our Russian lesson, asking me what the pictures represented. I made not a single mistake, as I had written Japanese letters under each of the pictures, which, I was amused to find, no one had suspected to be sound-symbols! I smiled to think that there may be some people who crib at an entrance examination, wearing a chintz suit with secret notes printed in Tibetan characters. While I was thus playing with the little ones, the mother clapped her hands and pointed out of the window. I noticed nothing unusual but the soil where snow had already thawed, which struck me as rather strange. She saw soil for the first time in six months, because she had been with her husband at his post in Irkutsk. Thus, my fifth and last day in Siberia has passed into evening.

§ 4

Moscow in Light Snow

I awoke in the Ural mountains. There is a well-known Japanese song, 'Beyond the Ural the wind is raging', so I had expected to see mountains a little wilder, but these slope gently. The tracks are now under reconstruction so as to be made double, so our train ran rather slowly. For the prisoners in servitude, the time taken by passing trains is the official period of rest, and they leaned on their pick-axes and stretched themselves, or leaned against the side-banks cut wider, and stood in rows with dreary faces. Watchmen with bayonets were standing near by the working places and around the barracks surrounded by barbed wire fences to prevent their escaping. Conspicuous among the prisoners were a large number of middle-aged and white-bearded old men. For what offences are they thus punished, these respectable looking persons? Are they rich peasants or Whites? Worn-out eyes stare after us. With a disagreeable feeling I was looking out of the window vacantly, biting my nails. Before I had noticed it, there had come into view a brook running westward. I stood up almost involuntarily, realizing that we had come to the slope on the European side. A flowing stream, bubbling with bright laughter, was pleasant to the eyes that had seen rivers frozen into sleigh-roads, and the stiffness of my heart was relaxed. The wheat gleamed green. The buds of the sallows on the river were glistening in soft warm fur. I stretched myself, glad to think that Siberia had at last been left behind.

The proportion of fir-trees in the forest had gradually

increased. They stretched their branches almost from the earth, rising upward in the shape of cones, half-covered with snow. The sight had been familiar to me from Christmas cards. Horse-sleighs came up and down frequently, and the drivers cracking their whips were standing like so many Santa Clauses out of work.

Towards evening, delicate colours appear, reflected from the setting sun upon the snow. Biting the sunflower seeds which I had bought in Peiping, I enjoyed the sight to my heart's content. To-morrow we shall be in Moscow.

All was in winter attire again. We crossed the Volga, but the frames of the iron bridge obstructed our free view of the river. At to-day's *abyede* (dinner), we were served, owing perhaps to the shortage of food, only one dish, pressed caviare, which was black and sloppy; so much so that Mr. P. made a sarcastic remark, 'This is not caviare; it's shoe-black. Yesterday's beef-steak was shoe-leather. They match each other perfectly.' Caviare means a dainty dish, but this seemed to have been of very inferior quality, without any flavour. With that dish alone, we gulped down some sour rye-bread, and made our stomachs full for seeing the city of Moscow. In a handbook of Japanese-Russian conversation, a talk like this is found, and betokens much foresight on the part of the compiler: 'Does the train get to Moscow on schedule time?' 'No, it arrives five hours late.' 'Then shall we be in time for the train to Stolptzy?' 'Oh, yes, it will be waiting for you there.' Our train, too, found the outskirts of Moscow three hours behind schedule, and arrived at Yaroslavsky station at half-past five in the afternoon. Following Mr. P., a young Englishman and we two went out sightseeing. Powdery snow was dancing in whirls

over the streets, but we daringly advanced, calling it
'Napoleon's march'. There were four or five miserable
motor-cars near the entrance of the station, and droskies
were running. Tramcars were overflowing, many passengers
hanging over the sides of the conductors' platforms. Mr.
P. said, teasing me, 'That's exactly as in a certain country.
Doesn't it make you think with longing of home?' I saw
that one of the shop-windows had a large single pane,
reminiscent of better days, but it was miserably broken and
held together with iron hooks, and the window-panes were
all covered with dust and blurred like frosted glass. Peering
through the dusty pane, I found absolutely nothing within
but a solitary bust of Lenin. The window next door was the
same. Two or three other shops were the same, and the
next two shops had windows that contained enough to
show that they were, respectively, a book shop and bedding
shop, and the next one had again only a Lenin bust. It is
probably useful as a charm for keeping burglars away from
the windows; it doesn't look as if it had been placed there
out of any passion for Lenin.

I came across another book-shop. It outclassed other shops
in liveliness. Cooking, cattle-breeding, children's stories,
machinery, sports, and all other branches of knowledge and
sciences necessary for life had been put into elementary
books like simplified guide-books. They were all thin, but
in great numbers, and so popularized that even we could
understand them by the pictures on the covers. As it was
past six o'clock, all the shops were closed, but every grocery
was full of people with tickets in their hands, waiting for
their turn. I understand very well that they were not
'customers', but 'buyers', but what I cannot understand was
why the 'salesmen' looked so superior, as if they were

'almsgivers'. I wonder if equality is a thing so difficult to maintain in practice.

I peeped into the next shop, wondering if it too had Lenin, but it was an ordinary shop with more than a dozen sturdy workmen studying something very eagerly before plain wooden tables. The teacher, who was lecturing and drawing a circle on the blackboard, was also unkempt. There was a church, something whose existence here I had not expected, for I had been told that all churches had been changed into meeting-houses and club-rooms, but this one was keeping up its life. We entered. It was a very distressing sight to see simple spiritless votaries moving in the depths of gloom, stagnant with superstition and heavy with candle-lights, under disorderly but showily glittering lights and canopies. Ancient stories teach us that unless one is poor, one cannot be dutiful to one's parents, and unless one is persecuted one cannot experience true religious ecstasy, yet when, at the end of the Ching dynasty in China, that country was in disorder, not many faithful subjects appeared, and so here in Russia, no martyr-saints have yet been heard of. This is a world in which things do not go as prophesied in olden days.

At last we came to the 'Red Square'. The Kremlin held its towering head from behind massive walls of red tile, and there were surprisingly narrow little gates on either side. Occupying the left quarter of the square there are domes shaped like a leek-head, and with small cupolas, one behind another, twisted like barbers' poles, a great cathedral in the Byzantine style squatting like a big mass of gold and green rust intermixed. The right quarter is taken up by a protruding wall separating the next division of the town from the square by forming an arch having as its background

Lenin's square mausoleum in maroon and black, heavily rooted in front of a rectangular area with a wide frontage.

This mausoleum of maroon and black stone is shaped like the Roman numeral I I I I, and looks as firm as if growing up from the ground. In front of the ponderously closed iron gate, two guards stand face to face, in grey woollen overcoats, as stiff as metal, and two other guards in the same uniform patrol the wall of the tomb right and left, keeping step with the regularity of a pendulum. The maroon, showing the inwardly seething passions; the black, showing the unshakable confidence; the grey, symbolizing dispassionate reason; the straight lines, reminding one of the power of decisive action; surrounded by all these, how appropriate the tomb of Lenin, like a square crystal, appears! In this connection I pity Napoleon for his tomb in Paris which lacks individuality, squeezed into perfect milk chocolate.

If it were summer, it would pain the marrow of my brain to see the cenotaph with these strong colours in front of the red-tiled castle wall, but fortunately I saw them all to-day through white snowflakes flying around, and what a beautiful sight it was! It is a merit of this spring snow that it makes me feel calm and gives me the leisure to think, standing here in the centre where the suffocatingly serious thought and practice were born, that Hiroshige chose a snowy day to paint our Asakusa temple lacquered in red.

By the side of the square, however, there stood the angular statue of a workman about twenty feet high, clutching the handle of a switch with all his might to compress the Five-Year Plan into Four, and looking for all the world as if he were sneering at my easy-going temperament.

We could not enter the Kremlin because it was too late. That was quite obvious, but Mr. P. went up to the bayoneted guard to negotiate with him. Flatly rebuffed with a 'Nyet!', he said, 'Spaseebo' (Thank you), adding reverently, in Japanese, 'Not at all'. Though the soldier had a very ferocious look, he was good-natured and saluted Mr. P. Then we ploughed through knee-deep snow, sometimes barked at by dogs, and walked through the park beside the Palace. We came to the bank of the Moscow river. Notwithstanding the snow, a soldier was sitting as if waiting for somebody on a bench which he had cleared of snow. He must have warmed up a bit the last time, for regardless of the climate he had promised his sweetheart to be at the bench in the park next time, and with this in mind, I thought him a very nice boy.

In the lead-coloured water of the river, large flakes of snow dissolved and vanished, and on the opposite side a many-storeyed building of the Soviet Government was half-finished and the sound of riveting echoed on the water's surface.

Soon afterwards we made for Tverskaya Street, which is the Piccadilly of Moscow. All the people walking along the street impressed me as being labourers. I saw many young girls looking very healthy and intelligent, though not yet highly educated, with their eyes bright with the desire to absorb as much as possible. I looked back after them with a tender heart. In the train, too, I had seen a young working woman in a greasy overall and trousers. The girl had very smart manners, and pleased me, for she looked as if she felt life worth living; nor was her bearing at all coarse. But on the other hand, the faces of old women who have been entirely broken formed so extreme a contrast that although I saw them very seldom, I feel that I cannot leave them unmentioned. The tramcars were always crowded and were flying red flags on the roofs, with propagandist slogans written thereon. The roads are paved with cobble-stones, and very slippery, filled in at this time with ice.

At every corner of the street droskies were waiting. Old cabs, drooping horses, heavily-bearded, bull-necked old drivers, smiling at us, asking us if we would care to ride — they were so alike that at first I felt that I was returning to the same corner over and over again. We were famished, and entered a public restaurant. Having no tickets, we feared lest we should be refused with a 'Nyet', but an elderly waitress who looked like a good housewife arranged matters for us and served us. *Borshchi*, which is something intermediate between soup and stew, containing chopped cabbage, was rich in rural flavour, like the soup boiled in a big pot hung over the fire which is served in our own rural districts. Russian pickles, which are made of vinegar and cucumber, had an excellent taste. I asked the way to Byelorusky station, from which the train for Poland starts. The waitress said, 'There is no such station'. I was puzzled at this answer, but she drew us a rough map to indicate Alexander station. This is the old name under Imperial régime, which the Soviet Government has changed to Byelorusky in accordance with its spirit. These alterations seem to be generally unpopular, as this incident shows. When leaving our seats, I wanted to tip the helpful waitress, but she refused it. This was quite a noteworthy occurrence during our travel through Europe. In such a country as France, the tipping system is formidable, and at a reception by the President, the usher in the cloak-room suggestively displayed the paper notes, given him by previous guests, to serve as an example for us foreigners. How disagreeable it was! So in theatres, of course, there are many idlers who know how to say, 'Tip for me!' in English, while they don't know even 'one, two'. You call a taxi, and they hold out their palms just for opening the door. In the age of the Czars, French customs prevailed, and Moscow was notorious for its beggars, so that this abuse must have been very great, and I was much struck by the conduct of the waitress, thinking that this was really and truly a public restaurant under Soviet rule. I know that the waitresses in the dining-rooms of Japanese department-stores accept no tips. They gently say, 'Well, but I should be scolded for this'. What made this waitress refuse the tip? Did she think that it would be a loss to her if she should be discharged only for twenty or thirty cents, or did she decline it with pride in the true spirit of Soviet principles? I had no means of ascertaining her motive. I left Moscow, looking forward to the time when I should be able to return for a closer inspection, but the Manchurian disturbances broke out within six months, so that my intention to get home through Russia had to be given up, and I was obliged to return by sea. Therefore, Moscow, in my mind, remains for ever as a town where snow is incessantly falling and the streets, although uneven, are slippery. At nine in the evening our train started and I lay down soon afterwards.

§ 5

Moscow to Paris

After arriving in Berlin we had a bath, after a long interval a glass of Rhenish wine; *Rigoletto* at the opera-house. The country of the Soviets was now left far behind in my thoughts.

The next day, we saw the Kaiser's Old Palace, which struck me as rather uncouth and unrefined; we climbed to the top of the high tower of the broadcasting station, visited the zoo and two department-stores, and then walked along the streets. President Hindenburg was just coming out of his official residence. A single day in Germany is enough to show the hostile feeling of the Germans against the French. There is a three-mark coin upon which is inscribed 'The Rhine is Germany's river, not her border'. This means that the true natural German boundary is far west of the Rhine, and Alsace-Lorraine is German territory. I wondered at the audacity of expressing such a sentiment by means of a coin everywhere current. It is a spirit of revenge etched upon both metal and soul. A child in kindergarten says to its father who is humming a tune, 'You will be scolded for singing that'. It is 'Deutschland über Alles', which was prohibited because of protests from other countries. On the other hand, the business depression is increasing the number of 'houses to let' in the principal streets, and hotels hang diagrams and notices on every door to show that they cannot help raising the rates, because of heavy taxes, compared with those of Switzerland.

Early next morning, we arrived at Cologne. As we had an hour before the train started for Paris, we were preparing ourselves to visit the famous Cathedral by donning over-coats, when suddenly I felt an ineffable yearning for my children. I suppressed that feeling as best I could, saying to myself, 'You fussy emotion, don't come up at this busy time, but be still, be still'. As we came out of the station, we heard the morning chimes of the Cathedral melting into the air above the city in the smoky spring rain. Strangely enough, before the chimes reached my ears as sounds, they had stimulated my lachrymatory glands. Two grand towers rose into the whitish grey sky above the dome, while the misty rain was falling, and the iron-coloured solemnity was softened in the drizzling morning rain, just like an etching of a landscape. It stood aloft throwing its shadow faintly upon the wet pavement, and that picture was clearly taken by the camera of my mind. I consider no cathedral superior to this. Inside there was as yet utter gloom, and I felt like a blind man feeling a big elephant's leg when I walked around a pillar thirty-eight paces in circumference. After walking along a street for a little while, where there were many eau-de-Cologne shops, we returned to the station. On the doors of the toilets standing in a row at the station, several charges — ten, fifteen, and twenty pfennig — were marked. After using the ten-pfennig one, I wished to try the toilet twice as expensive, just to see what the equipment might be like, but I felt shy of the woman in charge, and refrained.

On the book-stands in the station, I found quite a number of serious books, some bearing the swastika or Hitler's picture and others bearing the title, *Awake, German Youth!* There was a row of guide-books, which made me think that they must be all reliable in every way, since it was in Germany that *Baedekers* originated, and it is also here that people are most fond of travelling and of accuracy.

On entering Belgium, we noticed that the manners became quite French. Our train ran through a region of peaceful farms and pastures, and then through a coal-producing district dotted with mountains of slag which looked like pyramids suffering from the Black Death. We came to France, and soon arrived in Paris.

CHAPTER III

PARIS, THE FLOWERY CITY

§ I

First Impressions

GREY, sooty, solid-looking buildings with narrow, winding streets in between. If you pop out from them, you emerge quite unexpectedly into a very flourishing quarter. This usually happens in Paris, and our hotel was situated in a thriving section in a by-street, not far from the Théâtre Français. It was like dwelling behind the scenes of a very brilliant show. The first thing I felt about Paris was that it would be very thrilling to tear up the paving-stones, and begin street-fighting with them. The hotel was a small one, where only breakfast was served. A bald-headed porter, who shouted 'Bonjour' at us in a head-voice and wore a red-striped black waistcoat and a green apron, brought in our breakfast. He seemed to think it an expression of courtesy to guests to show a flurried manner when he brought newspapers in. This is a Latin way of showing hospitality. Breakfast was delicious. When I tasted the sweet coffee, weak but not watery, in this cheap hotel, I realized that I was indeed in France. I realized this again when I went to the Panthéon, where we saw pictures by Puvis de Chavannes, who achieved such intensity of effect with such light colours. The group image of the Revolution was also very good. The beauty of these statues can be easily appreciated by Japanese masters of flower-arrangement. All the styles used in that art seem to be applied naturally to these statues. The rooms in the basement containing coffins have offensive bars, like those of prison-cells, but I was charmed by the relief on Rousseau's monument. It represented a strong arm holding a flambeau protruding from a slightly open bronze door.

The *marronnier* trees in the Champs-Elysées were beautifully fresh and green. The people passing there were unlike the Germans, who are entirely arrayed in one colour, for these, although they wore pepper-and-salt, yet sprinkled it with red and blue, just like a magpie, which displays a brilliant colour in some corner of its wings. Thus they show their individuality in their clothes, and this makes scrutiny interesting.

Face-powder sold in shops is divided into five colours, so we often come upon a woman who gives us a gentle shock with her excellent make-up of purple and green. Food is very good in any and every restaurant without exception. Wine is sweet yet inexpensive and in some restaurants, even if you don't drink wine with your meal you have to pay for it nevertheless, so that you will soon grow accustomed to the use of alcoholic liquors. A typical article of food is *bouillabaisse à la Marseilles*, a rather salty soup, with such fish as chopped lobster or gurnet and shell-fish in the shells. It smells of the Mediterranean, and invites me to go to the southern shores as soon as possible.

I sustained a pretty severe blow to my self-confidence as amateur critic when I visited the Louvre, because it was borne in upon me that I have no eye for pictures. I am for this reason disinclined to say anything about them. But I should say, in passing, that though the pictures of San Sebastian in which he is represented with his neck and breast full of arrows and gazing heavenwards, may give an effect to ordinary people of his face being in ecstasy, yet to me it seemed listless and phlegmatic. I simply have a feeling of intense pressure when I find myself between great master-pieces in a comparatively narrow corridor: works which represent a reeling steed foaming at the mouth, an armed warrior nearly crushed by it, and the like. I am not affecting a horror of cruelty, for I am sometimes fascinated by bull-fighting, but I am worse than swine having pearls cast before them, and my heart aches when I see such pictures. A woman painted by Rubens was nauseating to me because she looked as if she would melt into thick fat if she were squeezed. I expected to like Greuze's girls better, but, oh, those eyes, like rotting gooseberries! Generally speaking, the Louvre Art Museum is justly proud of having collected many famous pictures, but it seems to lack any real love for them. It is very difficult to see the pictures clearly because of the glare, for glass is used without modulating the sunlight upon them. Sometimes my face reflected on angels' faces. In one place I saw a very modern-looking girl standing before a picture painted in the seventeenth century, and eagerly moving her face this way and that. I looked at her enviously, wondering how well such a modern girl could understand the beauty of the old picture. After a while, however, she began adjusting her hat, and I realized that she had been using the glass as a fashion mirror. I thought, 'This, too, is French!'

It is very common in France to rearrange one's facial make-up openly before one's husband or paramour, it doesn't matter which. They wipe off the old rouge and apply new rouge, and men look earnestly on, continuing to talk with them. This made me think that they find pleasure in the process of creating facial beauty, and it is not strange that women should show men how to rearrange their faces, because that art is worth boasting of. To us Japanese, toilet means transformation, and it is considered offensive to see the fox-demon hiding its tail hurriedly as it assumes human shape. But these French women do it frankly in the sight of God and man, and we have to change our ideas on the subject.

To-day being Sunday, I visited the Madeleine. It is a pleasing and quiet church, and the music is splendid. The congregation numbered, I think, two or three thousand, all serious, most of them past middle age, but even young men were crossing themselves every time the priests went up to the altar. The collection of money, however, was extremely disgusting. Women who looked like housemaids came up during the service holding out their hands to us to collect offerings, in a manner by no means reverent. They carried paper-notes, displaying them to all. As they were so persistent, an American girl, wrapped entirely in panther fur, blushed in spite of herself, possibly because she didn't carry with her small money. The collection-women went up to late-comers every time any entered but 'gleaners' of money are not at all a good subject for a picture. The jingling of the money, as the presiding priest put it into a bag, was also disagreeable, interrupting as it did the splendid chorus. Hallelujah! — Jingle! Hallelujah — Jingle!

I went into a department-store. The manner of the women who pick up articles they don't ever intend to buy is something like that in Japan. After three or four days' observation, I find that women in this country whom I thought merely beautiful at first, are really thrifty. They try to buy things cheap, even a few leaves of vegetables, so as to save up the money with which to buy stockings. They impressed me as being very fidgety.

Thus we stayed in Paris till the end of April, when the young leaves of the *marronnier* trees began to shoot, and girls, thirteen or fourteen years old, dressed in white for confirmation like child-brides went along shaking their thin white clothes. When we were in England the *marronnier* trees were in full bloom, but there they are called by the rustic name of horse-chestnuts. In June, when the trees began gradually to throw their dark shadows on the roads, with their fruits like green comfits, flickering among the dark green foliage, we came back to Paris again.

§ 2

Plays and Revues

Of the plays, the one I saw in the Théâtre Français, very like a play of the 'new school' in Japan, had a regular plot like our 'Namiko'. A girl who has a lover marries a *parvenu* for her father's sake, but her lover loses a great deal of money, and she supports him by selling her jewels. In the last scene, the lover enters a room and the girl wants to follow him, but the door is locked. A revolver-shot is heard. The curtain falls on the heroine crying and knocking at the door. Even such an oldish plot draws full houses. I saw a long queue of people at the entrance, and saw among them girls with their eyelashes pasted up chewing bread. In the theatre there occurred an interesting incident. A silver-haired queen-looking madame was sitting near me. This was the first time I had seen the beauty of an old woman carefully made up, and as I looked at her I thought that I should have to extend the age-limit of feminine beauty. But the madame had a bowl-shaped cap of black velvet, closely fitting her head, which the attendants repeatedly asked her to remove. She persisted in wearing it, but the attendants, on their part, were very obstinate, although the hat was no hindrance in any way to the people behind her. At last a person uniformed like a gaoler came and spoke to her. Then the 'queen' got up in anger, and went out, and the face of the monsieur who followed her was indeed worth watching. All the people cheered them standing up and sitting down skittishly several times. They clapped their hands noisily and their manner was frivolous and offensive. I found this incident very interesting, seeing in it the European habit of paying too much attention to the matter of hats and caps. In the churches, women are not allowed to enter hatless, and I have heard that a Japanese lady in native dress (which is never worn with a hat) was refused admission at the Milan Cathedral. I think it must be very annoying for men that they should have to take off their hats when a lady is in the same lift.

Carmen, which I saw played at the Comédie Française, was interesting. Although the part of Carmen was played too 'saccharinely', like an over-ripe persimmon, yet for us who were going to Spain, it was a very fitting preparation, and had much tragic beauty in it. After this we saw in the Théâtre Français, *Le Cid*, an historical play with a good deal of solemnity and massiveness in it, which impressed me as another good preparation for travelling in Spain. The two indeed made for us a delightful combination.

The gestures of grief used by the male operatic stars were

too stereotyped. They spread their hands palms up, protruded their chins, tottered forward two or three steps, bent their arms violently, and with the force of grasping their hair, they tottered backwards again. It seemed that this was the whole gamut of their histrionic art.

The Grand Opera was as splendid as I had expected. In these three theatres — the Théâtre Français, the Comédie Française, and the Grand Opera — Mr. Kahn had reserved a box for us, which we used. The box was especially magnificent, being near the centre of the dress-circle. It had an adjoining space which was covered with scarlet velvet, and was furnished with a large mirror. Seated luxuriously in a comfortable chair, I felt — but only during the dimming of lights — as if I were the eastern princess in *Monte Cristo*, sitting in the private box of Monte Cristo. The structure, stairs, and ceilings, all have an imposing grace which distinguishes this theatre from all others. Generally speaking, French palaces — Fontainebleau and the Palais d'Elysée, and others — are all very gorgeous, but true to the French type, are not as gorgeous as the rings on a *parvenu's* fingers; but there is something about the lightness which smacks of tawdry fragileness when you scrutinize them, and one marvels at their getting such a good general effect, in a piece of architectural work so superficial. Superficiality cannot be avoided in such buildings, but this theatre, paradoxically, becomes more beautiful the longer you look at it. In the darkness while the play was going on, the dark gold lustre of the pillars and ceiling rose along the convex and concave curves, and as the music swelled like a fountain, the gold became softly brighter, and as the music sank, the colours, too, seemed to fade away. Absorbed in this observation, I was apt to be attracted by the ceiling, and watched it.

72

The gold that sinks into the noble obscurity is very dignified, but not oppressive. It is weighty, but not heavy. If you shift your eyes a little lower down, you will find a row of boxes covered with dark scarlet velvet, each divided by a protruding frame having a soft but masculine curve, like the back of a harp. The dark ruby colour has a purely European beauty, like a passion suppressed. On the stage, in the light composed of very strange phantasmal moonlight-blue and purplish silver like that of the desert of Siberia in the setting sun, the shadowy figure of a girl in a white veil was gliding with a wavy motion to and fro. The music, instrumental and vocal, was also soft and soothing. I thought it peerless luxury to let my eyes wander freely from the structure to the stage and back again. The cosy feeling, as of bathing in a hot spring, created a lasting impression in me, making the night an outstanding one of relaxation during my otherwise perpetually tense sight-seeing trip. The intervals between acts are interesting, because you can see the beauties walking leisurely round and round in the *foyer*, seeing and being seen by others. They are indeed different from the ladies whom we often come across in the streets, and whose smartness seasoned by grotesqueness attracts our attention: most of those in the theatre seemed to be the very essence of beauty. There were among them beautiful persons so languidly lovely that they gave no after-taste and made little impression upon us. The people who were cruising aimlessly in the great hall — no, not aimlessly, for they had the serious aim of exhibiting themselves — moved around naturally in one direction, and many persons leaning over the gilt rails on the upper balcony, regaled their eyes by looking down upon them. The sight rather put me in mind of an aquarium or a bowl of goldfish, and I felt like saying, 'Look, another beautiful one has just swum into view'.

It was also amusing to let oneself be amazed, like a fresh *étrangère*, in the Casino de Paris. Girls dance here more than four hours without intermission, changing the dances incessantly, gorgeous and glittering. Amid the general soft tones of colour, Josephine Baker, the most popular dancer in Paris, appeared, and the grey skin, in which is mixed a large proportion of Negro blood, her nails dyed gold, and her eyes that seem to have come out from an Egyptian wall-painting, were very fantastic but strongly impressive. Sometimes she rushed in wearing only diamond-studded shorts, and sometimes she appeared with her head swathed in white peacock feathers. Sometimes she would dance like one who was itching along her whole spine with flea-bites. Her long face and long fingers and the metallic lustre of her swarthy skin had an Indian charm and she looked like the female demon who appeared to disturb Buddha's meditations with her allurements. Thus I found in her dance quite a strange interest. Covering the whole stage, a curtain of lace came down, and figures, which had appeared in the stage-light to be part of the curtain's design, suddenly began to move, some getting on swings and others performing on tight-ropes. While the première danseuse was dancing on a high balcony before a curtain representing a blue sky, more than twenty well-tamed white pigeons flew about from one T-shaped pole to another, which two dancers were holding at the ends of the stage, and the première danseuse seemed as if she were flying up into the sky stepping on the white clouds of pigeons. In one of the dances of various countries, Baker danced on the back of an artificial camel, and after finishing the dance the camel began to step it too, which was cheered with roars of applause. The audience in the Casino, however, was not so interesting to observe as in the other theatres, because we couldn't see any young girls or any students who give plausible excuses for going to such resorts by saying, 'We who use our brains need occasional diversions of this innocent sort'. The young people are bored unless they show themselves to, and are in turn seen by, others as young as themselves, and here the audience was composed of older men and women and foreign tourists.

§ 3

Mr. Kahn

When we came back from England to Paris, we took one of the rooms in the club-house, built on Mr. Kahn's grounds. Mr. Kahn's residence is near by, but we had first seen him in his office. It was on the second storey of a building in the central quarter of the city. We entered Mr. Kahn's room, going up the dark, narrow stairs and walking past people at work as in an office. There was only one desk in the old empty room, before which Mr. Kahn was writing. He was an old man well over seventy, of a ruddy complexion, and his appearance on the whole was that of a Santa Claus without beard, but the impression he gave me was quite different because of the spiritual power hidden within. He spoke quite light-heartedly, sometimes saying that he paid special attention to such disturbed countries of the world as Russia, Germany, and Spain, and sometimes asking us how the thought was changing in Japan. He also said, 'It is up to the government to offer expenses for making scholars study abroad in order to promote the knowledge of the various branches of science which they pursue. What I want you to do is to look around the world not as a professor of English literature, but as an amateur apart from your speciality and merely as a man of culture. So I should like you to see the less-known parts of Europe as much as you can. Don't settle in a great city. Well, I am giving a suggestion not very welcome to Madame, eh? You can't do good shopping in places like the Balkans or Finland.' And, he shook his finger awkwardly and added in laughter, 'This is indeed a bad old man to say such things! But while you are staying in Paris, I'll let you see a lot of plays instead'. Even for small matters, he went into the next room himself to attend to them, saying, 'Just a minute, please', without ringing for a secretary. His veins and skinny hands betokened that he had for many years battled on the tempestuous sea of life. When he left with awkward motions and shuffling steps, I examined the room he had left behind, and found that his wicker chair with wooden arms had no cushions in it and that one of the handles on the desk had come off. The wall-paper of the room was peeling off in places and so was the leather of the chairs for visitors. He didn't look at all the millionaire who gave up tens of thousands of pounds to enable foreigners, with whom he had no personal relations at all, to travel all over the world, by creating the Kahn Travelling Fellowships in many countries.

But he was too human and interesting an old man to be looked upon simply as a venerable saint, who cared very little about himself. His was the proud lack of vanity that no timid person knows, who is sensitive about other people's opinions of him. Most Japanese millionaires fall into one type by thinking it one of their duties to resort to luxury as evidence of their respectability, regardless of their own interest in so doing. This duty each millionaire shares with his fellows, as a member of the united front of millionaires, to demonstrate the strength of their class. Compared with these millionaires, how clearly distinguished Mr. Kahn is. He had bought Rodin's 'God's Hand' and placed it quite casually in the photographic studio of the club-house, because he wanted to do so. His residence was next door to the club-house. The entrance was the same for both, made of iron bars, entangled with ivy, and his goings and comings were quite simple and unobtrusive, although he had a big villa near Nice in southern France, because he liked the place. But more than such trifling details of his life, the liberality of his outlook on the world made a strong impression upon me, opening my mind wider than the seeing of some countries did. He lacked any narrow nationalism, seeing the world as he did as a member of humanity; and when he shook his head, dissatisfied, and said, 'This is a little strange', I saw in him a very interesting spirit. He amassed great wealth, rising from extreme poverty, and has spent it without stint, creating a travelling fund for a better understanding between the nations even though the direct effect is not immediately apparent.

Entirely free from any biased national attachment, and from any love of fame and vanity, he was doing as he liked, in the true and best sense of that phrase. He was deeply faithful to his sentiments, and since he was born on the earth he wanted to make it better, however slightly. In this intention of his, I perceived an interesting, inflexible spirit, though I had expected to see a wealthy man, ordinarily dignified. He could have contributed part of his enormous wealth to the country for the national defence of France, before making efforts to promote the peace of the world. He was indeed an ideal millionaire. I had thought that he was interested in peace, because France would be also unhappy without it, but while I was now seeing Mr. Kahn face to face and looking at the tip of his ruddy nose my thought was entirely changed. It may be a bold dogma, but this man did not seem to be interested in contributing to help the national competition of elbowing other countries, and in spending money merely as a fee for retaining his respectability even when he lost his interest in such a cause. He was a great free person, who gained his wealth by his own hand, without any support of popularity, and he spent it just as he wished. Looking at his nose again, I muttered to myself that a great Jewish mind was like this indeed.

As we were leaving, Mr. Kahn saluted, saying charmingly and light-heartedly, 'Sayonara!' When I was coming down along the dark, narrow stairs, I said to my husband breathlessly, 'I am very thankful that I have come with you into the wide world'. There are things worth seeing in the middle of the world other than those mentioned in guide-books, though I had looked forward very eagerly to the Swiss Alps and to the English people.

§ 4

Staying in the Club-house

To-day a number of guests have come since morning, because of the twenty-fifth anniversary of the Kahn Foundation. When it was time for dinner, which was held in the hall, I was called up by Mr. Kahn to sit next to him. I tried to decline, pleading that the seat was too exalted for me, but he took me and seated me at the main table, saying, 'Never mind. I have not had time to hear about your grandfather, Viscount Shibusawa, being always busy, so come up beside me. The German *chargé d'affaires* sitting next to you says the dinner tastes better when he can see a girl wearing kimono than when he sits next to an old man like me. Everyone knows very well my ways of doing things, so no one will be angry. Come on. Your grandfather is a great man,' he said, with his face close to mine. 'Yes, I know that quite well.' To my regret, there seemed to have been much of the Japanese smile of embarrassment underlying those words. He waved his hand wildly, and said, 'No, no. He is ten times greater than you think. Like this,' he said, spreading his arms wide apart. His small round eyes glared, and the corners of his eyes twinkled, as if to say, 'Only a great man can appreciate a great man. Don't say impudently, "I know that". You are only a little girl'. His smile shot through my bones like an electric shock. 'Yes, I would like — to become — a great — woman — to understand perfectly that my grandfather was . . .' I stuttered, joining my broken words. As he was very understanding, unlike the English, he said, 'All right, quite all right,' and asked, 'Is your grandfather feeling well?' When we had visited him before our departure, my grandfather said, 'Mr. Kahn made me ride in a motor-car for the first time. I felt very nervous, and Mr. Kahn, amused by my fear, said jocularly, "I am entrusted with your life", and forthwith drove even faster. He is very mischievous, even though he doesn't look it'. I told him this story and said, 'I am not afraid of flying even if you make me do that, unlike my eminent grandfather,' and laughed. But with my poor English, I could not explain how my grandfather praised Mr. Kahn in his usual solemn tone before he told me that anecdote. He said to me, 'He is a great man of peculiar ideas. He doesn't easily trust other people, but when he *does* trust a person, he trusts him with money as well as work, large-mindedly, and never does anything to interfere. Other people are afraid, thinking him uncertain in his ways, but he never wavers and says, "All right, my eyes are never clouded". Such a thing can never be done by a man unless he has strong perspicacity and self-confidence'. While he was saying this, he repeated the words two or three times, 'He is a strange person, really strange'. I felt that the words were words of admiration, but I heard them without paying much attention, but now I suddenly remembered them powerfully and I looked at Mr. Kahn's profile, feeling that he was a great and strange person indeed. Mr. Kahn, like a restless old man, moved his glass from one place to another, and kept on making a ball of his bread without eating anything at all.

Representatives of all the countries where the Foundation operates stood and made speeches. First my husband got up and made a congratulatory address in French, and both the German *chargé d'affaires*, who looked just like Dr. Eckener, and Mr. K. Yoshizawa, our Ambassador, also spoke. Mr. Kahn made no attempt to make a speech of thanks. Wiping his face with his handkerchief all the time because he felt warm, and often breathing deeply, he simply said, 'There are too many people here. I like very much to have friends one by one, but I hate seeing people together like this'. His cuff-links were made of cheap mother-of-pearl. I had been told many stories about him. At one time he bought an expensive plant for the garden of his villa near Nice. He often ordered his gardener to move a tree from one place to another, but the gardener didn't do as he was told, thinking that the tree would die. Mr. Kahn said to him angrily, 'I have paid my money in order to have the pleasure of making a garden, not to have a rare plant looked after, or to make other people admire it by keeping it in perfect trim'. He never paid money for unreasonable things. When there was a mistake in the charge for a berth in a train even for one night, he waited till midnight to make the conductor correct it, and never said, 'It's only a small loss'. I was also told that he was fond of music. He often listened to music with a few friends in a darkened chamber.

After dinner we took a walk in the garden. It was divided into many gardens of different styles, such as an English garden of lawn, a section of firs with mossy stones lying about, a copy of Mr. Kahn's native home, a garden with fences of rose and pear trees, the branches of which were bent in the antique French manner, and a Japanese garden, which was the most attractive of all. The latter had a house with two rooms, eight and six mats wide respectively, surrounded by verandas, and had at the porch a latticed door, and a detached tea-room. In the stream were scattered stepping-stones showing a severe taste, and, going through a wicket made of twigs, you would find yourselves in a real Japanese world. The pines and azaleas were indeed remarkably well-kept, because they had been looked after by Japanese gardeners before French gardeners had mastered the art of tending them. If you stepped out of that garden, you would find a rock-garden of Alpine plants, where white edelweiss and glacier-gentians grew, the latter such a deep blue that they looked almost black. It was perfectly marvellous. In one part of the garden there was a studio, where natural colour pictures were taken and projected, as this was also one of Mr. Kahn's hobbies. My husband and I had our photographs taken, too.

The club-house, where we were staying, was situated in this garden. It was on the considerably upper course of the Seine. If we got up late in the morning, we could see reflections of the June sunshine, quivering like jelly, on the ceiling above our bed. When we came home late at night, hurrying along the road beside the river, the pale gaslight of the street-lamps making a long row, of which every second lamp went off at twelve o'clock, made us feel that it was very late. We felt the wicket-gate, hardly distinguishable from the next door, covered with ivy. In our club-house we had a housekeeper named Madame D., and a married couple as servants. No one could speak a word of English, but they were all pleasant and helpful. Madame D. was a widow. I was told that she stood on her dignity, because her husband had been Prof. D., but she was to me nothing more than a good old lady. She kept speaking in French quite indifferent to my ignorance of that language, and talkative as I was, I staggered sometimes, but I felt quite at home with her. At one time, being told that Madame came from Serignan, where Fabre lived, I delighted her very much by saying that I was an admirer of his *Book of Insects*. Often during talks on this subject she would begin to sing a folk-song of that district, showing that she came from the south, where the people are easily excitable. Her face, like that of Fabre, seemed to show coarseness of skin and also a rural sort of beauty. When I returned from Spain, I told her that I had seen bull-fighting, and she asked me whether I liked it, awaiting my answer with a great deal of interest. I was afraid that I should be prayed over by an old woman, 'God save this cruel pagan's soul!' and I thought it would be better

not to offend her. Hating, however, to tell a lie, I said
boldly, 'Oui, oui. Très joli. Très bien'. To my surprise, she
tapped my shoulder and said, with an air of satisfaction,
'Well, you are sensible'. I should have known that bullfights were very popular in Southern France, and those seen
in the Roman ruins at Nîmes were very famous. Madame D.
then told me, accompanying her tale with gestures, the story
of an affected woman who went to see a bull-fight. At first,
she couldn't endure it, but the second round she watched
merely for the curiosity of seeing horrible deeds, and her
interest was gradually aroused during the third and fourth
rounds, and at the last round she stood up and applauded,
clapping her hands violently. Madame D. divided the story
into six rounds, and showed the woman's change of emotion
with light and witty gestures.

French things are all light and witty. The annoying language, with its distinctions of gender, was a jargon to me,
but even from my wholly ungallic mouth there sometimes
slipped out very naturally and spontaneously, 'comme ça'
and 'n'est-ce pas?' and I often blushed secretly at my
audacity. Madame D. never stopped knitting by the window.
Her grandson, who was about seven years old, was leaning
on my knee and kept coaxing me for another paper-doll. I
unconsciously said, 'comme ça', when I pressed a crease in a
piece of red paper folded into a triangle. I didn't know
whether I could use it in such a place, but it was an expression pleasant to the mouth. '*Quoi, quoi, quoi?*' was like
our '*koa?*' (What's this?), and the French '*fermé*' for 'closed'
was very much like the Japanese word *hērmé* (may not go
in), and '*Oui, c'est ça*', pleased me, for it had the same lightness as our '*Ai, sōsa*' (Aye, that's so). To be frank, there was
a funny story about my French. At one time when I hurried

into a *métro* train, the automatic door shut smoothly, leaving my husband outside. I looked around me upset and found the conductor standing at the farther corner of the carriage. He could not have understood me, if I had simply pointed at my husband. I had to say something to him. The words that I hit upon just at that moment were '*mon bon père*'. Delightedly I shouted aloud 'mon père'. The conductor nodded and pushed the button, and my husband, who knew nothing of my perplexity, came in saying, 'All right now'.

When it had been decided that I should travel in France, I began to study French, which I had heard very seldom before. I clapped on the receivers every evening, anyway, like a good student, to listen in to the French lessons on the radio, intending to learn at least a few words of French. But as the lesson was given soon after dinner, and as I had a dizzyingly busy day of preparation for the unexpected travel, giving directions for the housekeeping during our absence, examining things, and receiving visitors, the lesson given by the teacher, who was known for his fluency, was a pleasant lullaby for me, and I began to nod soon after sitting down to listen, so that my weary ears always caught the first few words: 'Mon bon père (has a pair of shoes),' 'Mon bon père . . .' All I heard distinctly were these, the other words melting softly into my ears, so I used to throw away my receivers, fearing that I might catch a cold if I kept them on. But this small diligence plainly rewarded me, and I was saved from becoming a stray waif. However, I was a little proud of myself, without regretting my ignorance, for having dropped off the word 'bon'. Both in Japan and abroad, we always called each other 'father' and 'mother', but it was too elaborate to have introduced my husband as father in French. While travelling in France, I always considered myself a mute, so I enjoyed a silent laugh every time I was in a restaurant. The waiter gave me the menu, but as I couldn't understand it, I passed it to my husband, who ordered for me too. The waiter always looked at me, asking reverently, 'Madame, aussi?' (which of course means 'too' but sounds like the Japanese word for 'mute'), upon which I would nod gently, but it sounded cynical and made me smile.

§ 5

Receptions and Ceremonies

This is the first day of the fourth centenary of the Collège de France. It was one of our objects to attend it as representatives of the Imperial University of Tokyo. The university here is composed of neat little buildings, and the reception, which was given in the open place in front of the porch, consisted in talking idly while standing, tea-cup in hand, which required balancing in order to prevent its falling among the crowd, as it left no available space. I spoke with a venerable scholar, who told me that he was interested in Oriental studies. He talked and talked, beginning with Alexander the Great, about the influence of Eastern and Western art upon each other, saying, for instance, 'In the age of 'Ideyoshi . . .' I talked, too, as best I could, about the treasures in the Shōsōin on which many Persian designs are found, about the Piyün temple in Peiping where there was an image of Marco Polo as a Buddhist disciple (*arhat*), etc. etc. As I had expected that I should be forced to express my admiration of Paris in answer to the obvious question in the English style, 'How do you like this city?' I found it very interesting and stimulating, though rather hard work, to speak with the old scholar, who, repeating 'Pardon!' every time he was pushed by other people, made notes in his pocket-book of all I said.

In the evening we were invited to the Hôtel de Ville. When we had inquired about it, at the usher's office of the Collège, we were given to understand that my husband alone was to attend the dinner, and that I was to join the reception at half-past ten, so I went by myself late in the evening. At the porch an usher came out from within and asked me to enter. With a muffled sigh of relief, I followed him and found my husband among the crowd. He said that wives of the delegates had also been invited to dinner, but that the Collège de France had made a mistake and failed to inform us correctly. While I was listening to him, a trim little old man came to us and said repeatedly, 'It was not the fault of the municipality; it was the Collège that made the mistake'. As it was near the entrance, I thought him simply the chief usher, so I greeted him in just an ordinary way, and entered. After stepping up the famous wide stairs, we walked through the rooms noted for their wall-paintings by Vauthier and Puvis de Chavannes, and were greeted by a stout queen-like lady standing to receive the guests. She also apologized to me repeatedly for the mistake made in not inviting me. Though elderly, she was extremely beautiful. But an artificial mole near the corner of her eye, which was about a quarter of an inch in diameter, with the lustre of velvet, was tunnelled under every time she smiled by a crow's-foot from the corner of her eye, and made me feel a little uneasy; but notwithstanding its apparently precarious position, it still remained there. I was rather absorbed in observing this mole, but as I guessed her to be a great personage, I answered with due respect. When the speeches were given in the hall, I realized with surprise that the 'queen' was the wife of the man whom I had taken to be the chief usher, and that he was the host of the evening. The humility I felt when I remembered that he had come himself to greet me came too late to be of service. But when they apologized together like that, placing the blame at the door of the Collège in the effort to exonerate the municipality, anyone who didn't take it too seriously could see the pettiness of it all, for it made no difference whose fault it was. It's the fault of France, after all. The English never will make such petty and humble apologies.

In the meantime, the show began. Solo and chorus. The woman who played on the harp had beautiful fingers. The last on the programme was a Russian ballet. The firm muscles of the male dancer and the soft body of the girl, which seemed to melt when grasped, were beautifully intertwined and, forming a fine pose at each interval, they stopped for a moment to make an attitude, which in Japan would have been accompanied by a clack of wooden clappers. A dance called the Venus dance was an extremely daring one. But it was pleasant to see grave-looking old men, including the Director of the Collège, gazing intently at it, showing that they regarded the piece as a work of art. As I was coming out of the room, I caught sight of a handsome lady who wore an artistic happi-coat. On the ground which was all in the blue of the sky there was represented a picture of the Nihombashi bridge in the Hiroshige style. When her eyes met mine, she held up her slender hands, and, smiling slightly at me, winked, pressing her manicured fingers like cherry-bloom shells against the name of the fish-market dyed in Japanese characters on both sides of the neck. Her wink eloquently expressed her thought: 'Although I know that these letters are not appropriate to this place and occasion, I came in this robe, because the people around me, I thought, would be all in blissful ignorance. Don't tell them, for heaven's sake!' 'Eyes speak as eloquently as mouths.' I understood perfectly why men are captivated by the French women.

The next afternoon, the most important ceremony of all was held in the grand amphitheatre of the Sorbonne. This hall had Chavannes's famous painting on the wall, and in front of it, two or three tiers of chairs had been placed. Facing these were seats for delegates, in a space which, in a theatre, would be the orchestra stalls. People were overflowing in the hall, the capacity of which was three or four thousand, with two galleries. As the time for the ceremony approached, dragoons, in gold helmets, black coats with red decorations, and white trousers, stood at the front entrance and in other important places with drawn swords. Their black hair was drooping as if shampooed, and their coats seemed to be turned up at the back. In dignity and manner they were inferior to the English guardsmen, who boasted of being like dolls with steel spines. They bent their heads now and then while standing, and stared at some delegates in strange costume. All this was surely not to their credit, but when I remembered the English dragoons who completely suppressed human expression, I began to sympathize with the French guards, for after all, since they were only human they might as well act like men of flesh and blood. In the meantime, with President Doumer in the centre, President Bédier, and the Academicians in green dress with gold braid arabesque designs, seated themselves so as to face us. Amid all this gaudiness, the President of France alone was in a black coat, against which his white beard was beautiful, while the red ribbons of his decorations lent colour to his attire, which was admirably suited to a republican country. Through another entrance, two hundred and fifty delegates from all the universities of the world trooped in, each in his own distinctive robe. The sight was very gay and beautiful, with bright red, purple, green, yellow and gold embroideries and rims with white wool, some of them wearing caps like nursery lamp-shades. President Doumer took the chair, and the ceremony began with the national anthem. Four or five dignitaries gave addresses after the President of the University of Paris and the President of the oldest university in the world, that of Bologna in Italy, had made congratulatory speeches. After these, the other delegates handed written addresses of congratulation to the President, coming up in order of the seniority of their institutions. A man standing beside him announced the name of each university and its delegate, and when a particularly popular university was announced, the audience cheered. When it came to my husband's turn, he was cheered loudly. In the second gallery, an American lady sitting next to me sent round a piece of paper, asking people to applaud the Japanese delegate, so cheerful were the spectators. The delegate from Cairo was blind, and was led by his wife, so the people clapped for him with all their might. Coming out of the hall, I heard someone behind me repeating, parrot-fashion, in Japanese, 'Konchiwa, omedetaku, omedetaki' ('Good morning! Congratulations'.) I turned round and found two students of the University who had recognized my attire, saluting me in Japanese, and constructing Japanese sentences to the best of their ability. They told me that they were studying Oriental languages, so I said in Japanese with delight, 'Arigato! Sayonara, gokigen-yo!' ('Thank you. Good-bye and good luck'.) When I was leaving the hall, they followed me out and asked eagerly, 'We understand "sayonara", but what does "gokigen" mean?' After I had explained, they said, 'Sayonara, anata ga gokigen yo!' (Good-bye and you are in good luck'.) This time it was I who pursued them, to correct their Japanese, saying, '"Anata mo" (to you also) is better form'. In the evening, my husband alone was invited to dinner, and each of the thirty-four delegates present gave a two-minute speech. My husband had rehearsed in the morning, looking at his watch, so he was able to finish in the time, but some others exceeded the time-limit and were criticized by the Swiss delegate, who came after them. He said, 'I come from a land of precision, so I will stick exactly to the time allowed!'

The next day we went on an excursion to Fontainebleau. On leaving Paris we drove along a beautiful avenue, which, I was told, was the highway to Rome. And I realized with wonder that the expression, 'All roads lead to Rome', was literal as well as metaphorical. Tired of the long ride in the bus, scholars began to compete with each other by unfolding their status in the learned world. An American professor spoke to Dr. D. of Poland, white-haired and boyish in features, saying 'I am . . . ,' to which the other replied, 'I was once . . .' They had a give-and-take in this way, but at last the old man seemed to have mentioned an exceptionally honourable degree. The American scholar threw up his hands in despair and said, 'With whom am I contesting? I am no match for you, you are so much above me', and laughed, throwing his head back, for he was too straight-forward and candid to hide his embarrassment. Although the whole thing looked absurd, yet I felt something akin to esteem for him.

I again dressed up and went out for the reception given by the President of the Republic at the Palais d'Elysée. Amid the salute of the dragoons, we went up to the porch, and trooped towards the room where the President received us. We entered, one by one. The footman in fine dress, standing at the entrance, called out the names, 'Madame ——', 'Monsieur ——'. But my name, Ichikawa, was very difficult for the Frenchman to pronounce. He asked my husband how to pronounce it, so the President, seeing the trouble, merely said 'Mademoiselle', held out his hand, and greeted me. M. Bédier, who was standing beside him, made some remarks to him, and he grinned and said 'Madame', extending his hand. Thus, I had the honour of shaking hands twice with the President. His wife said, 'I am glad that you have come all the way'. President Doumer was seventy-five years old at this time, and made a very mild, elegant figure with his beautiful silvery hair, but in that mild look the corners of his eyes were sharply cut away. His appearance impressed me like a clear winter moon shining brightly yet lonely. Some days after that I saw in a magazine a picture of the President, black-haired, standing slightly sideways with a smile, at the end of a row of his five grown-up sons, ranged according to their height. Reading the words under the picture, I learned with surprise that he had lost four of them in the Great War. I felt that I somehow understood, now for the first time, what had given him his impressive appearance, and I looked at the picture again, as if in a new light.

He was at present in a position where he might truly compare himself, in the poetical language of Michinaga, to a full moon without a speck or spot; for he had risen to the exalted position of President from his humble station as the son of a poor labourer, but he was now shining lonely like a winter moon, and his natural modesty had no traces of artificiality. It had not come from suppressing his pardonable pride with that hand of morality called humility, but had a pellucid beauty all its own. Now I understood that his graciousness sprang from his having been washed in tears and sorrow, eradicating the human harshness. One day, after we returned to Japan, I was thunderstruck to read in the papers that M. Doumer had been assassinated, and I recalled that group picture once more. Young sons stood in a row according to height, and at the end of the row stood their proud father. The ominous association of their going down like ninepins was realized, for they fell one after another, till at last their father followed them. All of them had fallen, victims not of a disease that eats men's bodies, but of a social fever that spoils the health of the world.

Such being his personality, when I shook hands with him I was not so much impressed by the thought that he was the helmsman at the wheels of his state, as by the mental image of him as an edelweiss that adorned the head of a country called France. The French minister of public instruction was an interesting contrast to him. He was just about my height, and was a wild-looking gentleman with a shock of hair. If he had joined in a strike, he would have cheered the rout with 'Go ahead, give it them!' He was anything but polished, whether in a good or a bad sense. As he found me in Japanese dress he beckoned to me, and I went up to him to be examined from head to foot, in about three separate sections. But this attitude of his rather pleased me, because it was so naïve and entirely ungallic. What did annoy me was the method of an old lady who took out a pair of *lorgnettes* in the shape of a mantis's forelegs, and scrutinized me through them. I nearly wanted to shout, 'Hey, I'm no worm. I'll have none of this'. I was delighted, on the other hand, to have a chance of speaking, among the standing crowd, with Dr. Maspéro, a scholar of Oriental art, about the *Bukkoku-ji* temple of Korea and hear him express his admiration of *Keishū*. At tea even the President was elbowed by ladies with glasses of ice-cream in their hands, who merely said 'Pardon', and he had to step backwards and forwards while he tried to talk. All this impressed me with the free-and-easiness of a republic.

CHAPTER IV

ENGLAND AND WALES

§ 1

Arrival in London

THE Channel steamer was small and crowded with passengers, and the deck benches were high in the English style, so that a small person like myself had to cross the Channel, shaken all the time with my feet hanging in the air. When I looked up, thinking that we should soon arrive at Dover, I saw raging waves breaking against, and springing back again from, the foot of the cliffs, which stood coolly upright like a concrete prison wall. When the boat stopped, I wanted to ask a porter to carry our luggage, but there were none who could easily be distinguished from idle sailors. They were quite unlike ordinary porters, who have those watchful ferret eyes. A porter who looked like King George responded to the waving of my hand, and approached me quite calmly. He took our suit-case, carried it lightly, and went ahead of us. Though he was just taking it easy, he was quick and, following him hurriedly, we grinned because our suit-case suddenly seemed smaller. It didn't look the same thing which, an hour ago, a French porter with a short round neck had carried into the boat with short, heavy steps. This didn't matter much, but what made me smile when going into the train was my fear that I, like that suit-case, might also look smaller. Going into the dining-car, we were told that it was only for the first-class passengers, and those in the second class had to eat their meals in their own seats. The hop-fields which we saw from our window looked something like our cucumber fields with supports for their vines, and besides those fields, there was nothing but a succession of meadows. The first impression of England that I got was that the people there would starve if their navy were not strong enough. The country seemed somewhat uncongenial to us who were born and brought up among potato and pumpkin fields. The district was full of low hills, and I saw a lot of cuttings where primroses were in full bloom. The flowers had no cream-coloured warmness but were pale as they are often described. Approaching London, I saw, at the back of a factory, some workmen who, after finishing their toil, were playing football in an unoccupied plot of ground, and I saw also small back-yards of closely-built tenement-houses, where housewives were taking in their dry sheets, and where the masters of the houses, in shirt-sleeves, were tending their flowers after the day's work. The sight was just that of five o'clock in the afternoon in the suburbs, and soon we were at Victoria Station.

We put up at an hotel in the West End. It appeared grand but was very noisy. On the beams of the dining-room there were hung a row of shields, which had the coats-of-arms of various towns, and we were served with toast which was always overdone. Notwithstanding that it was such an unquiet hotel, we did not move out, although we were told that there was a group of better and quieter establishments near by. This was simply because we put up there only to sleep, rushing around all day sightseeing. Every day when we went out, locking the door of our room, we left the key at the counter. Hotels everywhere seem to be much annoyed by people who go away with their keys in their pockets, and they therefore attach big rings or heavy balls to them. The key of this hotel had a plate attached, on which was written, 'If anybody takes this key away, please send it back with a stamp here', and our key had a Yorkshire stamp which showed that some careless but conscientious man must have had to put the instructions into practice. As we were returning to our room, the lift-boy, who always stood up as straight as if he had swallowed a stick, asked us, saying 'Number, sir?' which was amusing, because it sounded just like the Japanese words meaning, 'What number, sir?' At the entrance also there were standing a number of boys scarcely fourteen years of age, and they all looked as prematurely old as if their growth had been stunted on purpose to curry favour with that human nature which loved aristocratic ways; and the sight of young urchins so pert gave me the same sort of unpleasant feeling as when one saw a lap-dog. But the old porter outside the gate was very much like King George again, and I felt it almost irreverent to trouble him by asking the numbers of buses too many times. What attracted me most in the streets were the policemen, for whom London is famous. As among dogs, Swiss St. Bernards; so among men, these policemen — both seemed strong, tender-hearted, strikingly big; and they really fascinated me. In the same category may also be put the London cart-horses. Upon their big shins they have super-fluous shaggy hair, and as they draw the carts their hoofs make a hollow sound like the tapping of a coco-nut on the floor. Each with its innocence and with abundant capacity seems not to be worried with its labour, and imparts a very soothing air to the streets. The women are mostly in brown, and high-heeled shoes are less in evidence than in France. This attracts the attention of those who have just come from there, and makes it seem as if the women were all school-mistresses. Their great merit is in their restraining them-selves from such impertinence as staring at people, but because of this, we could not find any chance of speaking to them in the train, much as I wished to. With old American women I used to become acquainted immediately I smiled: they would say, for instance, 'I have seen fifteen "Grand Hotels" already since I came to England. Let me know if you see one out of your window'. I was surprised to find that I felt awkward in speaking to English people in English. Therefore I, who in Finland went so far as to go to a Finnish bath to be treated by an old woman who did not speak a word except in her own language, did not have the courage, although I was urged, to go to the Turkish bath with which our hotel was equipped.

§ 2

Shakespeare Festival

On April 22nd we left London for Stratford-on-Avon at once, although we had come over to England just the day before. It was because of the Shakespeare Festival. When changing cars at Leamington, we came across Mr. M., and went together with him. After passing a number of local stations, I was asked, 'What station is this?' and I betrayed the fact of my being a stranger at once by answering, 'Bovril', which I saw written on the platform. Soon after-wards I noticed it was the name of a beverage, the advertise-ment of which was found at every station. It was quite natural that I should have made that mistake, seeing that it was written in big white letters on a blue board. In four hours we got to Stratford and went to the Shakespeare Hotel. We went directly to the Town Hall, and saw the chief of the preparation committee of the Festival. My husband expressed his wish to hoist the Japanese flag, representing the Shakespeare Society of Japan, but the man looked a little perplexed, and rubbing his clean-shaven chin with his long fingers, said, 'The man who unfurls the Japanese flag has been fixed upon, so would you mind unfurling the Danish flag instead, please?' Of course we had not come all the way to unfurl a foreign flag, so we said, 'Then we will at least stand beneath the Japanese flag', and we at once went out to see a matinée of a Shakespeare play. As the theatre had been burnt down, and was under reconstruction, the play was going on in a cinema-theatre. *Antony and Cleopatra* was that day's performance. The actors were very fine, and the leading actress was of a large build and looked beautiful; her only drawback was that she appeared somewhat hard, lacking in sweetness, like a mission-school mistress. For the night show, we saw *The Taming of the Shrew*, which was marred by the same fault, for the heroine was too dry. The English audience gave me the impression that they were more sombre than the Parisian. The women did not give so much attention to making their toilet in their seats, as in Paris, but instead they had tea and biscuits carried to their seats at the matinée. Although England is a country where tea is just as indispensable as the three meals in other countries, it does not seem good to have it in their own seats at the theatre, because it is rather disorderly.

On the 23rd, in the morning, we went to see Shakespeare's birthplace. The roof ridge and the beams were not hidden, and the rooms had whitewashed walls. It was rather a big two-storeyed house, but what disappointed me was that the interior was too much like a museum with exhibits and did not look like a private house. The room where he was born was walled with planks and made prosaic by attracting people's attention to such names as Carlyle and Browning scribbled on the window-pane. There was a garden outside, and we went to see it. The trunks of rosemary were as big as those of shrubs, while primroses and narcissi were very beautiful, blooming in abundance. But contrary to my expectation the plants had apparently been collected there without any system. I thought that they should have made, together with this one, a garden of another sort, in which we should be able to find a few specimens of each kind of plant that appeared in Shakespeare's plays, if possible with the passages indicated.

About noon, when the Festival was to commence, delegates of all countries came down from London, so that the town became more lively every moment. Then we returned to the hotel to dress up (I put on my Japanese dress) and we went out again. The streets were all decorated with curtains and ribbons of black and yellow, the Shakespearian colours. Among the flowers, which were also used for decoration, yellow daffodils of the season made the keynote. It was a beautiful colour which was quite suitable for England on the festival of the great writer, being bright and calm, and giving an impression that it was the golden light of shining hope. And it was indeed the perfect colour for decoration, clearly setting off the red, white and blue of the colours of the national flags which were to be hoisted by the delegates of all countries. I thought that the colour of the Japanese flag was favourable to distinguish itself, whilst the German and the Belgian flags in black and yellow lost much against it, and while I was thus thinking a schoolgirl came running along, and put on our breasts small sprigs of rosemary which were tied up with black and yellow ribbons. While waiting at the Town Hall, I saw the Siamese consul among the many guests. I looked with fellow-feeling at his sallow Oriental complexion, when a portly gentleman, who resembled Mr. Matsudaira, the Japanese Ambassador, but was taller, came in. He was speaking English so fluently, and behaving so charmingly, that it made me think that he would never have the worse of any Westerner in his attitude, but afterwards I found that he was the Chinese Ambassador, Alfred Shih, who later played a very active part at the Conference in Geneva following the Manchurian affair. In the meantime, the mayors of neighbouring towns appeared in black gowns with big mayoral decorations, consisting of large gold medals in the form of a chain, hanging on their breasts. The first of them was the Mayor of Stratford. Led by the troop of mayors, all the other people followed, and went out into the main street. There I found flags of more than seventy countries. They were rolled up and hung from the tops of poles, and stood in rows in the middle and on either side of the street. Before them all stood the Union Jack, and the Japanese flag took the fifth or sixth place down from the head, just in front of the Red Horse Hotel, where Washington Irving is said to have put up. We stood and waited at the foot of the flag-pole, in the middle of which hung a golden shield, representing the Imperial crest of the chrysanthemum. As Mr. Saito did not turn up in time my husband unfurled the flag. Presently the Mayor gave a short address, and at the first note of the band, they tugged at the flags and unfurled them. The whole city became gayer, and there came the music of 'God save the King'.

Then newspaper reporters came and took photographs, and
I was asked to come forward because I was in Japanese
dress. I was looking on with a smile, for the cameramen of
the newspapers were competing with each other to get ahead
in photographing me, but at the same time other people were
clicking their cameras incessantly. I thought that they were
amateurs, but in reality they were the picture postcard
makers of the town, and I was much surprised to find my
portraits on sale the next day, some smiling, and some peering.
Then the band went ahead, and preceded by a harbinger in
a coat of red wool decorated with gold braid, the Mayor
went along with a wreath in his hand, and we trooped along
each with flowers in his hand, and went to the poet's grave. I
proceeded with a wreath sent from the Shakespeare Society
of Japan, which was made of purple irises, interlaced with
laurel leaves. It was quite right that my Japanese dress
should be very much admired, but while my hands were
occupied with the wreath and my umbrella, I had always to
pay attention to my skirts, to see that they did not fly in the
wind blowing just a little violently, and at the same time I
had to keep step to the music with my sandalled feet, so
that I spent more energy than if I had been doing some fairly
strenuous exercise. Added to that, every time I was asked,
'Why did you choose that flower?' or 'Is it because that
colour matches your purple kimono?' I wanted to answer in
all the English that I knew, by saying, 'Because in summer,
in Japan, the riverside where fireflies float is filled with these
flowers'. Thus I had to spend much care, and again and
again that disquieting wind blew. But I thought with a
cheerful heart that this strong wind would be good for the
Japanese flag we had just hoisted, for while the other flags
fluttered gallantly in the breeze, to our great annoyance ours

drooped down forlornly, since it was six yards across, far larger than the others. The simple and impressive sun-flag, among the flags of all the nations, gave me great joy to gaze upon, but it would be no good unless it was flying bravely, even because our national character is like a peppercorn, small but hot.

The procession of four or five hundred people marched to Trinity Church, becoming all the time the target for snapshots from the human fences that had been formed by spectators the whole way. The church had a very graceful entrance, with an avenue of lime trees intertwining their branches like colonnades in a Gothic church. It was a trim church, and in the north wall of the chancel was inlaid the Shakespeare Monument — the monument with which we are well familiar through photographs. The poet's tomb is just beneath it. But on that day it was covered with so many wreaths, that the famous epitaph was buried among them. It was useless to stay there long, because visitors poured in one after another, so that we went out through the exit at the side, and found the churchyard very quiet, as if we had come into another world. Mossy tombstones were standing aslant in the shade of yew trees, and the only sound that fell upon our ears came from the stream of the Avon that flowed, washing against the stone banks.

After lunch, in the ball-room of the Town Hall, with the Mayor in the chair, addresses were given by Irish and Greek delegates, Mr. Drinkwater, Miss Lilian Braithwaite, the actress, and other noted people. Every speaker began with, 'Your Serene Highness, your Excellencies, your Worships, my Lords, Ladies and Gentlemen'. Would any high personage of rank so addressed be angry if any one of the appellations were omitted? On the main table there were placed side by side, a microphone, and the gold mace, which had on the top a gold crown that was the emblem of a mayor.

In the afternoon, on the lawn garden of New Place, where Shakespeare spent his later years, old folk-dances were performed by schoolgirls, and a man with a broom in his hand danced what was called the 'broom dance'. Here, there was the famous mulberry tree of Shakespeare, and the Wishing Well, which is said to fulfil people's wishes. At about four o'clock, a reception was given in the Town Hall, and among other entertainments a lady rehearsed Juliet's stage soliloquy. We had dinner with Mr. and Mrs. Drinkwater that evening. Although I heard he was a famous writer, he looked just an ordinary gentleman, whereas Mrs. Drinkwater had richness in her expression and in her physique, and had some of the features of the women of southern climes. The night play was *Winter's Tale* with a very entertaining, picturesque ring-dance in the meadows.

On that day the theatre was full, and the tickets had been sold out very early, but they managed to get tickets specially for us, so we were fortunate enough to be able to see the play. The next night *Measure for Measure* was produced. Four Shakespeare plays in three days was considerable labour even on the part of the audience, and I thought it must be a great trouble for the actors to learn those long stage speeches, performing different plays every day, and I was very much impressed. When compared with Gielgud's *King Lear*, which I saw in London later, their performance seemed to be a series of beautiful illustrations of the plays rather than dramatic presentations, and gave impressions of shallowness, but they were an indispensable company, having ideal actors both as Falstaff and as a meagre and comical servant who were such good foils for each other. It was almost unpleasant to notice that one of the servants of our hotel was just like this servant, both in build and in manner, which struck us as if he were born to be a servant of men.

On the 24th, in the morning, we saw the grammar-school which Shakespeare attended. It was one of the houses in the main street, and I was surprised to know that the two-storeyed house, with bare beams in ebony-black, which I had taken to be a construction reserved for historical interest only, had even now two hundred pupils. This special charm of the staid, quiet English manner had always been affecting me. To give another instance: I was told that yesterday, while the festival was going on, a piece of paper was found on Shakespeare's tomb, on which was written, 'Here lies the spirit of Francis Bacon'. One of the committee had picked it up, and quite calmly put it aside, not particularly flurried, nor crumpling it into a ball, and looking as if nothing had happened. Such behaviour might well be called graceful, and excite our envious admiration. When told of this incident, I visualized to myself an elderly gentleman, who had a long narrow chin, clean-shaven, disposing of the piece of paper quietly and cynically, without so much as moving his eyebrows with a smile of confidence in the sober wrinkles of his cheek.

Then we went to see the Memorial Theatre which was under construction. This was being built on the site of the burnt theatre in a style modern but quite fitting to that town. They all said to me, 'As we are having the opening ceremony next spring, come again to attend it'. After rambling on the half-constructed stage, we visited the Shakespeare Museum next door, and in the room next to the entrance, we found, in the central case, copies of the Japanese edition of

Shakespeare's plays, each exhibit opened at its title-page. They occupied a prominent place, kept in the same place with Irving's hair. The walls were entirely covered with books, among which was found an adaptation of a Shakespeare play by Toshimaro Hamura, produced in the Hongōza Theatre in Tokyo, and its programme as well as one out of the three printed copies of its translation by an English lady. This museum and the theatre under construction are both on the Avon. Swans were floating on the river, dim in the spring rain. When the theatre is completed, people may enjoy boating near the antique stone-arched bridge, and near where the slim spire of Trinity Church throws its shadow, and afterwards they may leave their boats near the entrance to the theatre and enjoy classical plays.

Then we visited Anne Hathaway's Cottage. We walked across the meadows where daisies were scattered like hailstones, turned off, following a blackthorn and hawthorn hedge, and strolled about a mile. The cottage was an antique one in every way, for the thatched roof had the eaves cut out a little to make room for a window higher than the rest, and the red brick chimney harmonized well with the straw roof, moistened darkly by the rain, while the foot of the white walls was buried in flowers. It was all too trimly arranged, and made me think of a Christmas present, in which chocolates, done up in silver paper, were kept. But it is a good thing to preserve an old country-house like this so well. In the interior also, the butter and the cheese rooms were found just as they were a long time ago. On the way back, we passed along the village highway, and heard the shuffling of the hand-looms from the houses, out of which dyed threads were hung to dry. We came across a peasant, who, meeting us on the road, said amiably, 'Good morning'.

This greeting reminded me that it was very late in the morning and suddenly I felt hungry, so we dropped into a teahouse and had our lunch there, consisting of some meat, Yorkshire pudding, and cauliflowers, boiled without any seasoning.

When we came back to the town of Stratford, the tulips and forget-me-nots were very beautiful in the front-garden of each and every house, and I thought it was a sign of rustic peacefulness that those houses had name-plates upon which 'Primrose Cottage' or 'Mountain-Ash House' was written according to the plants which they had at the entrance. They had no numbers, but letters were delivered according to these names.

§ 3

Wales

Just at midday on May 8th, we started for Wales. Our train, passing through Rugby and Lichfield, ran through green meadows as usual. On the bank of a canal overflowing with water, a horse was walking quietly, tugging a boat along by a rope. Although it was a very calm and peaceful scene, we who had not taken our luncheons with us, simply had to turn our heads away from the smell of roast chicken, which a family in the same compartment were having for lunch, and had to pretend that we had been attracted by the charm of castle-ruins and cathedrals. Passing through a number of stations, all empty, we came near to the river Dee, along which our train ran. It reminded me that I was made to learn the Miller's poem by heart in my school days, but what I most clearly remembered was my tomboy life in those days rather than passages from the poem. The sandy beach at the estuary was widening like a trumpet, and on the sand of the ebbing tide were scattered sea-weeds, making the view cold and bleak. The sea also had no charm for me at all, since it was dull white, seeming to have shallow water close to the shore, which was cemented into a promenade. At about five o'clock in the afternoon, we arrived at Carnarvon, in North Wales. We took a bus to Llanberis as we were advised to do. There was something strange in the air. Suddenly I noticed to my surprise that the other passengers were talking in a language that I did not understand at all.

Although I was told that Wales was a land of the Celtic race, I did not expect, as it was only four or five hours' ride from London by train, that Welsh, which was entirely different from English, would be so widely spoken as this. Carefully observing them, I found that the Welsh were more meagre in appearance and of slighter build than the English. Their way of speaking was rather like jabbering. Our bus, carrying all these passengers, gradually went up into the mountains. To my eyes, which had been seeing only un-dulating hills smooth and green, rocky mountains were quite new. There were slate-quarries here and there, and while we went along in view of those curious sights of rough mouldering heaps of coal-black slate, we came to the edge of Lake Padarn. As we drove along the shore of the long narrow lake, a beautifully shaped mountain began to appear in the distance. That it was Snowdon was obvious, rising clear-cut above all the other hills. It is the second highest mountain in Great Britain, and the first in beauty of shape. In short, it is the Mount Fuji of England, but it is only 3,600 feet above sea-level. We got out of the bus at Llanberis to walk in the village. While we were walking, looking around, we saw with much interest some advertisement-boards on which a preposition was represented by the letter 'y' and the word 'avon' stood for a river. Then we came across a plate on the second storey of a tailor's shop, inscribed 'Public Library', so we went up the creaking stairs and found a room, dark with tobacco smoke, where two old men were reading newspapers. Among the papers scattered on the old plain table were those in Welsh, and some had the words 'National University of Wales', which made me realize that Wales was quite an independent district. At the Shakespeare Festival at Stratford, more than seventy flags were going to be unfurled, and I thought, 'There are only sixty-six countries in the world', but Wales was counted among the number just as much as the United States and Japan. In Czechoslovakia, I have heard, they take special care not to insert a hyphen between 'Czecho' and 'Slovakia'. I smiled at English magnanimity, comparing the English with this newly-risen nation so nervously wanting to unite the minds of the two races who have established a joint household. But it would be very inconvenient that their languages should be so different. When leaving the library, I wanted to say, 'Thank you' (Diolchi ichwi), which I had just learned, but I could not possibly articulate the 'chwi' of 'ichwi'.

Our hotel was situated on raised ground at the edge of the lake. It commanded a fine view, which made us laugh at the prosaic name — 'The Royal Victoria Hotel' — a name very common in England, but as it was not yet the season, there were no guests besides us. Looking down on the faint purple face of the lake, shining in the evening sunlight, I leaned back in a chair on the veranda. Everything was so calm and quiet, that I began to forget myself. Above the mountain beyond, the sun was going down, leaving what seemed to be only a foot between it and the top of the peak, lingering there for as long as half an hour before it went down. A cuckoo was calling somewhere. It sounded like the hiccups of some hermit. If I had got a full stomach, I should have nodded off to sweet sleep, but at the thought that a small trout of the lake might have been fried in one of the kitchen pans by now, my mouth involuntarily watered.

Next morning we went up Snowdon. The proprietress of our hotel said, 'Although it is now out of season, the mountain tram will be running just once in the afternoon, so you had better make use of it'. But I said, 'This is nothing for me. In Japan I used to climb mountains three times as high'. So saying we started, and on the way found a waterfall about sixty feet high. Even such a comparatively small fall is famous here as a 'big fall' (Ceunant Mawr). Soon we quitted the wood and came on to a grass mountain. Piles of slate-stones were used for the fences round the meadows, and both the notice-boards and the posts were made of slate broken up into narrow pieces. I thought I had discovered a fine monument that had fallen down, but on scrutinizing it, I found it to be a bridge across a ditch in which water might flow only two hours after a shower. The stony meadows looked very much deserted, and a wild waste of thorny gorse, half-burnt because they tried to burn it away, still bloomed with yellow bean-like flowers. The mountain-path soon began to ascend, covered with short grass and moss, and strewn with greyish stones. Here and there, and just in front of us also, we heard sheep bleating. They baa'd clearly, as if they were deliberately making fools of us, and it annoyed us for a while. Looking carefully, we saw a large number of grey-coloured sheep mingling with the boulders like a picture-puzzle. The parent sheep resembled stones with their protective colours, but the helpless lambs stood out distinctly, like white cotton-work. Their noses only were black, and they had quite innocent-looking faces, like those of naughty children, as they turned them towards us. I said to them, 'What would you do if you were taken away by a great eagle? Run back, run back!' and they scampered away, crying 'Baa!' One of 'those stones' over there might be their mother. Crossing a spur of the mountain, we saw the summit of Mount Snowdon, within hailing distance. Then our path went across a cog-railway. I admired *Baedeker* now because whatever small paths there were were mentioned so accurately that it was as if the scenery had conspired with *Baedeker*. If it states that there is no grass to be seen from here, the scenery just seems to have entirely lost grass and put stones instead. Climbing mossy crags, we found a little snow remaining, and suddenly the mountain took on the appearance of a mountain of about eight thousand feet in Japan, and we found ourselves on the top. Sitting on a crag, we ate our sandwiches and inhaled mountain air to our hearts' content, cleansing our lungs that had become sooty in London. The other side of the mountain sloped very acutely, and far away from our feet a gloomy lake was seen in sombre dullness among the rocky mountains. The peak next to ours was rising sharply, and the successive mountains continued like waves in the sea, one behind the other, while about a dozen tarns could be counted, near and far. It gave me the impression that we were indeed high up in the mountains. On the way back, however, we ran down without pausing for breath. The proprietress of our hotel asked, 'Well, how did you like Snowdon?' I wanted to say, 'It was a nice and trim mountain', but I could not translate my expression, so

I just said, 'Very nice', and nothing more, but to her question, 'You must be tired?' I said, 'Oh no! I could climb it again now'. Soon afterwards we took our bus, which was just starting. We had some lemonade in a village, and bought a few picture-postcards of a Welsh woman in the old style, with a hat on like a tall top-hat. While I was making these purchases I heard some village girls whispering to each other 'Chinee!' Although I suffered much pain in my feet (how big did I talk to the proprietress!) because the soles of my shoes had been broken by the slates, yet up to that time I had been walking with steady strides, keeping step with my husband. But now that I was taken for a Chinese woman, I gave up my posing with some sort of relief, and suddenly began to limp along. Such perseverance may be taken with a good grace as a manifestation of small patriotism, but I smiled at the curious working of my own mind, and when I fancied the villagers at supper that evening saying, 'I have read somewhere that Chinese women bind their feet, and really they do walk very awkwardly', I felt rather uneasy, for, might not some of my sightseeing notes have the same kind of inaccuracy? Added to that, in the train I had a slight stomach-ache, caused, perhaps, by that lemonade, but I could not even go to the toilet, as the English provincial train was a poor one, having been constructed in the 'nineties. It rumbled along, stopping at every station, dimly lighted with oil-lamps. At length we arrived at Holyhead, and up till two o'clock in the morning — the time when the ferry-boat left for Ireland — I sat writing my diary upstairs in our hotel, enduring my hunger, since I had to go without supper.

CHAPTER V

IRELAND AND SCOTLAND

§ 1

The Irish Free State

ON May 10th, when I got up, the breakwater of Kingstown was seen right before us. I had a sound sleep soon after the departure of the ferry-boat for Ireland from Holyhead at midnight, because I was tired out after having climbed Snowdon. There was a Customs House just where we landed, and the distance between there and Dublin, the capital of Ireland, was less than that between Tokyo and Yokohama. Dublin is a somewhat straggling city. Quite near the centre, there are the long prosaic cement walls of Guinness's Stout Brewery, and although the main street has some fine buildings, country women were walking along leisurely, wrapped up in big blankets. Things here thus gave an impression of untidiness. In the middle of the street, Thomas Moore's statue was holding up his hand. That place was now made into a safety zone, and surrounding it, tramcars with one pole sticking up in the air were running about with a screeching that set my teeth on edge. If the surroundings had been laid out properly, it might have been thought that Thomas Moore was celebrating the newly-gained independence of Ireland, but in that atmosphere he could only be taken tragi-comically, as a petrified policeman on point duty signalling to the traffic to stop. Trinity College is in front of the statue. Only in the premises of the college is

English quietness kept, like a solitary island. As it was Sunday, the college bell was ringing in the tower. Students were gathering in white gowns. Teachers carried on their shoulders cloths of different colours, something like shawls above their gowns. When all were assembled in the hall, the President came in, very ceremoniously, following a person who reverently carried a silver mace. Facing this hall, there is a memorial hall of the Great War. I was told that eight hundred students of the University went to the war, and five hundred of them were killed. While I was listening to this story, I had not only feelings of sadness, but also doubt, because that was also the time when rebellions of the independence movement were frequently breaking out. The first sign of Irish independence that attracts your attention in the streets is the fact that railway-tickets and notices of post-offices are all written in both Gaelic and English, side by side. But Gaelic is spoken only in secluded districts, and in this part of the country the peasants and old people with whom we came in contact could not speak a word of Gaelic, but used very poor English with a queer accent, articulating 'th' very imperfectly. But I was told that primary school children were now beginning to be taught Gaelic, which the authorities are anxious to revive. Thus the Gaelic movement seems to be a means of demonstrating their independence, notwithstanding that such a language could not possibly be practical. It may be a natural procedure, but I would like to keep primary school education from degenerating into an instrument of policy. A grown-up person may learn it if he likes, but if this movement becomes vigorous, only those who have either the best education or no education at all will be able to understand English, and in places where common education is the most popularized, you will not be able to make yourself understood in English. But the movement is beset with so much difficulty that there is no need of such fears. Those who could understand Gaelic wore gold-rings on their breasts, and we saw only two or three of them among the University students.

On our way to Glendalough in a charabanc, I saw a magnificent gate in a very long stone wall. The guide told us that it was the house of the President, who did much in gaining the Irish independence. Although it was a revolution, the impression was entirely different from that of Russia's. On both sides of our bus route, there were a lot of similar estates of wealthy squires. At the side of the iron gate with a coat-of-arms there was a lodge, and a passage of white sand in the avenue, slowly winding, seemed to lead to a stately residence in the far-away depths. Most of those estates are said to belong to the English gentry, and I saw them with much interest, as I thought they looked like Dorincourt Castle; but now I remember them rather with antipathy, for, are not the tenants of the gentry living very miserable lives, while their landlords own such extensive areas of land? Soon we left the outskirts of the city of Dublin, and drove sometimes across waste land where gorse was blooming rankly in noxious yellow, and sometimes over damp ground where dead sedges were growing. On a hill, low yet rocky, old rams were fighting with their horns, and near the stagnant swamp an old woman was standing, wrapped up in a black blanket, her greyish-white hair, protruding from the blanket, being blown in the wind — everything was just fitted to the background of a dark sky about to rain. It was so dark that it seemed like the end of the day, and with the fatigue due to a lot of sightseeing since morning weighing on me, I longed for supper, but in reality it was yet before lunchtime. Soon we got to Glendalough. As its name indicated, the water in the glen made a long, narrow lake, being divided into the upper and lower lakes. This is where, in the fifth century, St. Kevin lived a hermit, many monks flocking to him whose high virtues they esteemed, and living in the 'Seven Churches', the ruins of which still stand. The Round Tower, one hundred and ten feet in height, and seventeen feet in diameter, raising its head above the trees, is of a very simple shape, just like a huge pencil, and gives a characteristic mark to the scenery of Glendalough. As you approach it, walking among the grass, you see the Round Tower has an entrance at about ten feet high, cut narrowly above, and the top of the tower has four long narrow windows on the four sides, suggesting that there was a spiral staircase within in the old days. But now it is only a big round obelisk made of piled stones. At the foot of the tower there is an extremely simple stone cottage, the walls of which are also made of thickly piled-up stones. It was in mouldering decay or, forsaken even of decay, squatted in utter forlornness. It began to rain at last, so all the people left there and our guide as well, who leading the sightseers was saying, 'Ladies and gentlemen, this is St. Kevin's Kitchen. This stone cross is called St. Kevin's Cross. If a lady firmly embraces the foot of this cross, she will get luck. Will you try, madam?' All had gone away, and among the ruins scattered with mossy Celtic crosses, the sounds of raindrops were heard everywhere. Hastening along the highway, trying to get back to the hotel near the lake during a short lull in the rain, I found along the roadsides gorse closely laden with golden flowers, drooping over the road, wet with rain. The raindrops fell from them and the sweet fragrance of the flowers stimulated my brain, which had not had enough sleep. On the turnings of the roads, mossy stone Christs, so old that the corners of the crosses were rounded, stood dripping wet in the rain. In some ways, they were very much like our stone-images of Buddha, standing by the wayside among wild flowers, but in other ways they were very different, and their similarity and dissimilarity made that little piece of Irish scenery unforgettable to my inward eye.

When the rain stopped for a while, we, with some other passengers of the charabanc, hired a little boat, and rowed on the upper lake. The boatman was garrulous in the Irish way, and rowed along explaining the scenery rich in legends. Even the waves stirred by the oars being of an iron colour, the lake was dark and gloomy, and had a strange attraction, as though it was trying to draw us into the deep waters. As it was elongated in shape, we soon reached the opposite shore. On the cliff overhanging the water, there was a small natural cave. It was called St. Kevin's Bed, and was the scene of the legend which Moore wrote in a poem. St. Kevin, who was so handsome that he was called Fairborn, shut himself up in this cave, avoiding sweet Kathleen who pined after him. But, at last, Kathleen found out this retreat when looking for him, led by a little dog. The Saint awoke one day as usual, and saw a girl stooping over him, so he shook her off heartlessly, and threw her over the cliff. The girl was drowned in the depths of the lake. Then, at last, the Saint felt pity for her, and said, 'Heaven rest her soul!' and upon his blessing her thus, her ghost appeared with a smile on her lips. Saints are always at an advantage in such legends, and lovers dote even as ghosts. Now the cave was about forty feet above the water, in the side of a rock nearly vertical. 'Your wish will be fulfilled,' said our guide urging on the people, 'if you wish it in that cave. Well, ladies and

gentlemen, climb up.'. But the women on the boat were all
hesitating. Then I said, 'As I didn't embrace his cross for
luck, I will go in and get my wish fulfilled,' and jumped on
to the shore, this tomboy of the Far East. Climbing up the
cliff, I ascended along the cracks in the rocks, and easily got
to the cave. I entered with my husband, and there was no
room left at all. Under our eyes the water spread, and we
said, with a laugh, 'This is not St. Kevin's bed, but St. Kevin's
cabin'. After squatting for a while, we tried to go down, but
the rocks, wet in the rain, were slippery, and we found it very
hard to descend, in spite of the short distance of only about
forty feet. It would not have been nice to play the part of
Kathleen in the cine-cameras of the passengers in the boat.
Before the spectators I tried to show some composure, but
inwardly I felt very uneasy. Our guide gave us directions saying, 'Put your left hand at the rock corner, and put down your
foot in this hollow', but sometimes he said, 'Put your bottom
here', or something like that. I wondered what he meant
by 'bottom' and thought that he meant the sole of my shoe,
but doing that was inconvenient, as there was no foothold,
so I hesitated and he showed his posterior and tapped it!
'I am no tumbler', said I to myself, nearly bursting out and
feeling shaky in my stomach, which made me still more
uneasy. When we got back to the boat without mishap,
everybody admired me, saying, 'Brave girl!' and asked me
what I wished. I answered them, 'I have prayed for fine
weather while I travel through Ireland and Scotland'.
'Poor St. Kevin!' they all said with a laugh, 'He must have
been annoyed at that unexpected and difficult wish'. And
indeed we had no three consecutive days of fine weather
during this trip. Men-passengers of the charabanc had
drunk a bit in the hotel, so on the way back they shouted

from the bus to the peasant girls passing by the road, 'Hullo, dear! Why do you mince like that?' and thus they made merry rather boisterously. A mood like this which is similar to that of a 'cherry-blossom viewing party' in Japan is never found in England. Our bus ran over a goat, but our driver paid no attention to it, and drove on. Soon we came to the Vale of Avoca, and stopped at the Meeting of the Waters to which Moore took a great fancy. The great drawback of this place is the poor colour of its water, and the beauty which is found at the meeting of mountain brooks in Japan, cannot be seen here. Our coach started again and made for Dublin. A drunken passenger fell fast asleep, and never noticed that he had dropped his hat.

§ 2

Killarney

On May 11th, in the morning, we started by rail from Dublin for Killarney and ran for about six hours, south-west, through Ireland. Nearly half of the scenery along the railroad was made up of barren meadows, and when they were first reclaimed, stones that stood in their way were carried along and made into fences. If I say, 'The meadows have stone fences', a Japanese reader may think the Irish extravagant. But the fences which I saw before my eyes, were the monuments to show to what degree the exploitation was difficult. The other half of the land, which could not be turned into meadows, was waste land, dark brown as if scorched. It is called 'bog', and is cut out into pieces the size of a brick to be piled up to dry and made into 'turf'. It is generally used here as fuel, but it must be very smoky and sooty when burned. Few houses are visible. They are all rectangular stone buildings, the roofs being either thatched or slated. Just a single house on a treeless hill, with the stone-wall simply painted white, and not even the shadow of a person to be seen, the only creatures there being ducks floating on the pool of water that gathered in the hole where turf had been dug out — was a very solitary and cold sight. My husband told me that he had put up in a cottage like that when he travelled last time, and was attacked by fleas all night. And no sooner did he manage to doze, towards the dawn, than he was awakened by the quacking of the ducks which came into his room. In this part there was no wood and though Ireland is called an agricultural country, even wheatfields were very seldom met with, and there was an endless stretch of waste land. And the cutting of turf seemed as if the skin of the earth were being peeled off because there was no help for it. A country which is suffering from the chronic disease of famine is indeed wretched. When I heard that place was Tipperary, what I felt was not a traveller's sentiment that we had come 'a long, long way' even from London, but rather the doubt whether they really had a Molly or Kathleen beautiful enough to make them say 'Good-bye, Piccadilly'. Irish girls are called 'colleens'. They have big round eyes and plump red cheeks, and the way they wrap themselves up in blankets is ineffably charming, but I could not find any such girls around here. When I arrived at Killarney, coachmen noisily vied with one another to get their customers, and this sight was rather French than English. With much trouble, we managed to hire a jaunting-car with a very old driver, and started at once for the lakes. The jaunting-car was so constructed that the seats are put facing outwards and looking towards the wheels, so that the passengers sit on both sides with their backs to each other. First of all we visited the ruins of Muckross Abbey, beside the lower lake. The roof having entirely fallen in, and in the wall only the window-frames being left, covered all over with ivy, it looked a pattern of ruins. When we went back again to our car, my husband got in first, relaxing his mind because we were in the country. But he was checked by an old sexton's 'Look here! Ladies first', and he shrugged. Soon afterwards we went along a narrow peninsula which divided the middle lake and the lower. There were a lot of rhododendrons there, most of the blossoms still in bud, but I could imagine the beautiful sight when they should all open. There were many holly-bushes, and from between the trees there was seen a piece of water shining beautifully. Just at the end of the peninsula, there was a small island. As the stream from the upper lake, and the water from the middle lake came down all at once into this lower lake, there was a strong current here for a very short distance, and over that current a bridge was built, called the 'Wishing Bridge', under which you could be taken in a small boat to make your wish. In Ireland, a great many things of this kind are found, and in the Castle of Blarney, if you kiss a stone near the top of the tower, so the tradition goes, you will become talkative, and people who go there, holding fast to an iron bar and getting a guide to hold their feet, hang down like acrobats and lick the stone with head downward. My husband did kiss it last time, so the miraculous virtue of the stone can easily be imagined. As our car ran up the bank of a stream, that led to the upper lake, the scenery became more rough and wild. The guide said, 'That mountain over there is called "The

Eagle's Nest", and on the top of the peak on this side, there is a weird pond called the "Devil's Punch Bowl".' Half-way to the upper lake, we decided to return, and took a short rest. At the far end of the long narrow lake like a river, there were mountains rising from both sides, which seemed to overlap each other; and the dark blue of the mountains gradually became fainter, until it died away in the distance, and that wonderful sight filled my heart with yearning to follow after it to the world's end. The mountains near by, showing craggy rocks covered here and there with moss and heath, revealed a gloomy but wild beauty of strength, resembling the tautened muscles of the shoulders of a northern barbarian, who carelessly hung skin-clothes on them. This sort of savage beauty is not to be found in Japan. Sometimes we would pass by a person proudly walking homeward with a salmon about two feet long. At length we came back to the lower lake and entered the Lake Hotel. A little finger of land jutted out from the shore, and there were the ruins of a small castle standing on it. Two pine trees that had finely twisted branches, rather rare in Europe, were overhanging the ruins, and lilacs of white and purple were blooming beautifully. The scenery was almost too perfect, and I thought with a smile that the shops in Japan would give anything to have such a lovely landscape printed on their fans, which they distribute for advertisement. While I was walking, I met an American from our hotel, and I asked him from what part of America he came. He answered, 'From Chicago', and added in a grumbling tone, 'Nowadays Chicago is supposed to be the nest of hold-ups, so I feel rather small'. A swan was sitting near the sandy beach a little way off, and even when some hiking tomboys approached it, it only flapped its wings, and would not move away. It remained in the same position when I looked out of the window after I had had supper. Was it hurt? The long day was at length becoming twilight, and the scenery, which had much turbidity in the colour of the water, was gradually getting darker and stiller like a Gobelin tapestry, and stars began to twinkle. Everything was dark, except for the swan that appeared white as though in relief, and, thinking that evening had just set in, I looked at my watch and found to my surprise that it was already ten o'clock. The hotel was so old-fashioned that the maids brought us water in a jug for washing, and we found hot-water bottles in our beds.

Next morning we had another walk. All over the grass, beneath the sparse bushes, bluebells were blooming. Squirrels were playing among the ruins, and the morning was fresh and clear. The swan was very likely hatching its eggs. We went back to Dublin by train, and the return trip gave me a splendid opportunity of filling in my diary of the journey.

This week the music festival (Feis Ceoil) had been held in Dublin. A contest of amateur musicians had taken place in several halls and hotels, and the judges gave the winners cups and prizes. We wanted to attend the harp contest, but unfortunately it had finished the day before. We went to the Y.W.C.A. and found a competition of songs in progress. The first one was a chorus. Schoolgirls stood in rows on the stage with faces as if they expected the ill-humour of their master in case they were beaten, and a schoolmistress was nervously arranging them in good order — in fact everything, I thought, was just the same as we see in Japan. In due time this came to an end, and next there was a solo contest. They sang such songs as 'Sands of the River

Dee' and 'The Milkmaid'. I had expected Gaelic songs, but they were all sung in English. A man, just like a tailor, was found among the singers. Sometimes he sang with the expression of a shadowy, slender girl for 'The Milkmaid', sometimes he sang with the very erotic expression of a voluptuous beauty, and all was highly interesting. After that, we went to hear the band in the public hall. A performance was just ending, and the music sounded so loud that it seemed as if it would burst the hall. After playing, the musicians returned to their seats among the audience, and another band went on the stage and played the same piece. All the musicians were in clothes rather the worse for wear or in workmen's apparel, and some had their hats on. As there were many competitors among the audience who had their own rendition for that piece of music, they were all in earnest, beating time with their flutes or bows in their hands. In the end, the judges came up to the stage and criticized them. These judges were all in ordinary suits, unlike England, where they invariably wear decorations on ceremonious occasions. The people who listened intently, craning their necks forward, were also rather rough-looking, and the concert was more like a workmen's conference to decide whether or not to go on strike, than a musical contest, but it was not entirely without its charm.

§ 3

Ulster

On May 13th we drove about a hundred miles from Dublin to Belfast. It took four and a half hours by motor-coach. There were fields here and there along our route, but they were all very barren stony wheatfields, and when I thought of the fact that they change into black beer what little wheat they do raise from those fields, I remembered, with an unpleasant feeling, the big advertisement, 'Guinness is good for you', often seen in the London Underground. All the villages which we passed through looked poor and miserable, but invariably had public-houses. Without seeing any signboards, we could tell at once that they were public-houses, as there were always three or four people in workmen's clothes leaning against their white walls, with dull expressions on their faces. In these parts, all the men generally had reddish-purple noses, while the young Celts possessed pale dingy faces, having, instead of the young pink colour, veins spreading over their cheeks like a net, and the nearer you see them, the more undignified they look. The colours of their hair were all different, some being whitish, even to their eyelashes. Is it, I wonder, because of their Celtic blood that there were many who looked like Frenchmen in uniform? Peasants' houses had entrance doors divided into upper and lower halves, which opened separately. Sometimes they had at the door wagons with raised edges made of splinters woven like a basket. Some taverns had signboards written BONA FIDE on them, which means that they do not sell on Sundays, except to those who come along on foot from afar. Every sight and scene were exactly like those in Synge's plays. Soon we came to the border of Northern Ireland. An asphalt highway was running through an undulating meadow, and there was a Customs House on the roadside where they examined our luggage, asking whether we had cigarettes or not. Although there was not even a chalk-line to show the border from English territory, the money which was current up to that time could no longer be used. What fascinated me in the Irish Free State was its coins. The design on one side of them was a harp, and on the other side poultry, pig or rabbit was represented in bas-relief suggestive of a peaceful country. They were quite different from the coins of other countries, which had king's heads or crowns on them, but we could not use that money any more, and felt much annoyed. Soon we arrived at Belfast. At the first glance it seemed to be a thriving city after the style of London. The things displayed in the shop-windows, the men coming and going in top-hats in the main streets, the rows of cars left in such places on the outskirts as cricket grounds and golf-links — everything showed quite a different turn of mind in the people from that in Dublin, and the town seemed far superior in point of real efficiency. After spending a short time in the town, we went to see the Giant's Ring, about four miles away. We only managed to find the place after asking several times, here and there. Inside a ring nearly a mile in circuit, made of a slightly elevated mound, there was a grassy space, and in the centre there was a dolmen of seven big stones supporting a rock like a table-top. I was told that this was the grave of a chieftain who lived about four thousand years ago. There was nothing exceptionally curious about it, but it was a very rough structure, indeed like the work of a giant. I could more easily imagine giant-children playing with mud, clapping their huge hands with laughter, saying in front of the pile of stones, 'Now it's finished', than imagine, archaeologically, that a chief caused it to be made by oppressing and forcing many tribesmen to work. Climbing up the mound, we looked over the wheatfields outside, and heard a grasshopper singing in the grass, making a big creaking noise.

From its noise and the name of the place, the insect must have been a giant grasshopper, though for all our diligent search we failed to catch even a glimpse of it.

A great many emigrants went over to America from Ireland, and naturally we met a lot of American tourists here. On my return trip also, an American couple smiled at me in the train, and said, 'We've got an Irish maid who is always yearning after gorse, so we had expected a beautiful flower. But ... !' They laughed and complained that England lacked fresh vegetables and fruit. People like these soon take out photographs of their own houses to show them to us, and this couple was no exception.

While I was waiting for a train in the station of Portrush, I looked round and found a thing like a peep-show, in which, if you put a penny in the slot, a house was set on fire, or a doll of a criminal was hanged on a scaffold. Some of the posters had pictures of guardsmen in beautiful uniform with, 'Smart Irishmen are required', or 'Join the army; good diet and dress will be yours', which seemed almost to suggest that the authorities would like to have added, 'You will look very smart, and captivate the lasses' hearts!' And another had, like the posters you would see in a tourist bureau, a picture of scenery in Egypt, with 'Join the army and see the world'. There were five or six of those posters. Irish people sometimes have a very fine physique, and I was told that the men often become London policemen, but all those posters would look very strange to those who come from a country where a conscription system has been adopted.

At about six o'clock, we returned to Belfast, and at once boarded a boat for Glasgow.

§ 4

Scotland in Three Days

On May 15th at about five o'clock in the morning, I awoke and, looking out of my cabin porthole, saw the side of a big ship slowly passing before us. Thinking that we had already entered the River Clyde, I dozed for a short while and then peeped again, and still saw rusty ships' sides, and factories built of concrete. I slept again, thinking that it was quite natural, since this port was a large one and two-thirds of the English steamers were made here. When I lifted my head from the pillow for the third time, there was still . . . ! At last I went out on deck, and found that we were just near the Glasgow Bridge. Directly we landed, we started for Ayr by train. It was a seaside resort patronized mostly by the people of Glasgow. Passing before Burns's statue, we came to High Street. Mingling with old buildings, such as the Tam-o'-Shanter Inn, which still carefully kept its thatched roof, and the tower where Wallace was shut in, there was a Woolworth's sixpenny store. It was selling bathing-shoes, for sixpence a shoe, and selling also Ayr souvenirs of chocolates in a fancy-box of Scottish tartan, with white heather made of beads. All these articles seemed to be waiting for the season. We went as far as Alloway in a rattling train, and saw the Burns Monument. To anybody's eyes, the structure was not in keeping with the surroundings, and by its side were stone figures of Tam-o'-Shanter, Johnny, and his wife, while below the monument they were selling purses in the shape of tam-o'-shanter hats just by the side of Burns's hair — everything was such as to disappoint ardent admirers of Burns. A girl who was standing at the back of a stall to sell purses and other souvenirs, did not even say anything recommending those articles, and so when we were getting out of the place where the monument stood, I said, 'That girl must simply be a guard for Burns's relics there', but the girl of the souvenir-shop at the entrance of the park was also standing with an air of indifference, like a living doll, only just keeping her shop. This seems to be the English way. The only thing which I thought was worth our visit was the river Doon and the picturesque Brig o' Turk. The distant view of the arched bridge, simple and sturdy, made a strong grey bow against the bright, fresh foliage. Under the arch there flowed a stream, one half glittering, the other half dark in the shadow, slowly like the rhythm of the song 'Bonnie Doon'. A robin redbreast was perching on the low rail, which was like a stone fence, and suddenly to my disappointment it flitted up, but soon came back down at my feet, and looked up at me with its beak turned upwards. On our way back we dropped into Burns's birthplace. It was a rustic cottage with his bedroom next to a horse-stable, with a partition wall separating the two. When we came back to Glasgow, we began our sightseeing with the museum. We were very busy, for we were trying to see the second largest town in Great Britain in half a day. In the museum, we found a primitive pair of shoes which they use in the Shetland Islands off the north coast of Scotland. They were made of cow-hide with the hair still on it. We had a pair at home which my husband had bought as a souvenir of his trip to the Aran Islands, but a dog carried them away and they were lost. At the time I showed my regret only out of politeness, because they smelt all the year round, being covered with mould, and when they were lost, I was not without a feeling of relief.

On the 16th, we started from a station where the platforms were built under the ground, and trains came and went belching forth black smoke without restraint — a station so sooty and smoky all over, that I felt a rather stimulating delight. Soon we arrived at Balloch, where we were to cross over Loch Lomond. We crossed the lake in a boat carrying a party of about one hundred and fifty passengers, although it was not yet the season. As the boat sailed, the peak of Ben Lomond rose above the clouds with a mass of snow shining like a brooch at its breast. A sudden shower came on, and young people who looked like Scottish lads, playing bowls with oranges on the deck, ran down below. After the rain-cloud had passed over, the mountain was seen pretty near and there was a waterfall on the craggy side of it, giving a fine view. But the colour of the water was like that of beer, which of course added a slightly bitter-sweet taste to the scenery, but the waterfall of Inversnaid where we landed was so miserably discoloured, that it was not worth seeing. Yet Englishmen's curiosity would seem to be satisfied if they just saw water flowing downwards, perpendicularly. Here we took a coach. The four-in-hand stage-coach had such high seats for sixteen passengers that we got on to them by a ladder, which gave it a good countrified effect. Running up a zigzag road, we came out to a heathy moor which appeared very much like a plateau.

Highland cows stared with round eyes after our coach. We were already familiar with their faces through the advertisements of 'Oxo' seen all over England. We crossed Loch Katrine by steamer. Against the rocky peaks of Ben Venue fresh green Ellen's Isle was floating, and the sound of a bagpipe came droning from the shore. Then we drove along the shore of Loch Achray. As it was Saturday, there were holiday-makers come from Edinburgh, and it was a delight to see young couples or old women enjoying their tea, with thermos-flasks beside them, their cars left by the wayside. But so few children were seen that it almost worried me. We arrived at Edinburgh at about half-past five. According to Scottish custom, in a second-class, commercial, hotel, we were served with a simple supper of only about one dish, with bread and tea, and it is called 'high tea'. We fortified ourselves with some grilled salmon, and started off at once to see the city. The Castle was indeed magnificent. It may be said that the upper part of the rocky mountain, which looks like massive iron to the core, has changed into the castle, or that the base of the Castle has been transfigured into the rocky mountain. What charmed us was that the piled-up stone skirt of the Castle firmly merged into the rock. Princes Street, which is one of the main streets, has buildings only on one side, while the other side is lower than the street, and made into a park. At the far end of the park is the rock wall of the Castle mountain, and trains run at the foot of the mountain, puffing smoke, making the rock still blacker. The Scott Monument has a spire like a shoot of asparagus just growing up, so often seen in picture-cards of Edinburgh. It was a flag-day as well as Saturday, and people in fancy dresses went about collecting money for hospitals, and gipsies were dancing in the cars, and there were ice-cream and other stalls. It was because of this that the streets were strewn with waste paper, the untidiness of which had attracted our notice. When I saw the first star in the sky, it was half-past ten. We returned to our hotel fatigued, and throwing myself into a chair in the hall, I found the seat very hard. Observing it closely, I found it was made entirely of deers' horns. It was not in good taste, but very Scottish.

On the 17th, which was Sunday, I saw groups of soldiers out in the streets. They wore tartan kilts of red and blue, like closely-pleated skirts, and underneath them bare knees were seen, the stocking tops being in a red and white check pattern, and they wore white spats. The big pouch which hung in front was covered with white fur, with two black tassels attached to it, somewhat like the head of a badger, and the whole attire was very elaborate and gallant. I saw a picture in a newspaper with the title, 'Topsy-Turvy', in which a man in this attire and a hiking girl in khaki shorts stood hand in hand, and indeed most of the soldiers seen were walking arm in arm with girls. Then we went towards the older part of the town. A few months ago Shakespeare's *Second Folio* was offered for sale at a book-shop in this neighbourhood and we sent an order from Japan to buy it, but it had been already sold. As it was Sunday, however, that shop and all other shops were closed, and although we wanted to try haggis, a food peculiar to Scotland which was like a sausage stuffed with the insides of animals, they were only to be seen in the shop-windows. The old town was made up of battered houses of four or five storeys, with a great many poles protruding from the windows for hanging out clothes to dry. In this city there were a number of public-houses, and we saw last night a middle-aged woman lying in the street, helplessly drunk, and jabbering incoherently. But to-day children were flocking to the Cathedral, dressed neatly, though in worn Sunday clothes. We followed them, and listened to the morning service. Then we went to the Museum and the Botanic Gardens. The hot-houses were magnificent. What was interesting to me was a bed of

131

plants, which in Japanese are called 'champa-giku' (*Macleya cordata*), and here labelled 'Japan'. This rank weed was planted also in Bergen in Norway, and labelled as a Japanese plant, just as in museums, gigantic salamanders and king-crabs are exhibited as representatives of Japanese animals. This was amusing, because it made me wonder how Occidentals would imagine Japan, trying to harmonize these curious animals with the Japanese scenery, which they have seen on porcelain or fans with Mount Fuji, cherry-blossoms and *torii*. We next visited Newhaven at the estuary of the River Forth. As it is a village inhabited by fisher-folk of Scandinavian origin, the women's costumes are said to be different, but it being Sunday there were very few people about, and we came back and climbed Calton Hill. The monument of Dugald Stewart was again like that of Burns, somewhat awkward in its surroundings, and sure enough it was a copy of the monument of Lysicrates in Athens. So much for the 'Athens of the North'. And what is worse, I was told they built this unfinished monument modelled on the Parthenon to commemorate the Crimean War. I couldn't understand their psychology at all. Another monument was erected in memory of the Boer War. 'For such a war!' thought I. Such morose reflections may have been due to fatigue. I had not enjoyed any sleep the whole night, disturbed by the noise of the trains, and the ox-tail soup which we had had for lunch having been digested a long time ago, I was feeling hungry. At last, I appealed to my husband, saying with a complaining note, 'Let's go back to the hotel'; but although this was the only appeal that I had ever made in this trip abroad, he would not agree, and said, 'Let's go and see the Forth Bridge'. I got sulky, saying to myself, 'England annoys me because they have built a structure in which they used as much as five hundred million tons of iron, as they don't suffer a bit from a shortage of iron'. I got into the bus, wishing with a spiteful mind, that the lingering sun would set quickly. A Japanese hero is said to have called the sun back from setting, but now I wanted to press the sun's head down below the horizon and drown him. But while I was gazing at the extraordinarily big bridge in the blowing wind, the fatigue completely left me, and when I took my high tea in the hotel, my appetite was not satisfied, and I went out to buy some apples for myself.

CHAPTER VI

ENGLAND AGAIN

§ 1

The Lake District

On May 18th we left Edinburgh by train for the South. Even on such a short trip, we met with an old man in the train who would make friends with us, saying, 'Scottish custom is much more like yours than English, in that we celebrate the New Year much better than in England'. Our train ran among wheatfields and meadows. We caught sight of many rabbits, and it was lovely to see them scuttle into their holes showing their white tails. Taking advantage of the spare time between changes in Carlisle, we went to see the Cathedral and the Castle, and the dungeon of the Castle, made of red-brown sandstone, which seemed to have absorbed men's blood, was so gloomy and forbidding that it was sufficient to take away our appetite for three or four hours afterwards. The watchman guided us, saying, 'Be careful! There are two more steps'. Farther down a dark subterranean corridor, there was a space about fifteen feet square, with wall, floor and ceiling, all of stone, and an electric light was shining dimly. A long narrow slit in the wall was open, so that we could see there was some ventilation, but when the light was switched off, the place was pitch-dark. In the wall, there were a large number of holes in a row. When they tortured a criminal, they hung his head here in an iron-ring, so that he stood on tiptoe. The stone floor under his feet was maliciously devised into a slope, and it was slippery because no sunlight penetrated into this dungeon. If he slipped, his neck was, wrung, so he had to stand on tiptoe without even being able to doze in the dark, or to relax his tense feet by an inch. It is a most merciless form of torture. The criminals confined in this dungeon were not even given water, and they licked part of the wall where water oozed out, and there were sinister signs of their thirst in the sandstone, for by continual licking they had made grooves in the wall.

At about four o'clock in the afternoon we arrived at Keswick, and as there was a stone-circle in the neighbourhood, we went to see it. There is a hill named the 'Saddleback', so called from its shape. It was quite spring-like with green and brown mingling, and the peaceful songs of larks were heard below. As we climbed up the road, perspiring slightly, Derwentwater spread beneath, and on the top of the hill about thirty big stones were standing in a circle, the biggest being about eight feet long. The sight of those stones lying on the grass in a ring in the evening sun of late spring, filled me with warm yearning, because it made me think that, even in the Stone Age, which somehow gave me a gloomy feeling when I thought of it, men and women must have had a peaceful spring-time, and a heart to love the genial days on such a quiet hill-side. It was indeed a fine sight. After a while we went down to the lake, and walked to the end of the promenade of the promontory. This is called Friar's Crag, where Ruskin's monument is erected. While I was reading the epitaph on the pointed monument which appeared like a natural stone, the wind whistled through the pines quite unusually. This monument seemed to harmonize well with the place, and in Japan, they would probably have inscribed a 'haiku' of Bashô, the poet-traveller. The view of the lake, which was smooth and quiet, was specially beautiful farther away where there was a small island with the green leaves of its trees so luxuriant that they overflowed the whole island. On the water, the colour of which looked a little dark, the bright green of fresh young leaves was reflected, and allured us to row around in a boat.

On the 19th we started from Keswick in a motor-coach, and went along a mountain road that looked down on Thirlmere. Near here, we now and then came across old shepherds driving flocks of sheep with a long staff called a 'crook', the head of which was in the shape of a '?'. A sheep-dog, which looked very clever but unable to get fat on account of its nervousness, walked round and round the flock, and scolding them with its barking tried to keep them in a group which, however, kept scattering, but he made them keep away from cars, as if to say, 'They give me a lot of trouble'. On seeing the sheep greedily eating grass on the way, and, cowed by the dog, bleating, I did not feel we could compare ourselves to the sheep of God. God himself would not like us to have such sluggish meekness as that, although it might be convenient for pastors. We got out of the coach by the side of Grasmere, and had a look at Wordsworth's Dove Cottage. I was amused to find that the path leading to the arbour, built on something like an artificial hill in the back-yard, was strewn with stepping-stones, which appealed to the Japanese taste. Then we visited his grave. It was a very simple tomb, so simple that we bowed to the poet only after we had referred to our guide-book, because there were two tombs of the same size upon which 'William Wordsworth' was inscribed, one standing on the left of the tomb of Dorothy, the poet's sister, and the other next to his brother's, on the right. Once again we took a bus, and went to Windermere and climbed Orrest Head, the hill at the back of the lake. The lake stretched far away like a winding stream, and the island in the centre seemed floating as if in danger of being blown aside by the wind. Far in the haze, there was the sea. Dreamy-coloured sunbeams filtered through in streaks between the mouse-grey clouds, which brought showers every now and then. The colours of the things seen in the strata of the air in dim, mild and pale hues enchanted me and somehow made me realize I was indeed in England. Looking into *Baedeker*, I said, trying to be clever, 'Isn't it absurd not to put an asterisk against such a lovely place as this?' because I thought I had caught him nodding. 'Why look! There are two asterisks put before the word "View",' answered my husband, and I was humbled. Indeed the Head itself was a poor hill, and *Baedeker* was right. We descended the hill, and went to the lake on foot. Soon afterwards, we once more took a train, and passing Lancaster and other stations, we came to Manchester and drove by car through the streets rich in monuments. We went into another train and entered the Peak District, the highest place in England, composed of limestone. Going along the bank of an unusually large ravine, we arrived at Buxton. This is the highest town in England, situated about a thousand feet above sea-level. We came here because it was supposed to be one of the most fashionable places for mineral springs. Indeed, there were a number of big hotels, the hotel where we put up having about two hundred rooms; and there were four musicians playing to the best of their ability to an audience of only seven or eight. The guests were quite different from those we had seen at Keswick. The hotels in the Lake District were full of tourists. The lounge was also noisy with joyous and simply-dressed people, some tracing on their maps the places which they were going to visit the next day, and others writing postcards, asking, 'What was the name of that waterfall we saw just now?' But in this hotel, they were all formally dressed and all were old and looked bored, never forgetting to clap their hands when the music stopped. Spas out of season seem to be patronized by people out of season in life. Anyhow, the important thing was the hot-springs, but the only words that even suggested hot-springs in a guide-book of Buxton, which was kept at the office of the hotel, were 'blue water' without any description. The rest was all about golf and dance-halls. When I asked the manager, he only told me to go to the bath of the town, and appeared to know nothing about it.

The next day we went up to the source of the mineral water. In a corner in a café there was a tiled well which looked like a bath-tub, and, indeed, bluish water was flowing over the edge. A waitress scooped some into a glass for me, and I found it lukewarm and tasteless. It gave me an uncomfortable feeling, because I felt as if I was drinking bath-water. I was told that the bill for drinking this water for three weeks was three pounds, and the charge for having a bath in the establishment built opposite this house was actually ten shillings each time. But the baths as seen in a picture were not a bit different from ordinary ones.

§ 2

On the Beach at Yarmouth

Our train ran through a plain bright with the yellow flowers of cabbage fields. After coming into England I saw for the first time cultivated ground stretching continuously away on both sides of the railway, and the thought came to me that at last we had come into fertile land. But then no small part of the land was used for beautiful flower-fields like those which we see in printed mousseline. Since they make so light of vegetables, it is natural that the humpback should be called an English disease. In my diary, deaf people and stutterers have been mentioned more than once. But how is it that so few people wear spectacles? Is this not a country where sunlight is scarce? 'It may be good for the eyes to eat so much meat,' said I. Upon this, my husband took out of my bag a pocket dictionary and said with a sigh, 'It may be this little fellow that makes Japanese near-sighted'. Killing time with such talk, we arrived at Yarmouth after dark. Having come to the South, I found that the sun set remarkably soon. The coast was an ordinary English bathing-place with a row of hotels, the beach being well paved, with a pier jutting out into the sea with a recreation ground and cafés at the end of it. The Yare, running into the sea near the bathing-place, clashed with the seawaves about a hundred yards away from the shore, and the white surf ran across in a straight line. I realized now the meaning of the 'bar' in 'Crossing the Bar'. Although the sea did not make a bay, it was calm on this side of the bar, but the river emptying itself into the sea made it turbid.

Good hot-springs and fine sea-scenery are found only in Japan.

On the 21st, we went by bus to Lowestoft, the town farthest to the east in England. A distributing centre of herrings, it had rows of large warehouses near the sea, with piles of barrels, and throbbing oil-engine boats were coming into the canal one after another. The bridges were split in two in the middle letting tall-masted boats through, and cut the traffic for a while, filling the ends with bronze-coloured sailors and fishermen. Most of them wore black sweaters and trousers, which hung down from their necks, being used as aprons at the same time, and over their trousers they wore boots, not for the mud as in Japan, but perhaps for wading through the heaps of herrings. Every workman looked busy and idle at the same time, and though the air was suffocating with the smell of fish and grease, it was not dead as in London, but alive and impure as in a fishing-port. We asked our way to Ness Point. It was on the coast near the mouth of the port, and was pebbled with stones as large as hen's eggs. Turbulent waves came rushing over the beach, and drew back, as it were, rattling their throats. A broken pier which once had a lighthouse on it is the most easterly point of England. My husband, on his last tour, stood on Dunnet Head, the northernmost end of Scotland, and also on the west and south ends of England, so now he finished the four corners of Great Britain. On the wild beach on this dark windy day, an old woman was seen gathering driftwood with a basket in her hand. I also picked some up, and put it into her basket when she came across towards me. Looking after her walking zigzag driven by the waves, along the beach, her black ragged shawl flying in the wind, I began to fancy that the wood which I had picked up for her might have been splinters from a wrecked ship. What sort of porridge would she cook with it, I wondered.

Just turning back towards the port mouth, we found an interesting shed. It was a shanty about six yards wide, but had two quaint wooden female busts double the life size, fixed to the front of its red roof. Their cheeks were coloured red and their dresses green, reminding one of a macaw, but both the colour and the shape were childish and naïve, and not at all loud. These busts had once been attached to the bows of an old ship, and made me imagine the olden days when a boat sailed raising them above, or driving them through, the tide wave after wave, as the sailor who held the rudder managed the boat. On the roof there was built a look-out, and both the weather-cock and the chimney smoke were indicating the violent west wind. An old fisherman opened the upper half of the door, and began to gaze, lengthening an antique brass telescope, at a fishing-boat that was going towards the port. Approaching him, we asked whether we might enter, whereupon he nodded and opened the door. Within there was a fire burning, and on the wall above it was nailed a pair of wooden shoes, which in Holland are called 'sabots'. They were coloured in red, white, and blue, for holding pencils or tooth-brushes. On the mantelpiece were reverently placed, I know not why, cups made of chocolate tinfoil. The four or five fishermen gathered in that room were all old men, and had strong bony fingers. 'Who made it?' I wondered. It was the more interesting, because if it had been a London club, they would have hung Japanese *no*-masks on the wall, or placed some golf-cups on the mantelpiece for ornament. The simple seamen were playing cards in silence, and beside them on the table there was a wooden board in which they had made holes, just like a series of dominoes, putting in them used match-sticks. Wondering, I asked them what it was. They simply replied 'Crib-board!' and nothing more. It seemed to be the scorer in the game of cards, but they gave no explanation. They were not, however, cold to us, and one taking his pipe from out of his mouth pointed to the wall and said 'Japan flag', and smiled, showing wrinkles at the corners of his eyes. It was this taciturn old fellow's way of showing hospitality. Looking up, I indeed found flags of every country in the world, a picture of a shipping company, a time-table of tide and ebb, and a list of flag-signs — all kinds of papers that showed the life of these people were pasted on the wall as well as such a picture as a three-coloured one of a naval review of the English fleet. In the middle a lamp was hung which reminded me of my early years with many sentimental memories, and in the oil there was a wick in coil. Presently one of them stood up and opened the trapdoor above the stairs to the second storey, perhaps meaning us to go up. The garret, used for mending nets, was scattered with creels, and in one part of it there was a look-out protruding. Thanking them for their silent hospitality, we were going out, and I wanted to tip them, but there was something which made it rather difficult to do so. This was the real value of their character. But fortunately, I found a box for a sea-disasters relief fund, so I put some money in it and left them. In this town of Lowestoft there were between houses many long narrow passages called 'scores', leading down to the beach from the streets, so we tried the narrowest one which was in some parts about a yard wide, running between two- or three-storeyed houses for nearly a hundred and twenty yards. More than a hundred of such narrow passages were also found in Yarmouth, and there they are called 'rows'. After returning to Yarmouth, we walked down one of the main streets. It looked typical of a bathing resort, and they were selling 'Yarmouth rocks' as souvenirs. Imitating the 'Edinburgh rocks', they were silly cake made like candy-sticks of white and pink, with a scented flavour. It is also absurd that they should sell these rocks everywhere, whether in the Lake District or in Buxton, naming them after the place and calling them 'rocks'. Those of Yarmouth, having in them shapes of fish, were made a seaside souvenir. Among cakes, the most abominable was the cheap liquorice in strips. It looked just like a bit of coal tar, and to me, it tasted just like it, so I spat it out.

We started from Yarmouth at about one o'clock, and soon we got out of the train at Norwich, to see the Cathedral there. The sides of the roofs being rigid and huge like a house for keeping an elephant in, it was rather repulsive on the external view, but the inside, with Norman arches, was very fine. When we went to see the Norman water-gate, they were playing a football match in a school-ground beside it, and people were pouring in one after another. Considering the number of factories there, the town was not at all rough and seemed rich, while the townsfolk seemed happy and peaceful. We had our tea in an hotel which is said to have existed for several centuries. Just as the old-time inns in Japan had unfloored grounds where the travellers took off their sandals, so the construction of this house, having a courtyard for the people who came on horseback or by carriage, was very antique. The inside of the room showed signs of trading on antiquity. We took our train again for Cambridge. In the seaside districts, the round stones found near the beach were used for plastering into the outside walls of houses, and the walls in which flint stones, made into about three inches square, were used, were usually those of churches or manor-houses. But as we gradually came away from the sea and approached the place where those stones were quarried, ordinary houses were of flint. Even in places where there was very little worth seeing, we could find many interesting things if we were careful, but for fear that my diary would get into arrears again I began to write shaking in the train. If I was not careful, my diary would leave me far behind, and it was a great pity that it was impossible to write about my sight-seeing ahead when I had leisure! We saw town halls everywhere, in Leicester, Yarmouth and Lowestoft. Each had an underground dungeon and exhibited instruments for cutting one's head off. After seeing those town halls one after another, my memory was muddled, but the chaotic state of my mind gave me the conception that ancient cities and towns of England had each its own power, independent of one another.

The places which our train had been running through were mostly composed of marshes, so this district, I have heard, is called the 'fen' district, and wild rabbits were plentiful. Now and then, bluebells were blowing in the shade on the meadows, and when our train flew past, the grass looked beautiful, smoky as if a purple mist had been spread over it. The heath that covered the waste land was still a brown, dead winter colour, and those two or three days were as cold as March. But on the way at a small station, a tottering old woman came in, after embracing an old man who had come to see her off, opened the window wide and never thought of other people's comfort. They are generally careless about the cold. At this time of the year the sheep in this part were shorn and they seemed slender and rejuvenated, but I sympathized with them, thinking from my point of view that they might catch cold.

§ 3

Cambridge

We arrived at Cambridge and put up at the Bull Hotel. On the 23rd, as school began at about ten at the colleges, we had a walk in the 'Backs'. Large horse-chestnut and beech trees that made an avenue along the river, were intertwining their branches bearing young leaves, and the air was filled with the fragrance of invisible flowers. At the tips of the leaves of grass by the roadside, the dew-drops were changing red and blue like so many opals. The streets were narrow, and the students came and went on bicycles. They looked rather like trades-boys carrying books in baskets fixed to their handle-bars, but their faces showed that they had no mental troubles and their soft white skins looked very much softer helped by the soft nuance of the colours of their suits, their coats being reddish-brown and their flannel trousers being mouse-grey. Among Japanese students, no one can be found who might provoke the appetite of an old cannibal, but even I might have been able to eat such young men as they. I believe their bodies are trained very well by exercise, but their white skin is faintly-coloured pink, which reminds us that they lack sunshine during the long winter months. Some of them are extremely tall, but they are rather slender, just like asparagus cultivated under glass. We now visited Trinity College and then the King's College, one after the other, each having its own chapel like a big church. We were greeted with such great names as Newton, Thackeray and Wordsworth. When I had listened to our guide mentioning great names at Oxford, I had thought that only mediocre people were left in Cambridge. But in Cambridge too, I felt that they were telling me of all the great men in England, one and all.

I could not make out where and when the students attended the lectures. In the grounds behind the colleges, cricket, tennis, and other sports were being played. As usual, I was jealous of the beauty of the lawn, but the tending seemed to be an awful business. They were driving horse-drawn lawn-mowers, and self-supporting students were seen mowing here and there. The students always stood aside politely and opened doors for me. This custom of the placidly polite English people is indeed a good thing, but suppose you visit, for instance, an old castle by charabanc. When you think you would like to stay in some room to enjoy the sight from the window a little longer even if you were left behind, some gentleman is sure to be standing upright by the door, waiting for the ladies to leave first. As it is too unnatural to stay in spite of them, we often go out reluctantly. Sometimes I felt so irritated that I wanted to shout, 'I am not a baby. I can walk quite all right by myself'. I wonder how Western ladies feel about this old conventional respect to them, in which they are treated as if they were impotent people. Then we saw the old mulberry tree that Milton had planted in the garden of Christ's College, but its buds were still firm. I was told that it bears fruit, which the students eat, but I thought the tongue dyed purple with mulberries would be more suitable for the country children in Japan, where the sound of weaving-machines is heard coming from the houses. In Cambridge they have 'fellows' gardens' besides the College gardens open to the public. They are gardens set aside for College dons, and we walked in one with Mr. Lowes Dickinson, a fellow of the King's College. He was a critic of civilization and once came over to Japan, and also published anonymously a book called *Letters from John Chinaman*, by which he had attracted the attention of the reading public. He was an old man who looked as if he had a peculiar character, and the Chinese skull-cap he had on, with a red button at the top, became him very well. He also wrote a book about the civilization of two thousand years ago. In answer to my question as to what he was writing now, he replied, 'I am writing about the civilization of two thousand years hence', and looked quite nonchalant, as if he were writing about the flowers around him. On the beautiful lawn in the garden, there were lying some bowling balls, and the lilacs were smelling sweet, while laburnums were hanging their bunches of flowers like golden wistaria, and upon all, the sun of early May was shining, and the young leaves of copper-beeches were glistening with beautiful lustre. The copper gloss was quiet, giving a very English local colour to the garden. We saw Mr. Dickinson again in Paris at the twenty-fifth anniversary of the Kahn Foundation. He attended the ceremony as a representative of England, and he was still wearing his Chinese cap except on special occasions. At the tea given by the President of the Higher Normal School in Paris, I heard him speaking in French, not very fluently, to a man whose hair suggested a poet, but who looked somewhat important. I thought that that man must be a person of importance because the aged English scholar seemed to have been stammering out French words, and I found out that he was Paul Valéry. When I heard some time ago that Mr. Dickinson had died, I wondered with a sad heart whether the critic of civilization who rebuked modern materialism based upon science, had gone to heaven where no noise of motor-cycles is heard.

Then we called upon Mr. Cockerel, the head of the Fitzwilliam Museum. Eighteen years ago, my husband found a copy of the *Life and Letters* of Ch. Darwin with his autograph letter in the window of a bookshop and bought it. Mr. Cockerel asked the shopkeeper who bought it, and on being told that a Japanese student had bought it he told him to tell the purchaser to come round and see him when he next saw that Japanese student. In this way, we came into contact with him. He showed us a place where the letters of famous Cambridge graduates were arranged according to the Colleges they came from, but he seemed very busy with the business of enlarging the building of the Museum, so we parted from him without staying long. Then we visited Heffer's bookshop, but it was closed. As I was familiar with the too frequent 'closed shops' in Japan, I was surprised to find it closed at midday. But the next moment I found that it was the custom to take a rest from twelve to half-past one, by locking the doors of the shops, and I blushed to find insular pettiness in my way of thinking. Speaking of bookshops, we met the keeper of a bookstall named David, who was keeping a booth at a square in Cambridge. The old man saw my husband, who knew him eighteen years ago, and held out his trembling hand in salutation. He said to himself repeatedly, 'Time passes quickly indeed', shaking his head. Consulting our watches, we went back to Heffer's. It did my heart good to meet sensible business men like Mr. Heffer, or Mr. H. of Oxford. The latter spoke in an unflattering tone, and criticized some Japanese customers without reserve. To my husband he said, 'You have entirely grown up in eighteen years, haven't you?' and ringing up a professor of the University, he talked in a friendly way, saying, 'Hullo! Having a nap?' This must be because he was intensely filled with a sense of self-regard for his own profession, and such a tone seemed to me to be entirely natural. He had a very upright carriage, having no superfluous flesh or hollows. His way of speaking was positive and incisive, and both his mind and body seemed firm. Indeed he can be compared to the square style of Chinese writing, and when I saw such a firm, steady person, I felt uplifted and thought that I would also walk bravely in this life.

Then we called on Mr. B., a linguist. The space in front of his study was laid out something like a greenhouse and the sight of not very uncommon flowers there gave us an easy comfortable feeling, as they were put in such a way that suggested they were kept with love. As his wife was just weeding in front of the hall, I helped her while I was waiting for our car. Even though it was only for ten minutes, Cambridge, where I had a chance of coming into contact with the earth, is recollected with much more familiarity than Oxford. The power of the earth is indeed remarkable.

§ 4

Spring Events

I saw May-day in London. The day before, I went by myself to a tea-party of the Royal Society of Literature. As lectures were going to be given by such authors as Drink-water and de la Mare, I was a little afraid of attending them, but contrary to my expectations, I found the audience were mostly ladies past middle age. Hearing me say I had a child of fourteen years, a quick-eared old lady said, with admiration, 'Oh! It was marvellous of you to come to England when you are so young, only fourteen'. I corrected her mistake and said it was my son's age, to which she replied, without showing even a smile, 'You must send him to Oxford'. When I said, among other things, 'As to-morrow is May-day, I hope it will be fine', she remarked, 'But May-day is gradually dying out, and such a splendid one as we saw in the old days can now never be seen'. May-day only reminded her of maypoles. Surely those old ladies had never been worried, as Japanese women have, about their sons' and grandsons' contagion by the dangerous left-wing thought.

Indeed, as we had heard that in London a maypole was actually to be erected only at Walworth, on the outskirts, we went out there to see it, but unfortunately, the festival had ended early in the morning, and everything had been taken away. According to what I was told, the top of the maypole is made to revolve, and five-coloured ropes hang down so that they weave beautiful figures, when children dance each holding a rope. But the ropes had already been coiled up, and the flower-cart, which carried the girl chosen as the Queen, was broken and left in a miserable state. The hall there, however, being on the site of a church where Browning was baptized, was called Browning Hall, so that we were able to see in the library the photo of his study and a lock of his hair, one of his hats and some other relics. The hall was further used as a home for poor old people and as a consulta-tion-room for weak children, and the ultra-violet-ray lamps placed there made me think of the definite relation between the sunless misty country and young hunchbacks. In the afternoon we went out to Hyde Park to see how May-day was going on. I found this park very interesting at any time. The part, from the hillock where wild rabbits are fed, to the statue of Peter Pan, is the territory of children looked after by their mothers, and scenes such as a pigeon, perched on a smiling old man's shoulder, fed from his mouth full of peas, and a girl who seemed to come here every day to give crusts to the sparrows, were common peaceful pleasant sights. Along the pond where Peter Pan's statue stands, we walked and soon came to Kensington Gardens next to Hyde Park. In spite of the fact that they form really one big park, the quality of the people in the two parks is quite different, and the people in Kensington Gardens are more high-class. Sometimes we see nursemaids who have newly-ironed caps on their heads pushing perambulators, and sometimes an Indian nobleman's child accompanied by his stolid tutor can be seen taking a walk, with his dark face looking pale seemingly through the difference of climate. On a Sunday, it thrives with smartly-dressed people rambling about on their way home from church, and everywhere chairs are placed for them to rest. And those chairs are mostly placed close together in pairs, as if they were embracing each other. We sat together complacently, saying that Japanese who come to study in England away from their wives, might feel reluctance when they have to take one of a pair of chairs, leaving the other empty. But soon we were approached by a person who charged for the seats.

We went round the pond where a model yacht was sailing, and criticizing the prosaic bulkiness of the Albert Memorial, we came back again to the east side of Hyde Park. Here it is mostly covered with grass, and the place near the gate by Marble Arch is always occupied by unknown speakers who gesticulate with their fists on rostrums, surrounded by crowds of spectators. The slope farther on from there is scattered with big trees which throw pleasant shadows on the grass, and young men and girls are lying down leisurely, embracing each other, looking at the sky or whispering, and are enjoying themselves peacefully. In a book of travel, written by a Japanese who came to this country accompanying some prince, the author reproaches them seriously, saying, 'What a strange monster with two heads and one body!' but they only made me smile. From of old, this place has become, somehow or other, a rendezvous for lovers, and it is amusing to see a sort of distinct localization, as in plants and animals. Now as the May-day procession was coming to this lawn on the eastern side of the park, a considerable number of lookers on had gathered at about three in the afternoon. Presently, near the entrance, red flags appeared over the waves of crowds, one after another, and the procession came in watched by mounted policemen on both sides, every sixth rank. I thought it was rather strict, but when the people scattered in the large park, the policemen soon began to stand and talk peacefully with each other and the tenseness was soon dispersed. The leaders of the procession stood up on the carts which had been placed here and there, and at once began to make speeches, the spectators gathering round them as thick as ants. Their minds were intense, like those who gather to listen in to the wireless before a radio-shop, but their attitude was like that of the people who listen to the news of the events of the world far away, so that the speakers who had intended to agitate them must have felt discouraged. A man was shouting before a flag upon which was written the name of some league in the East End, and a middle-aged woman was crying, 'Give independence to India!' But just behind the human fences which surrounded those people, young men and women were lolling leisurely on the grass and some nurses came pushing 'prams', so that, frankly speaking, the sight was so calm that it made me feel dull. Their speeches sometimes tended to be violent, but as policemen did not take them seriously, they seemed the more ineffective. Nevertheless, about four people were arrested by the police. It was while we were listening to a priest before a red flag with the device of the hammer and sickle, shouting, 'Does Jesus approve that a priest should not stand up afraid of the anger of bishops?' and just when he was getting considerably worked up, there was some disturbance behind us, which attracted everybody's attention. A man was being skilfully driven away among the crowd of people by a mounted policeman with the nose of his horse. He stepped aside five or six steps and turned back and, finding the long face of the horse just above his head, he reeled backward. The sight was so funny that everybody burst out laughing, and while his friend was making a fuss, saying, 'Give him back!' and was only irritated being unable to face the police, he was taken away by two burly constables, who took hold of him by the arms. As the constables were also laughing, turning their heads aside, it was difficult to tell whether they were giving a hand to a sick man or arresting an offender. Though they were laughing looking aside like that, they were so enormously big that there was no fear of the man's getting away. The priest who had the audience's back turned on him, did not lose the chance and said, 'From this high place I will tell those who cannot see the scene what is going on . . . Now the horse has blown through his nose on the man and he is frightened . . . !' Thus he entered into the spirit of the thing together with the audience, and then finding a chance again, 'What causes such a sight as this? . . .' In this way he skilfully drew the hearers' attention again to himself, like a very trained speaker. I was very much struck by the way of the authorities who made people's minds exhausted and tired, wasting their energy to no purpose, instead of suppressing their discontent simply to enhance its explosive power. But just because of this, it was a very insipid and dull May-day for us.

May 30th fell on Chestnut Sunday, and posters were put up in the Underground stations, so we went to Hampton Court and Bushy Park. On the way, we passed people going hiking. It was not a rare sight to see a girl in shorts, or riding on the pillion of a motor-bike, clasping the man round the waist, but we sometimes saw a bicycle which had two sets of pedals and seats in front and behind, the distance between the wheels being longer, and man and wife riding on them. It made me smile to see them go up a slope with joint efforts, because it seemed a sample of a couple working together for a living. Hampton Court was beautiful, with trees on both sides of a long narrow moat making a little dense wood, but I personally did not like the general taste of the Court. Beside an Elizabethan garden called a knot-garden made of pruned shrubs and flowers in patterns, there was a vine planted in 1768, completely filling the hothouse, the base of the trunk being six feet nine inches in circumference. An entrance-fee was charged to see this vine. The inside of the Palace was filled with paintings and tapestries as usual. I thought it was rather silly to hang a tapestry on which a picture of circumcision in life size was woven, no matter how much the sight of the circumcision might be an object of religious faith.

§ 5

The Derby

The Derby was held on June 3rd. As it is such a great occasion that they say, 'Don't speak of the English character until you have seen the Derby', we planned not to cross over to the Continent until after we had seen the race. Fortunately it was a very fine day. In the morning, we went to the motor-coach stand as arranged, where we found an old couple who had a bundle done up in a cloth having the mark of a well-known Japanese shop. We went up to them and found that they were Prof. C. of the Commercial University, and his wife. The race-course is at Epsom, at some distance from London. There was a grand-stand near the finish of the U-shaped track, and thousands of buses were ranged on both sides of the fences. The rear rank is occupied by double-decker red buses, and when you look at them from afar they look like rows of houses standing close around. Crowds rolled up one after another. I heard that three hundred thousand people had gathered the year before, so this year it would not be less than that. Our coach held thirty-five passengers and was in the second rank from the front. At the back of the ranges of coaches, there were bookmakers' booths in a row, and behind that row, in the open place enclosed by the U-shaped track there were seen all over the area penny-rolling stalls and coco-nut shies, which we described, when talking about Bank Holiday, but as usual no toy stalls at all and very few food stalls were found, though there were some show-tents here. A big woman weighing half a ton, a dwarf, a curious dance — dancers standing outside the curtain, and when the show was going to start the curtain suddenly dropped down, suggesting by the gay noise of music something worth seeing happening within — these and the thickly-coloured advertisement boards were just like the shows which we see at the festival of the Yasukuni Shrine in Tokyo. We went into a tent to see boxing. It would be cruel to criticize boxing on such a low standard, but there was apparently no interest of piquant art, which is found in bull-fighting or Japanese wrestling; it was only savage and brutal. We also entered a tent where a dwarf was being shown. The head was as large as an ordinary person's, but the body was soft and small. It would be possible to meet with a dwarf, probably only a little bigger than this, any day in the streets of London. What astounded me were lavatory shops! Some were tents, while others were like police-boxes, and you gave a penny to use it, but there was nothing very strange inside. When a rival shop is opened near one of them and it does not thrive, the shopman goes inside, carries it on his shoulder and moves to some other place on the grass. And the people of this country think nothing of lying down on the same grass. How amazing they are! An old gipsy with a reddish black face kept her shop with a signboard upon which was written, THE PRINCE OF WALES HAS CONSULTED US. WHY NOT YOU? The shop was a carriage with a chimney, and on the windows there hung lace-curtains. This was a trimly furnished one among the rest, the others being tattered caravans drawn by horses or motor-cars. These gipsies wander from town to town, where festivals seem to take place — beggars playing on flutes and girls singing. Among the greasy middle-aged women, there were many who still retained the features suggesting that they roved from the South. Though they came originally from India, their skin was brown and rough like that of the American Indians. The crowds kept on increasing, and they made seas of human faces. Men, who looked exactly like boxes inlaid with shells, walked between cars, having shell-buttons all over their black velvet dress, which I learned was the full dress of old London cockneys, and men offering 'tips' on the betting for sixpence, walked round recommending themselves.

People now began to consider which horse they should bet on for the first race, and from the booths behind, they got their betting tickets for their horses. I have heard that in the case of a favourite, even if it wins, you are sometimes given only twice or four-fifths of the betted money, but in the case of an 'outsider', where there is very little chance of winning, you are given ten or sometimes a hundred times as much. Big betting seemed to be done elsewhere, but the people near us mostly betted one or two shillings. Mr. M. and Captain S. betted according to the forecasts of the newspapers. The only people looking on idle and leisurely were Mr. S. and ourselves.

Soon the King and Queen appeared on the stand. The sounding of the bell. When the start was reported, only the shouting of the people's voices came in waves, approaching like a gale, and the sound of the hoofs mingled with it. Immediately, the various colours of the vests of the jockeys who stooped low on the horses' backs, skimmed over the people's heads. While they were shouting noisily, 'Blue was first', 'Number seven', 'No, thirteen', a plate of numbers slipped up on the notice-board. Getting out of his car, the Captain shouted, 'Mine's won! Mine's won!' and went to get the money, so I followed him and saw five shillings jingle into his hand, which held out his ticket. It was five times as much. It was rather disappointingly simple. Thirteen or fourteen horses ran at a time, and there were six races. To-day there were very few surprises and the newspapers were correct in their forecasts, so amateurs won to a great extent. In each of the six races, the Captain betted on two horses, and one of the two won without fail, and he made quite a profit! Accordingly, the betting booths had to pay out considerable sums, a few of them even having to close their shops, and there was trouble because of non-payment, and some people were taken away by the police, but on the whole I was impressed by their quietness, for I never heard harsh words. By degrees the crowds became engrossed in the races, and everything became very much alive as if it was boiling, aeroplanes and balloons flying and ascending in the air. Just before the third race, in which Cameronian took part, the noise of the people was exactly like a huge pot seething on the boil, and people shouted, 'Cameronian!' here, there and everywhere. Excited by the noise, Mr. M. lost his ticket for Cameronian, and very astonished, he searched all his pockets. Taking out his handkerchief, purse, boxes of cigarettes, which were indispensable to him, a match-box, a pocket notebook and penknife — everything, he searched every pocket of the sixteen, six in his coat, four in his waistcoat, four in his trousers, and two in his overcoat. The Captain, who was cheerful over his winnings, said, jeeringly, 'If you were an octopus, you would be able to search all your pockets in two goes, with your eight arms!' and I also joined in, partly because I envied him for his pockets, for I had felt like demanding the same rights between men and women in the matter of pockets, because the fashion in women's dress did not allow pockets and I was suffering much inconvenience. Being annoyed by our banter, he went to buy another ticket. All this was a cheerful and gay episode befitting the Derby! Soon the race started. 'Cameronian!' 'Blue! Blue!' 'Hurrah! Hurrah!' The shouting approached like a tidal wave, and indeed the blue-vested jockey came first and swept away at once. The sound of the horses' hoofs were soft because of the grass, and the horses were very toylike probably on account of the gay colours of the jockeys. I could hardly take the race seriously, finding it so trifling for such great betting. I have heard only of good luck, such as a workman getting three thousand pounds, or a man saying that he made a profit of one pound last year, but while on one hand this gambling is so openly done, there must be on the other hand cases where people buying furniture or clothes on the instalment system now in vogue, spend all their payment money on the horse races. If it should happen to be the landlord of a boarding-house, the bailiffs would come to the house and take the bedsteads and peel off the carpets, much to the boarders' anger and consternation.

It was five o'clock when the races ended. Like the ebb of the tide, motor coaches and people went home, and there at that time, the true character of the English was revealed. The rows of people were waiting for the bus like long snakes, and the last ones standing at the tails would not be able to get home until about eight or nine o'clock, and most of them had been on their legs the whole day. Their sense of public order was enough to astound us, but their physical strength and mental leisure were also enough to surprise us. They did not show any sign of awaiting their turn by suppressing their impatience, but they simply made a row with leisurely

appearance. We had an appointment for a dinner party, so
we were very much irritated within ourselves. On our way
back, in every village, children were seen scrambling for
coppers thrown at them. It is a tradition on this day, and
therefore, it is traditionally believed that to allow them to do
this will not do harm to their character. It would be almost
senseless to be too serious about this, but what I hate is their
attitude of taking it for granted that they will not go to
excess in anything.

§ 6

Dinner with the Binyons

Our hotel was near the British Museum, so I sometimes
went out by myself and walked in the Egyptian rooms to
enjoy a feeling of being away from the present day. Later
when we went over to Egypt and saw the ancient towns on
the Nile, the days I spent in those rooms proved very useful.
On the other hand, however, while travelling in Egypt and
Greece, I often experienced great disappointment, for every
night I read *Baedeker* in what little time I could find in
preparation for the sightseeing of the next day, and reading
it with the joyful excitement and anticipation of seeing
splendid sculptures and columns, I found at the bottom of
the descriptions, the words, 'Now in the British Museum'.
But Greece of the present day is too poor for us to cry, 'Return Greek things to Greece!' for Turkey lies next door, and
Italy advances into the Archipelago and Greece is too much
unsettled to be trusted with the treasures of the world.
Thinking somewhat like this, I felt I would like to uphold
England, because I was greatly fascinated by the atmosphere

of the Museum, which was quite suitable for ancient times. When I am alone in the Assyrian room, where a lot of sculptures are exhibited, such as a stone monument of a king with rich curled beard, and a dying lion pierced with an arrow, boldly done in relief, I am filled with joy as if I were gloating on my favourite things collected around me. It is more than cheap to get such satisfaction, without paying for admission, but I probably felt like that because the things exhibited were in comparative disorder, and being strong, they were not encumbered with glass cases. Upstairs, there are a lot of Indian things. Why is it that the Buddhist sculptures of India are strangely sensuous, giving out a stuffy air? In a hot country, where the blood is boiled, human desire congested because of unnatural asceticism seems to have burst out as pimples on the surface of the stone. They gave me an unpleasant feeling, which is half fearful and half cynical, and very much like the feeling which you get when something sits heavily on your stomach.

In one of the rooms, there were vases, and vases, and vases! Thousands of vases were displayed from the Greek age to the Roman age ... black ones, red ones, and white ones! It is very strange that it was only about these vases that I was made to feel, 'What plenty! They ought to give at least twenty or thirty to Japan!'

In another, the customs and manners of the natives of the South Seas, Australia, Africa and so forth, were shown. One day, we were looking round with Mr. M. and two or three others. In front of an exhibition-case in which necklaces made of stringed cowries, dried-up heads of men, a weapon made of a stick of a coco-nut tree with sharks' teeth embedded in it, and other such things were kept, a friend of his, an official of our Department of Communications, saying,

'Well, well! How horrible!' as if looking at the things of the inhabitants of Mars, was accosted by an old man who came up to us and asked him, 'Are these the things of your native country?' Mr. M. answered, 'We are Japanese, you know,' but there did not seem to be so much of the 'you know' about him! The question was, of course, well-meant on his part, so the man who was questioned, being all the more dispirited, turned on his heels, saying with a voice that sounded as if his stomach were empty, 'Let's go home'. The rest of us went on seeing other exhibits with the smile of a person who has eaten something sour.

It was two days before we left London that we were invited to dinner by Mr. Binyon of the British Museum. We came back in a hurry from the sightseeing and visits which took the whole day, and changing our dress, we went out.

Russell Square is only a small piece of land planted with trees, but squirrels were living there. Passing by the square, we turned one or two corners and came directly by the side of the British Museum. On the pavement there was a tattered hat beside landscapes drawn by a beggar. We went to the front gate, along the fence which is made of iron bars, strong and simple. It is a quiet street with a row of shops on one side only, and added to that, people in London never stare, so it was quite comfortable even in Japanese dress.

Going through the front gate, the building of the Museum stood in heavy grey with two wings protruding forwards, surrounding the open place before the front steps, and in the right wing, Mr. Binyon's family were living. Before the door of the drawing-room upstairs, we stopped and were gazing at some flowers arranged in a pot, somewhat in the style Japanese flowers are arranged, when Mr. and Mrs.

Binyon came out saying with a laugh, 'Welcome, Professor and Mrs. Ichikawa! Don't look at those flowers. It is only an imitation of your "ikebana". As we were fascinated by it, we sometimes try to copy it, but not to show to the people of its origin!' I sat near the window beside Mrs. Binyon. From the window, the portico of the Museum was seen aslant. Grand columns of the Ionian style standing like the trees of a forest have for their basis the lines of steps from which stretches a gravel road that leads to the gate. On both sides, there are rectangular green lawns, and the prospect which has depth in a grand way is dotted here and there with sightseers coming and going, who are in just large enough numbers to make it a good landscape picture. Mr. Binyon, in contemplation, would find it distant enough not to feel it annoying, when he wants to give his eyes a rest, casting them out of the window, and he would find it interesting when he feels bored, because his gaze would look upon the scenes as in a picture-scroll. There were a group of people who seemed to have come up from the country, gazing at the sculptures on the pediment with heads thrown back, one of them pointing to it giving some explanation. Some people were going up the steps to the library with quick paces as if on business, with big portfolios under their arms. The man who has just come out with a camera hanging from his shoulder and a *Baedeker* in hand, must be a Japanese. I gazed at the scene with breathless interest. It was just like seeing an etching of Hiroshige's landscape, and a flock of white doves flew down, scattering like flower-petals, softening the hardness of the scenery of the print. 'I really have taken a fancy to this window', I whispered. Mrs. Binyon said, 'Yes, my mother also used to sit here often all day, after she got weak in body'. Thinking that they must be living here for a long time, I was sitting before her, gazing on the scene intently. She was a gentle old lady, making one feel at home and easy, notwithstanding that she was herself thoroughly graceful. Preserving the faint charm of youth in her soft calmness, she reminded me of silvery grey velvet that flickers a faint purple in the sun. In the meantime Mr. and Mrs. Robert Lynd, Mr. and Mrs. de la Mare, and Mr. and Mrs. Ellis Roberts came one after another, and Sir Henry and Lady Newbolt were the last guests to arrive. The latter had come up to town all the way from Salisbury. Sir Henry was an extremely handsome old man and I should rather say that he was surrounded by a pearly atmosphere all over, than that he had pearly hair. If I say that I felt the room become faintly brighter directly he came into the room, anyone who knows this gentleman personally would never laugh, thinking that this was an exaggeration. I was simply charmed, thinking that genuine noblemen must be gentlemen like him, and I could not take my eyes off him. Lady Newbolt was also a graceful lady, but she was rather hard of hearing and listened to me through an ear-phone. An old lady like her is not rare in England, but as I had to broadcast my poor English into the mouth of the trumpet, I was a little embarrassed. Presently, the dining-room downstairs was opened and I seated myself between Mr. Binyon and Mr. de la Mare. I was rather frightened to be spoken to by Mr. de la Mare who evidently had little compassion upon my English. 'How do you like England?' 'What did you like best in London . . .?' I had resigned myself to these questions, with which I was always compelled to admire England by English people whom we met for the first time, but I frankly answered, 'What I like best in London are the policemen, cart-horses and Simpson's beef-steak. They are all strong and substantial . . . !' Then he asked again, 'Then what are the things you don't like?' I replied, 'Finnan haddock, which is served every morning, and the stuffy smell at the entrance of the Tube.' 'What do you think strange?' 'The tall hats of Eton boys,' I answered. 'What scenery do you like best?' 'What do you think of English women . . .?' I was asked, 'Where did you go to-day?' 'As we had trudged along doing so much sightseeing, the shoes of both of us were worn down, so we went to have them repaired, and then . . .' Thus I spoke expecting that he would think, 'Ha, ha, she is tired!' but he asked again, 'What book do you refer to for your sightseeing?' I answered, '*Baedeker*', and he said, 'That's no good. You ought to have a book made in England . . .', and he admired the Blue Guide, which seemed very like *Baedeker*. When he asked me again, 'What do you think the worst taste in our country?' I wanted to have nonplussed him, by answering, 'In our hotel, in the lavatory, an advertisement is printed on the toilet-paper, in which a lovely little child's face is drawn', but convention forbade me to say such a thing at dinner-table. So instead, I said just as I thought, 'That people make graves in the church which can be walked over, and that people "encore" in such a play as *King Lear*', and he said, 'It would be in the way if the graves were standing'. Oh! The best thing to do was to smile. 'Why don't you like "encores"?' I looked towards Mr. Binyon, sending him a glance of distress, asking for his help, and he at once took the conversation into his own hands and explained to him the taste of Japanese plays and *no*-plays. Being set free, I looked round and saw that the gentleman with a short jutting chin, in the Irish way, was Mr. Lynd, and the plump gentleman like a literary celebrity was Mr. Roberts. I could also now heartily appreciate my dinner at last. It was a carefully arranged dinner, though not too elaborate, and when people in full evening dress or dinner-jackets were having loganberry jam full of pips, I thought it was very English. But my husband told me that in spite of their ceremonious dress, Sir Henry Newbolt had been telling him, 'Lately, in England, they are getting gradually more and more informal'. Of course, he himself wore white tie and white waistcoat, and one would never have thought that he had been shaken in a train for nearly three hours. Mr. Binyon, the host, was also in full evening dress.

During the latter half of the dinner, Mr. Binyon spoke to me mostly. 'Just now,' said he in a quiet tone, 'you counted as one of the interesting sceneries Stonehenge with an aeroplane flying over it, and I thought the contrast between the two to be very nice. But since the neighbourhood of Stonehenge became a military training ground, we have started a society to keep the scenery from being spoilt by that,' and he added, 'The Eton hat seems very precarious, but the straw hat of Harrow is still more easily knocked off, the brim being very wide and the crown very shallow.' Everything he said only needed my saying, 'I see', and it gave me a good rest. I was partly delighted, and partly ashamed to think that he had been listening to my remarks which I had had to make up in my extremity. But thanks to him, my spirits were restored, and I even spoke of my own accord and said, 'I am going to see the Derby to-morrow leaving this country the day after. No! It's not that I'm fond of horse-racing, but because Mr. Nichols told me that I must see the Derby in order to understand the English character. You Englishmen are so enthusiastic about it, aren't you?' Mr. Binyon leaned close to me and said, 'I have never seen the Derby in all my life', and nodded three or four times slowly with his mouth slightly open. His mouth had every semblance of a laugh but no sound came, and this was one of his peculiarities. Since the time when he showed us round the Museum Library for the first time, turning round among the bookcases crammed with books, and saying 'Too much', I have noticed this habit of his several times. He looked softly into my eyes for a short time, as if to say, 'Well, you understand what I mean?'

§ 7

The Sights of London

It is very delightful indeed to walk in Westminster Abbey, looking up at the columns, leisurely, quite apart from the greed and duty of a sightseer. The Gothic columns that stand in rows, spreading outwards at the upper end, make high and loosely constructed tunnels above the aisles. If you look upwards, the lines of the branches of the columns shoot out from both sides, making beautiful designs of hemp-leaves, and up to the deep end of the altar, columns continue in lines so long that the end of the aisle looks very narrow. This style of cathedral architecture always reminds me of a beautiful avenue — not an avenue of thickly growing ever-green trees, but of lindens or elms with slightly yellow leaves, or bare of all leaves. This is also a road that leads to heaven, so it is not unnatural to regard the columns as an avenue. The air resting there looks green and smoky in the faint sunlight that peeps through the high windows; even the air has an intellectual grace proper to Westminster, giving the impression that it is mingled with the smoke of cigars of good quality, rather than mingling with the smell of a temple where incense is wafted. What I thought, looking upon those columns, was neither of the history of the famous cathedral, nor of the grand coronation-scenes of the generations of kings who had been crowned here, but was of the avenue of *keyaki* trees in the suburbs of Tokyo, which we had heard were going to be felled down, and I wondered what had become of those trees, with a sad feeling far away towards Japan. There is nothing in Japan that could remind one of a Gothic cathedral. Thinking of all the works of art in Japan, I could not think of anything that would even suggest a shade of this temple. Only the avenue of *keyaki* trees represents some aspect of it. 'Woodman, spare that tree! Touch not a single bough.' This verse made me yearn after poets, and I stepped towards the Poets' Corner, but I would like to say that the word 'corner' represents here rather the sense of smallness than of quietness which the word usually conveys, it was so much like a small blind alley. Just as we see, with admiration, every kind of food displayed on the shelf in a corner of a department-store, so we read, as we walk about, the names of all the poets one after the other on the wall, saying, 'Here's Thackeray!' 'There's Macaulay!' This superficial air of sightseeing was to me most distasteful, but it could not be helped, and on seeing the monuments on the wall, I said, 'Oh! This is Tennyson', and 'Look! There's Dryden', and I wanted to see their tombs, but I found other visitors standing on them. I thought that probably under that pair of brown shoes was the tomb that I wanted, and while looking at those legs, waiting for them to move, I began to think that spats were not yet out of fashion, for the gentleman wore them, or that those high heels were rather too high for English women. In this way, the sentiment which was beginning to swell up like a balloon in my bosom entirely collapsed, and I moved on without seeing the tombs, thinking it silly to follow only people's heels like geese. Browning's tomb has some peculiarity in that it is of a chocolate colour, and there is inlaid with gold a design something like cherry-blossom on the upper part and a conventionalized thistle-like design on the lower part. On the blue-black stone beneath it is inscribed that his wife is buried in Florence. Breaking the eternal love of man and wife, and detaching him from the clear blue sky of the country of which he sang, 'Open my heart, and you will see graved inside of it "Italy",' they inserted him between Tennyson and Chaucer, which made me think that this way of adoring great men was indeed very English. It made me think further that even the tombs of poets are used as instruments of the country to show that England abounds in great men, so much so that such chosen people as these must be pressed into such a tiny place as the Poets' Corner, and this impression made me dislike that nook. Another bad impression was given to my mind, when a priest in a long-skirted black robe answering to my inquiry as to where Browning's tomb was, pointed it out with the toe of his shoe which appeared a little under the robe, saying, 'Here it is'.

There can be no objection to raising as many monuments as they like, because they are quite different in nature from tombs, but the sight of the wall where those monuments are piled up one above the other, Shakespeare's standing figure, Longfellow's and Milton's stone images, Johnson's statue and so on, simply made me think that they are all, all very great, but the feeling left behind was one of sympathy for those poets who seemed uncomfortably confined and of anxiety over the fact that there was no more room left. I wondered if they were not going to care for the poets to come. Do they think that they will not have any more poets who are worthy of being set up in stone, or are they not going to carry the great poets into this place any more, thus abolishing the age-long custom? Worrying over this was very unnecessary, for if they thought it proper, they would squeeze them into the place by the side of Johnson or near Dickens. It is very ironical that people, who had no experience in life of being crammed into a train or a bus because they were born in England, should have to wedge themselves after their death into the hosts of poets with their shoulders rubbed together as in a crowded tram-car in Japan.

As I had been acquainted with the Tower of London only through the writing of Soseki Natsume, when I actually did visit it, I felt as if I were seeing the huge bones left in the soup of his writing, which is rich in flavour. Of course, I knew that his writing was born of this building, but as the soup was so delicious, I was greatly disillusioned as if I had attacked the bone of a chicken anticipating how sweet it would be. The Tower itself was indeed weird, the instruments of torture being especially interesting, for they were very primitive and practical at the same time. It keenly amused me when I thought that a man who needed a beautiful case with a lot of implements in it just for polishing his nails, could be beheaded with an axe and a tree stump, hollowed out a little in the middle. Up to that time, however, I had always associated the axe with a fairy story about the honest wood-cutter and had a peaceful idea about it, but after this my outlook towards it was somewhat changed. Why is it that I was strangely troubled by the thought that the axe might be firmly stuck into the block because of the force, and did not easily come out, rather than by directly imagining the cutting of the head?

Interesting was the 'Traitors' Gate', a gateway on the Thames through which boats that carried prisoners came and went, but the rest was too much like a museum; for instance, the scribbling of the criminals, being kept under glass before crowds of sightseers, inspired no creepy feeling. Every room was full of arms and armour. The armour of Europe, looking like robots or beetles with the joints bending like the legs of a cricket, was not artistic to see. When I saw the performance of *St. Joan* in Tokyo, in which silvery armour of this kind glittered, and clanked with an awful noise, I imagined the battle as one between aluminium lunch cases, and I felt entirely disgusted with European armour. Japanese armour is far more beautiful, the names even being artistic according to its kind, for instance, some are called, 'Little cherry-blossoms stitched . . .' and indeed I found here a suit of Japanese armour which was a gift from Mongolia. Is it booty captured at the time when the Mongolians invaded Japan in the thirteenth century? It was of a very practical kind.

What gave me a lasting impression in the Tower of London was the room in which the treasured crown is kept. Since it is labelled that it is the crown which is used for the coronation ceremony of the British king when he is enthroned, the jewels, which seem to be about half an inch in size, appear to be genuine. Another evidence of their genuineness is given by their being kept within bars like those of a cage of lions. If I say, 'It is treated like a fierce animal', the crown may answer, 'No! Not here. The fierce animals are on the other side of the cage'. Indeed it would be very interesting if you could see from inside the cage the faces of the people who peered into it. A Chinese proverb says that a small man commits a sin when he is tempted by a jewel, but when a big country is tempted by big jewels, it will surely be committing a great sin in such a place as the Transvaal.

Over the glass case, which is enclosed within the iron bars, an iron net is placed, and it is said that if anyone touches the case, the net automatically begins to work, arresting his hand, the door of the room is closed, and the bells everywhere ring. If they fear so much the possibility of its being stolen, they might have placed it on the shelf of the property-room of a revue theatre. No one would dream of stealing it.

In the garden, the Beefeaters were standing to attention in red velvet with gold braid, and four ravens out of the famous five were picking up the crusts that the visitors had scattered, spitefully driving away the pigeons and sparrows.

On May 7th, we went to the Houses of Parliament just to get a glimpse of the proceedings. Looking down from the audience-seats upstairs, the Speaker could be seen sitting in his seat that was as big as an altar in a church, the wood being carved all over. He looked very important with his white curly wig spreading over his shoulders. Near the other end of the table, a gold mace, the emblem of the King, was reverently placed. Resembling some Buddhist instrument, it is full of religious dignity. Apart from this, the table was littered with papers, which were only distinguished from other things by their whiteness, so dark was the inside of the Parliament. The rows of benches, placed on both sides of the table, rise up gradually in tiers, but you cannot easily make out whether there are three tiers or four unless you stare carefully at them. On that day, something about land-tax was being discussed, and probably because the subject was not very attractive, there were only seven Members of Parliament on one side and about a dozen on the other, and the newspaper reporters occupying the front seats upstairs on the opposite side, seemed peaceful. I was told that the place farther above the reporters' seats, behind an iron grating, was the Ladies' Gallery. As it was dark, I could not see whether the iron net was still kept or not, but at the time when the suffragette demonstrations were rife, it is said to have been stretched before the Gallery. In the members' seats, a member was standing at his seat and repeating, 'Farmers are . . .' He was a young man and looked to be straining every nerve within himself, but the ministers who were seated on the front bench and the man who seemed to be the leader of the Opposition party, as if by common consent, had their legs leisurely and comfortably stretched on the table, the tops of their feet shooting out two or three inches over it on the same level as their eyes. No one says that it is irreverent to the King because the King's emblem is placed on it. Everything in its natural home surroundings, even if it may seem to others to be rude and irreverent, must be expected to have its own individual and ineffable flavour. Now and then people around the speaker said, 'Aye! Aye!' or 'Hear! Hear!' but except for these, all was silent, and the 'Hear! Hear!' sounded old-fashioned, like the relic of an oratorical meeting of the 'nineties in Japan. The impression produced by the whole was like that of a temple, and I expected every minute that the sonorous music of a pipe-organ would shake the heavy air all at once.

The Houses of Parliament as seen from the Thames presents a broad and stately appearance with its numbers of parallel vertical lines just like a pipe-organ, and its unchallenged dignity, as the pivot of Great Britain, is expressed perfectly in those buildings.

The Law Courts impressed me as having the same antique air, when I entered. The Chief Justice in a black robe sat in a chair on an elevated platform. He was an old man of commanding dignity, and the white hair of his wig seemed natural. There was a seat for the prosecuting solicitor in front of him, and on the right there was, surrounded by a rail, the dock where the accused stands. Facing this, on the left side, there was an enclosed box-like space in which the jury were seated side by side. The front bench, facing the Chief Justice, seemed to be occupied by witnesses, and there were some women among them. Behind them, about three lawyers, in wigs and black gowns, were seated beside each other. The case was something about tons of sugar in 1920. It was dark as usual, and amidst the black, grey and brown colours of the court-room, the scarlet cordon, which the Chief Justice wore aslant from his shoulder, and the red tape that tied papers which were scattered on the desks, stood out distinctly. Red tape is used in the sense of excessive adherence to forms and formality in public business, and it is indeed a smart expression. Soon the twelve jurymen trooped in and seated themselves, and, after a while, they trooped out again. Then they once more came in, and the youngest of them asked a question, while the rest who sat behind him directed him, and being handed down some reference papers, they retired again, and that was the end of the inquiry on that day. Trials for small cases like this were being held in many other rooms of the Courts on that day.

Wigs are decidedly quaint things. My father was given a wig and gown when he became a Barrister-at-Law of the Middle Temple, and in his later days, when he had his portrait painted in oils in this attire, he said with a laugh, 'This does make my bald head itch!' Masses of hard white hair are implanted on a coarse cloth, one above the other in curls. When we were invited to dinner at the Embassy, Mrs. Matsudaira, the wife of the Ambassador, said to me, looking at the footmen standing behind her, 'Last night we invited Prince Arthur of Connaught, and these men wore wigs'. English etiquette may be orthodox, but the old footmen who clasped the Japanese soup-bowls eagle-fashion, as if to say, 'Any etiquette except English etiquette is not etiquette at all', had indeed faces which seemed to befit such wigs.

England is a country of antique formality in everything. At a dinner-party given by the Japan Society in honour of Sir Francis Lindley, the English Ambassador to Japan, the big waiter who seemed more than six feet high, stood straight behind Ambassador Matsudaira who took the chair — he stood bolt upright as if he had swallowed a straight stick, and looked so serious that if Charlie Chaplin had brought in Harold Lloyd on his shoulders, he would not smile. He struck the table with a wooden hammer with all his might and shouted, 'Ladies and gentlemen, grace will commence. Pray silence for the Chairman'. Every time a toast was given, he rose with his shout, the first being for the King, then for the Emperor of Japan, and the Queen and the Prince of Wales were toasted at the same time. Besides these, toasts were given for the Royal Families of both countries and other persons and things, including the Society and Sir Francis, and thus they awkwardly stood up and sat down about nine times. Though it was obvious that they would have to rise again for another toast, they could not remain standing all the time from the beginning. Although they did their utmost to avoid it, the scraping of the chairs made a strident noise because there were many people, but this also formed part of the etiquette. In China they call a most polite salute 'a salute of kowtowing three and nine times', and this Chinese etiquette seems to me to have some similarity to that of England.

The Whitehall Horse Guards are also something worth seeing. They sit like statues, riding on black horses, with large red plumes in their helmets, and resting their swords on their shoulders. They are so famous that people go on purpose to see the Changing of the Guard. One day, we saw a very interesting sight by chance. When we got out of the bus at Trafalgar Square, we found that something was about to happen at St. Martin's, for the steps of the church and of the National Gallery on the opposite side were buried under people. This was something to gladden our hearts, and we joined the crowd and asked the people near us, 'What's going on?' They answered, 'Something is coming out of the church!' and sure enough, twenty officers in full dress stood in two lines on the stone steps. The red plumes on the helmets pulled over the ears, the uniformly beautiful eyes and noses, the thick gold chin-straps so tightly pulled that they stretched just below the lower lips, the epaulettes glinting against the gaudiness of red wool, the white breeches, and the lustre of the long boots reaching up to the thighs! The sight of these guards standing in rows on the stone

steps from top to bottom was really gorgeous. In the meantime, buses and vans passed, and as it was very near to
Charing Cross where the traffic is always as thick as it can
be, when the flow of traffic stopped, cars stayed in front of
the church, so that the view of the people on the opposite
side of the road was obstructed. There was an advertisement
taking advantage of the space at the side of a van with 'Eat
Blank's bacon every morning. You won't catch cold', and
some man shouted, 'Get out of the light or I won't eat it!'
To a woman who muttered, 'Oh! The bride will come out
before you go away', another woman on top of a bus said,
'Well then, I will tell you about it from up here'. Everything was noisy like that. Soon, the soldiers drew their
swords all at once, and crossed them with those on the
opposite side, the door of the church opened, and the bride
in pure white, clinging to the arm of the bridegroom with a
flower in his buttonhole, came down the steps under the
archway of swords, her veil flowing after her. Her train was
held by four little children like fairies and some beautiful
girls followed them as bridesmaids. Everything was white,
and the white was beautiful against the gorgeous colours of
the soldiers' uniforms, who lined both sides of the steps.

This reminds me that when we visited Salisbury people
filled the place in front of the Town Hall, and we waited
among the crowd, expecting something to happen again.
Someone told me that the Justices of the Peace were coming
on that day to judge a murder case. With the thudding of
hoofs six dragoons came up, lifting their horses' legs high
as if making them jump, escorting the car which they
guarded. The straps of gold helmets, and uniforms rich
with scarlet and gold! They looked very gallant, mounted
on black horses with long boots of white leather, the red

plumes of their helmets flowing in the wind. Ta-ra, ta-ra!
they blew bugles to the sky, when they stopped still, in
front of the columns of the porch. On the long gold tubes
of the bugles were small bannerets embroidered with a shield
and a lion in raised-up gold threads. The Justice, who now
appeared, entered slowly in a wig of white hair and a scarlet
robe with gold embroidery. Now another troop of the same
kind arrived with a loud clattering of hoofs. While we were
looking at the white plumes on their helmets, another
Justice stepped out with a call upon bugles. He was in the
same kind of wig, but in a robe of black velvet with gold
embroidery. Seeing them trying cases in such attire, I am
almost sure, one could not help praising, 'A Daniel come to
judgment!'

All these things were too classical and super-temporal to
be called simply old-fashioned. They indeed made us mutter
for a few moments, 'That symbolizes the peace of the realm',
with a feeling of envy mixed with impatience. The English,
who are apt to produce only comedies on the stage, driving
classical plays out of the theatre, are quite comfortable,
themselves acting classical pageants in the ceremonies of
their daily life.

§ 8

Food

The taste of the English people for food is not well-
developed. Contrary to the salty taste of German food
English food is only boiled and not flavoured. Speaking in
their defence, they say it is a great thing not to lose the
particular taste of the food material itself. The foundation

of the taste of food is made by cooking, and the taste is controlled by the individual according to his liking by using salt and pepper, so English cooking may be said to have regard for individuality. You can say anything you like about English food, but still it is tasteless and wishy-washy all the same, and the variety of the material is limited, especially in the vegetable line, potato, tomato, cauliflower, rhubarb, asparagus, spinach, carrots, horse-radish, brussels sprouts, and lettuce—that's all! We are made to feed on an unending supply of meat, for the ox is utilized from its brain to its tail, making us think that England is, indeed, a live-stock country. Though she is surrounded by the sea, the flesh of turbot is so soft that it can easily be mashed with a fork, reminding us of the fact that those fish live in a grey sea which lacks sunlight. Added to this, fish which is half-smoked has the same smell as the air in the Tube. What I thought tasty among fish was salmon steak. Among delicacies may be counted the crackling bacon and eggs served in the morning, and the tortoise-shell-coloured marmalade!

The restaurants in London where the best food is served are either French or Italian, and first-class restaurants are indeed never to be forgotten because there we can taste once in a long while dainty dishes saturated with deliciousness, but the price is awful, being ten shillings for soup and one dish. The best English cooking is found only in the meat dishes. Specially to be mentioned is the Cheshire Cheese, which Dr. Johnson patronized. It is in a narrow alley off Fleet Street, one of the main streets of London. The alley, which seems to hide this shop of delicacies, is so narrow that if fat Dr. Johnson came out from the restaurant under the influence of drink, it might have been impossible for anyone else to pass him. At the right side of the entrance where, in

Japan they might hang a lantern, a round lamp, resembling somewhat a Japanese lantern, is suspended, on which is written 'YE OLDE CHESHIRE CHEESE. REBUILT 1667'. They are very proud of the building which was rebuilt after the Great Fire of London, and the room, still dimly lighted with gas-lamps, has, at the tables, clumsy fixed benches of oak with high backs that separate the seats from those behind, in which four or five people are seated as in a compartment. I was told that this was an old style which was called 'panel'. It is also an old style that sawdust is scattered over the floor, and that against the wall stood a grandfather's clock with a swaying pendulum, going tick-tack. I looked at it, thinking that the old second and the English second was and is so slow and leisurely. They say, standing upon historical dignity, that the usual seat of Dr. Johnson was in a corner, at the head of a table, while another seat was occupied by Boswell. Another seat was used by Dickens. The oak benches are fixed to the wall at one end, so that if you take the seat at the farther end, you cannot come out before the person who occupies the seat at the near end stands up. The special dish in this place is, they say, in winter, beef-steak, and in spring, when I visited it, meat-pie, so I ordered and finished a large dish of this tasty pie, which was served generously and rather in a mess. The crust of the fox-coloured pie, dipped in gravy like that of stew, was very delicious. Just at the side of the table, there was a cooking stove, and a big pot was boiling with a bubbling noise, and the lid of the soup-saucepan of red copper, beautifully polished, was being pushed up every time the bubbles forced their way up to the surface. It would have been unfit in summer, to drink deep or to discuss hotly in this place; especially the sight of Dr. Johnson, who wore a wig, besides being a lump of flesh which must have perspired a good deal, would not have been fit to be seen. The dirty part of the wall, against which they say his wig used to rub, is counted as one of the treasures of the house! My husband seated in Johnson's seat and Mr. S. in Goldsmith's, we had our meal leisurely, and after that, before we returned, they took us down to the wine-cellar, guiding us along the winding steps with such remarks as 'Mind your head here!'

The restaurant which rivals the Cheshire Cheese is the Olde Cock Tavern. This place was also shining sombrely with carved oak panels, and the floor was sprinkled with saw-dust in the same way. It is proud of being started in 1549, and advertises the fact that Tennyson came to dine here. It seems that English food can never be eaten without salt, and also without sprinkling the pepper which is called 'Old', better still 'Olde'.

Simpson's has got furniture in quite modern style, and when you order roast beef, which is the special dish there, a fat *chef* with a pleasant smile will come out pushing a table about the size of a perambulator, his white *chef's* cap setting off his ruddy face. If he takes off the big silver lid, a thick cloud of steam goes up, and a large round of beef, done to a brown colour, appears. It seems to weigh at least one and a half stone. After making the fire underneath a little smaller, the cook slowly handles the knife, and smoothly slices off the brown crackling and pink part, which has been moderately done, and placing a sufficient portion on a dish, he pours over it the gravy that came out of the beef, and adds a piece of Yorkshire pudding, which is a soft stuff made of egg, and some vegetables, and delivers the dishes to the people at the table with a look of self-confidence and charm, with his double chin flopping up and down. This is indeed a food which has all the special features of English cooking. It was so tender that it seemed to melt in my mouth, the fat was light, and I could not help admiring the elegant sweetness of good beef, as compared with the more artificial cooking of southern countries. The beefsteak which we tasted in the Strand was in English style, but it was rather tough, so that I might say it would be more suitable to the palate of a sailor. It was still sizzling on the plate, and when I put my knife into the brown surface, red juice was squeezed out a little. The more I chewed it, the more sweetness came out of it.

These things alone I found delicious, and all the cheap restaurants, in which tulips with their petals turned inside out were found on the tables, served us the same kind of meat without exception. I once took what was called Japanese salad, wondering what it was, and found it was salad with small chopped dried herring in it. Even such restaurants were very seldom open on Sundays. We also tried a vegetarian restaurant. Since it was called 'vegetarian', I expected cooking that intensified the special taste of the vegetables. But the food with which we were served was an imitation of the ordinary non-vegetarian food, as, for instance cutlet of brazil nut, and what was interesting was the fact that the customers there had a certain dryness about them which must have been caused by their biased diet. Chinese restaurants were thriving in London. This is because Chinese cooking has a substantial quality and it is skilful in taking in any foreign stuffs such as cauliflower, etc. But the Japanese cooking in London was insipid and poor, in that it only served to beguile the petty homesickness of the Japanese residents, so we did not especially want to eat Japanese food while in London.

Directly our boat arrived in France, after leaving England behind, we noticed a falling-off in the quality of the porters and other employees, but the food served in the dining-car was delicious as if in compensation. Thinking that two bad things never go together, I looked and saw an Englishman sitting near me sprinkling salt and pepper over his food, holding the pots upside down, without tasting the food first, because it was a rule for him to do so with a meat-dish.

§ 9

Two Poets

Both Mr. Blunden and Mr. Nichols are young English poets who came to Japan as professors of the Tokyo Imperial University. After returning to England, they have both settled down in the country to enjoy the peaceful life. We visited their houses partly to enjoy the grassy rural scenery of England in May.

Mr. B.'s home was in Kent. We got out of the train at Yalding and walked along the high road. Although the view was rich, with a large country river that moistened the plain, there were no vegetable or wheat fields. It was just a wide tract of grass, and the richness did not come from the fertility of the land but from the abundance of unoccupied fields. This richness was of such a nature that when you felt a little cross it would offend you, but it was pleasant to see the continuous green in the late spring haze. There was no fear at all of the fields being flooded with water, even if the river overflowed, and we walked on enjoying the sight of swans floating in unexpected places. On entering the village, we saw ladders left under the loft, which was over-full of hay, and from the stables to the river bank, ducks waddled along. Farmhouses like this continued up to some old stone buildings at the foot of a bridge, among which I found traces of windows filled in when windows were taxed in the time of George III. The bridge matches the houses in its antiquity. It had a thick rail, like a low stone fence, and what added some interest to it was the widening part of the bridge where one could wait for traffic coming from the other end. Mr. B.'s house was at the end of the road, where it widened like a square, and its red roof showed partly through the rich young foliage of a horse-chestnut tree. This house was once a grammar school where Mr. B. went as a boy, and the half of the house, which had been used as a classroom, was now closed. The antique windows, made of small diamond-shaped panes of glass joined together with lead, and the sloping rusty red roof, were distinct against the green of lilacs pruned in a round shape. Altogether the sight of the house in its entire quietude seemed to be like a scene from the Land of Memory in *The Blue Bird*. Mr. B.'s family were living in the right half of the building, which had been the private house of the schoolmaster when the grammar school was there. His parents were absent because they had gone out to see a cricket match, as English people are fond of doing. The only member of the family besides his parents was his sister-in-law, a German lady. Although she spoke English with a strong accent, I found her very frank and friendly. When I was told that she was born in Cologne, I pleased her very much by saying that the cathedral there fascinated me more than any other cathedral that I had ever seen.

One of the rooms upstairs was used as Mr. B.'s study.

Patting the wall which partitioned his room from the school, he said with a smile, 'There used to be a door here, and Mr. William, the schoolmaster, used to go through it into the classroom'. He probably remembered his school days when all the boys suddenly became silent with the warning of 'Ssh', when their schoolmaster entered. Going out into the backyard, I found a kitchen-garden for cabbages and carrots, and as I was walking along saying, 'Oh! Look at these gooseberries', and 'How successful you are with your beans', Mr. B. put his finger to his lips and took us to a little corner of the hedge. Looking into the middle of a hawthorn-bush, we peeped into a nest where four little baby birds with big red-skinned heads were squatting side by side. Soon we were called in for lunch. Mr. B. carved a large joint of lamb, with a bone, and offered us one portion after another, saying 'Another helping of this with crackling?' As it was his sister-in-law's cooking, I thought the best and easiest way of praising it was to eat, and I had several helpings of rhubarb and other things.

After lunch we went out for a walk in the neighbourhood. When we walked up a hill at the back, we found a horsetail as thick as a man's thumb and one and a half feet long growing by the wayside. I thought, with a smile, that cow-dung and sheep-dung went to the making of this monstrosity. From there we went to the upland meadow, trampling buttercups underfoot, and when we reached the top, we looked back and found a sea of endless green fields stretching away into the distance with woods scattered here and there like islands, the smoke of a passing train trailing along the sky. But what heightened the impressions that spring in the county of Kent gave me, was not the scenery itself but the clear transparent air in a kind of blue glimmer, which might

Le called the colour of eternity. We crossed the meadow. The patches of bluebells here and there looked from a distance like small pools upon which the blue of the sky was reflected. Approaching, we found that they were growing quite sparsely among the grass, and the place where we had stood a little before seemed even more blue all over. Enjoying the scenery, we came to a fence which kept the cows in. We all jumped over it except Miss H., a fat lady who had great trouble in getting over, causing us great amusement, and we went down to the village. When we crossed over the stile which was the border of the meadow, the apple blossoms in an orchard adjacent to it formed a tent of a light pink colour, and the trunks of the trees were all painted white with lime to keep off insects. The dull afternoon sun was shining, and the spring scenery somewhat made the blood mount to my head. We stepped into a barn of a farmhouse, but as we entered the thatched house with overhanging eaves so suddenly from outside, it seemed very dark, and as we came out of the barn before I could even clearly make out the wall, which seemed to have flails hung on it, all that I remember is the stuffy smell of the hay and the chilly feeling of the unfloored ground. Near the barn there was a hut where the hops were dried. It had a cone-shaped roof upon which another pointed roof, like an extinguisher, was put a little aslant, and when the wind blew on a bar protruding in the shape of a tongue, it made a dismal creaking sound, the upper roof twisting round. It had a shape, weird and comical at the same time, against which, if Don Quixote had seen it, he might have put himself in a posture of defence with his lance. Mr. B. said regretfully that they did not now dry hops any longer in this particular oast. Even the noise of the deserted oast-houses, like that of a man grinding his teeth, set off the peaceful calmness of that neighbourhood all the more, and spring penetrated the whole air of the village. The roads were made a little higher on the sides so that in case of flood the water might run in the middle and we rambled along one of these roads chatting. There was a church near Mr. B.'s house, and when we went through the mossy lych-gate, very much like a cross-barred gate of Japan, a yew tree stretched its branches outwards as is often seen in church-yards. On a grey stone in the gloomy churchyard, there was a face, like a mask used in *no*-plays, carved together with an hour-glass, both worn and weathered a good deal, which reminded me of Gray's line 'With uncouth rhymes and shapeless sculpture deck'd'. Near his house there was a little hut like a gamekeeper's lodge. It was used as a prison for the law-breakers of the village in olden times. The flow of time in the village which passed so quietly from generation to generation, seemed to be as stationary as in the hour-glass carved on the stone.

We went back to his house, and after tea we went outside into the courtyard again. Part of the courtyard was a lawn upon which a large cedar was standing. Mr. B. played with his father's dog 'Bimbo' which looked very much like a ball of waste wool, and sometimes he drove a big cedar-cone with a cricket-bat just for fun. His eyes looked beautiful when they followed the arched curve which the cone traced in the air. They looked like stars, but when I saw him so cheerfully gay, a feeling of sympathy skimmed across my heart like the blast of a cold wind — a feeling which we experience when we see an orphan absorbed in play. He was so kind to people and so sensitive, like glassware which could easily be cracked — so sensitive that he seemed to gnaw into himself with feelings of regret so that I imagined he would sometimes have sleepless nights when he would feel loneliness and misery, and I was worried by useless fears such as that the light in his study was pale, or that owls might screech in the tall tree. The spring sun had now begun to set, so we went out into the highway and waited for the motor-bus. Five or six cows walked up to us slowly and stopped to eat the grass by the wayside before being driven towards the village by a child. It becomes the coach in the country to keep us in eager impatience, seeming as if coming from another world. All of us stopped talking, listening to what seemed to be the sound of a horn, but we found it was only the cry of a cuckoo from afar. Gradually we talked less and less and stood in the evening fog, but when the bus eventually arrived and started again after picking us up, we felt as if we had something more to talk over, and we felt the regret of parting.

Mr. Nichols's house is at Winchelsea near the seashore. As the sea comes deep into the bay as though embracing the land, if you climb up the meadow where a deserted windmill stands, in the northern outskirts of the village, the bay is seen shining like silver far away. And if you walk to the cliff on the southern side where the wild roses are blooming fragrantly, the English Channel opens out into the distant haze, and the dull explosive sounds of the air-liner crossing to France lures you to sleep like the humming of bees. 'That aeroplane,' said Mr. N., 'shows that it is four-thirty, so let's go home to tea now.' But the late spring afternoon was so nice and quiet that I wanted to throw myself down on the grass of the meadow studded with daisies and buttercups. Walking half in a dream, I came to myself stung by nettles. On our way back to his house we inspected the ruins of a church. One half of the ruins was now being used and I was told that the stained-glass windows there were recently put in by raising funds. I have heard that the eagerness of Christians towards contributing to funds for stained-glass in churches is very much like the case of building bells for the temples in our own country both in religious passion and in abuse.

Mrs. N. who had been up to town came back. She is a graceful warm-hearted lady whom I like very much. After dinner we sat at ease in the parlour. In the long twilight Mr. N. talked and talked, as usual. Memories of Tokyo! Beautiful sights in Spain! His explanation to a bishop of Japanese *no*-plays in the *no*-costume made some time before. A play which he was now writing about 'Komuso'.

'Talking of Komuso,' he said with a deep sigh, 'Kyoto, Kyoto! There is no place so dear to me. Kyoto, Kyoto! I would like to go there once again ... !'

Now he put records on the gramophone. He nodded his head in time to the tune of a *samisen* in a Japanese play. He raised his shoulders with a soliloquy in another play, and burnt incense-sticks when he put on a record of the Japanese bamboo-flute. He listened to the music intently, looking at the smoke that rose slowly in the air and at the single scarlet spot in the darkness which had already come upon us as it was so late. He did look like a poet!

In the meantime, a man of the village, who walked leaning upon two crutches, came up and rested, sitting outside the fence, and then passed on. After the gramophone, he went on with his talks. 'I ought to have records of the cries of street-vendors in Tokyo — the vendors of seedlings in the early summer and vendors of Chinese spaghetti on the frosty night. Even in building a house, the chants sung by the workmen show the love of a lullaby caring for a new house and the mild and simple prayer appealing to the earth to be in peace. Think of the noise of the iron rivets being driven in by the pressure of air. Brrrr-rrr-brrrr!' He imitated the noise skilfully. As I had been comparing in my mind his way of talking to the rapid firing of a machine-gun, I felt a little amused myself.

Although the furniture of the bedroom allotted to us was simple, the small *kakemono* of a Chinese poem hung on the light-blue wall near my head, the indigo teacup with a small spray of a gingko tree and azalea in dawn colour thrown into it, picked from among the many flowers in the garden — all these deeply delighted me because they showed Mrs. N.'s superb care full of delicate taste. I looked carelessly out of the high window and gazed at a large hawthorn tree standing in the backyard. It was covered with white flowers on the crowded branches pruned into a round shape and looked as if it was floating in the air through the half-darkness of the night. Looking up at the *kakemono*, stretching myself in bed, I read the first two lines of the poem, 'Through the half-open window, there was seen the morning moon that shone upon the plum-bloom. In the dream I clearly saw a beautiful lady'. I slept well and had a peaceful night indeed befitting a person who came to stay with a poet.

§ 10

Oxford, the Old School Hat, and a Ticket to Boulogne

It was on our way back from Stratford-on-Avon to London that we visited Oxford. A chill spring rain was falling and the reeds were not yet budding in the marsh, where on the cold face of the water swans built twiggy nests and seemed to be hatching their eggs. A middle-aged gentleman in the car gave me a cutting from a newspaper about the Shakespeare Festival, and it said, 'A charming lady in Japanese dress attended'. I told him that I had come through Siberia, and our conversation at once changed to the dumping in Russia. In the papers, there were many articles about the dumping of wheat and timber, but dumping was not only confined to Russia alone. I was told a Member of Parliament made a speech a few days ago in Parliament, saying that the dumping of cotton things made in Japan was the enemy of the Lancashire cotton industry, and he brought out for inspection some stockings made in Japan, which cost threepence a pair. Approaching Oxford, we found that the fields were divided into small partitions called 'allotments'. They were farms that the Government suddenly encouraged people to make in the suburbs of many cities when England experienced food difficulties because she was cut off from food supplies by German submarines in the Great War. They were cultivated by amateur farmers from the cities, but as for their end in view they could do no more than relieve their conscience for a time. Really, they are nothing more than an advertisement that their ordeal did not pierce them to the quick and that they are dreaming again the peace of a naval country, because a danger passed is forgotten, and it simply drew a sour smile from me. But it will surely benefit the citizens, giving them health and interest in farming at the same time!

Arriving at Oxford, we put up with Mrs. W. to see what it was like to be paying-guests, although we could stay only for one night. She was over eighty but full of vigour. I have heard that she had had a lot of Japanese as guests, and she took great care of us with her creaking voice, like a machine that wanted oiling, and short gasping breath. We went out to see the town in the rain, but it being in the holidays, very few students were found and only one or two girl-students in square cap and gown were to be seen. We were taken to kitchens with primitive stoves where forty legs of mutton could be roasted at the same time, and many other things like that in Christ Church, Merton College and so on. In the dining-room of Magdalen College, we were pointed out the approximate position of Prince Chichibu's seat. When going round those gloomy chapels and halls, it was necessary to say to yourself about once every thirty minutes, 'This is a school. We are not visiting a temple or an historic place, but we are seeing a school. This is a factory where the future is brewed'. My mind, instead of being attracted by the things which were before me just now, such as the scrawls of the great men of the world, was only recalling with a yearning heart things which my father told us when I was a child. He came into contact with the atmosphere of this place in the 'seventies and was entirely enthralled, and he told us about these dining-rooms with such enthusiasm that it seemed as if he thought they were fairy wands which could magically produce true gentlemen. I recollected his stories along with the fragrance of a cigar, and the sound of quadrilles and cotillions. Whenever my father spoke about the life at English universities, it appeared that he was keenly anxious to transplant in Japan the mood of the students there, and he spoke with such passion that he seemed he wanted to draw it nearer to ourselves, even if it were only one or two feet, tying the mood with a piece of rope. In his impatience, he used to look rather severe with his Roman nose and moustache. I leaned against his knees, childlike, and listened, playing with the strings of his gown, and wondered why he got angry in spite of the fact that he was discoursing on a subject he loved so well.

Opening and closing our wet umbrellas many times, we went round from college to college. In the libraries, the catalogues were only arranged in the authors' alphabetical order, and the names of books were written down on slips of paper and pasted on the catalogue book, which was about two feet in length, so that many rows of shelves were taken up by these cumbersome catalogues. Most books were in Latin, and in one library we saw a valuable book tied up with a clumsy chain like that for a dog. The electric lamps looked rather out of place in these surroundings and seemed to be used there with much reluctance and regret, and the lamp-shades were no different from those used in the ordinary boarding houses. The red-painted fire extinguishers which I used to see in girls' schools of the early twentieth century in Japan, and thermometers, which chemists in Japan present to their customers at the end of the year, could be seen in the extremely dark and sombre-coloured rooms. Each college had its own beautiful garden where the flowers were now at their best, and the famous Addison's Walk, a beautiful promenade that ran beside a stream, had daffodils in a wild state under the trees, where deer nibbled at the grass and rabbits frolicked. After walking there, we went back to see the Colleges again.

University College is where Shelley wrote 'The Necessity of Atheism' for which he was expelled, and where, now, stands his monument. It is a marble statue of his nude body. The drowned corpse of the young poet, lying limply as if it had just been taken out of the water, looked so vivid and realistic that it seemed as if some seaweed was entangled in the hair and body. It was striking in that there was, in this neighbourhood, nothing of tender, romantic charm at all. The very disharmony of the statue and the building was fitting in an ironical way, for it was from here that he was expelled because his temperament clashed with the principles of the school. But what was regrettable was that the monument seen through the lattice from the passage seemed like looking into a cage of seals in an aquarium, almost making us feel that we ought to throw it a fish or something. Shelley's hair, soft-coloured like the feathers of a brown pigeon, was kept in the Bodleian Library. Sophocles' poems, which were found in his pocket when he was drowned, were also kept there. It was on July 7th, 1822, when, according to an Eastern mythology, two stars in heaven came for a rendezvous, but the sudden rain-storm not only came in their way but quenched the star on earth. There are, however, emerald waves in Spezia Bay. If I were to be drowned, I would choose the southern seas. I hate the tasteless, grey seas around England.

Then we paid a visit to the library called the Radcliffe Camera where enormous numbers of books were kept, and also to Blackwell's, a book-shop, before we returned home. At the dinner table, we were (like paying-guests) served with portions of food such as roast beef by Mrs. W., who was seated at the head of the table. Besides us there were a middle-aged lady and four or five young ladies including two Russian girls who were living on her as dependants. They were all extremely timid in that old lady's presence, and when she left the table, they suddenly began to talk noisily as when the lid is taken off a boiling saucepan, and when she came back to her seat, the awkward silence returned to them. The conversation in her absence was not so innocent as the mice who played when the cat was away. One girl said, 'I said that I would like to have some more gravy but you didn't ask for any for me, Flora', and Flora replied, 'Oh! I didn't hear you say that'. 'But I did all the same.' It was a useless quarrel of this kind. Miss Flora V. was one of the Russian girls, easily distinguished as such. She was about twenty years old and had a face like a damson. When the talk at table veered round to the travel through Siberia, Mrs. W. said, 'Oh! Russians! They are absolutely insensitive to dirty things. How can they be like that, Miss V.?' Such questions made her very downcast, so when she handed me a cup of tea, I said, 'Blagodaryoo vass', using the Russian for 'Thank you', which I had picked up in Siberia. At this, her face suddenly brightened up, but we said nothing in particular to each other. But when I was alone in the drawing-room, sitting with nothing to do, she came in wiping her hands and asked, quite abruptly, 'You don't like Russia, do you?' After talking a little, I said, 'Borshchi (Russian soup) is indeed delicious, isn't it?' Tears suddenly came into her eyes, and she said, 'Yes, it warms you . . .' Her voice was trembling as if she had never met with a warm heart since she had left Russia. Presently she took a photograph album from the shelf and asked me, 'Look at this, and wait a while for me, will you?' and then she went away in a hurry to see how things were going on in the kitchen. When she came back she sat down and said, 'Come on, tell me all about Moscow'. Saying, 'I learnt a song like this from the conductor on our train', I sang a song of the Volga, and she said, with tear-filled eyes, 'Every summer while I was living in Moscow . . .' Not finishing the sentence, she stood up abruptly and went towards the kitchen. While I was wondering over this strange action, Mrs. W.'s creaking voice said behind me, 'Do you play bridge?'

As our room was too cold for me to retire, I talked with Mrs. W. beside the fireplace about one thing or another. In Oxford I found that bottles of milk were left outside the door and did not seem to be stolen, so I admired this, saying, 'The poor people in Oxford seem to be wonderfully honest'. 'No!' she said, 'the poor people in this place do have thieving minds, but they know what they are and they don't come into town. The slums are placed in the east of the town'. Her proud tone of explanation seemed as if she meant that the pride of the town was the dishonest people who knew their social standing, rather than honest people. As I listened to her all the time just saying meekly, 'I see, I see', she was very pleased with me, and taking me into her room, she gave me an ash-tray of china, saying, 'As this tray bears the coat-of-arms of this town, I will give it to you for liking this town'. Her room was scattered all over with half-made artificial flowers. Flora and the other girls were probably making them by her order, for the use of some charity bazaar.

Next morning a comic incident happened. I locked the lavatory door, comparing the creaking noise to the landlady's voice, and while I was in, some lady in the house came after me and pulled the handle, thinking that it was not locked, and the key jammed and would not work. The lady outside felt sorry for me and brought various kinds of keys, saying through the keyhole, 'Don't worry, because I will open the door in a second'. It was all right, but what I could not help smiling at was, 'You must be cold in your gown. Warm yourself by doing exercises so that you don't catch cold'. When I was finally set free we all laughed heartily. Hearing

the news of my imprisonment Flora came running up to the
third floor, two steps at a time, and when I saw her curly
head beneath the stairs, I said, 'Dobr ootro' (Good morning!).
Hearing this, she jumped up clapping her hands with joy.
'What a happy day to-day will be, because I have heard a
Russian salutation early in the morning', and she continued,
saying coaxingly, 'I would like to thank you in your language.
How would you say "I love you"? Would you please write
it down?' So I gave her a postcard of a Japanese country-
girl, saying, 'This is a Japanese girl-labourer', and I wrote
'Thank you', 'Good-bye', and so on, but I was at a loss when
I tried to translate 'I love you!' into Japanese.

In the morning I visited St. John's College and, after
having lunch with Mr. K. and other people, we came home
in a great hurry, took our baggage and started. Flora said,
'Sayonara', and I said the same in Russian. She never
spoke Russian before the old lady. I heard that she was a
Russian refugee, so I took pity on her. We hastened to the
bus stop near the cattle-market and just managed to catch
the motor-coach for London.

I may criticize Oxford in several ways, but the memory of
it floats on my mind, whenever I face the busy workaday life
of the world. In the University town, the curfew sounded
every night, and the students were preparing for May-day
to sing Latin hymns, setting up a maypole. In Japan I have
often seen people in cinemas where Soviet pictures were
given, who showed their approval by clapping their hands
whenever tractors appeared. I am almost inclined to pile
up into a lump their frippery moods and put the bronze
weight of Oxford on them with a thud.

I could not help liking Oxford in the end, although I
did not acknowledge it at first owing to a sour humour, but

I felt a considerable antipathy against Eton. This may have
been because I have a son of about the same age as the boys
in this school. It may seem too fastidious to be critical about
such trivial things as their top-hats, but why on earth do they
put on the heads of young children as lusty as spring horses,
who are on the turning point from childhood to youth, top-
hats which, like hot-tempered young lords, are bright in
lustre but easily exasperated if rubbed the wrong way? 'Why
tie the horse to a blossoming cherry-tree? When it prances
the blossoms scatter.' And when the boys run the hats roll
off. I forgot my manners and looked back at a young boy
running after his older friends. Sure enough, his hat was
wobbling about on his head so he had to run holding the
brim with his hand. Why, is it not in itself an ornament to
this world, the head of a boy of this age, boldly stepping into
manhood with some last remains of a crust that belongs to
sweet childhood? The mysterious round heads crammed
with things that are growing up and going to open out
slowly and gradually, whatever they have got on the outside,
whether golden hair or short black hair! Upon those lively
globes you should only put light hats or caps that are fit to
protect them. In our abusive language we call a head a
'hat-stand'. I sympathized with the Eton boys who are
forced to serve those hats of vanity as stands for them. The
mind which wants to put a yoke on the head, which is more
than fetters and manacles, shows that it is going to put a
yoke on the spirit at the root of things. When we went
round to see the schoolhouses, what was pointed out to us
with pride was the fact that it was started in 1440, the
pillars which were made of the timber of Drake's boat, the
anecdote of Salisbury and the scrawl of Wellington . . .
This is all very well, and the scrawl of Gladstone is surely

worth seeing, but the guide who stands reverently before some
scribble saying, 'This is by the son of Gladstone and that is
his grandson . . .' tries too much to impress the value of such
scribbles on us, and therefore we feel unconsciously offended
by it. More than ten Prime Ministers were produced, he
told us, and it is indeed amazing, but what would they do
with the children who had a talent for science? When they
are old enough to go to the University they choose their
own course, finding out what they should follow, and in
Oxford the departments of science are not imperfect, but
it seemed to me that in this school they were only going to
teach the boys fresh from preparatory schools how to become
Prime Ministers. At least, they seem to astonish the weak
minds of visitors by that impression; but people should know
better. It is not without reason that I get so critical about
these things. While I was in Japan I felt that we were
suffering from the lack of fair play in every field, and I
knew of more than one person whom I wanted to inoculate
with the spirit of fair play of Eton origin. I wanted to get
it all for them, but I was very disappointed when I realized
that it was quite impossible for me to get even a half-portion
of it, since it was too expensive if produced only in this way.
I thought I might be depreciating the school in a mood like
that of the fox who said, 'The grapes are sour', and I reflected
over it well, but still I was unable to appreciate plump
children's top-hats and morning coats. In Japan, too, on
one of the festival-days of children, we see figures of the
same kind in the Shinto shrines. The children who are used
as instruments through which parents want to show off their
wealth under the cloak of the education of children's piety,
and the children who are used as advertisements of an old
tradition under the high-sounding name of gentlemanship,

both go along with cumbersome accoutrements as in a sack-race. What a gorgeous tragedy it is!

When we left England, we crossed over from Folkestone to Boulogne. It was a very fine day and the chalk cliffs of the English Channel saw our boat off with all their bright charm. We often spoke unkindly of the English, saying, 'They are stolid', or 'They are too composed', but now I felt it hard to part from them. It is strange, but only England made me feel a little lonely when I was leaving, as if I had left behind about a fiftieth part of my soul.

As soon as our boat arrived at Boulogne, French porters came up into the boat, competing with each other, and stared at us looking out for a customer who could give them a generous tip with bulky yet light luggage. We arrived at Paris and left our luggage in an hotel, and when we made a little purchase in a shop, we asked the shopman, 'What is the best way to go to the Eiffel Tower from here?' 'The best way,' he answered, 'is to hire a taxi.' In England we never received such answers but instead, if you asked an old man out of breath, 'Which is the shortest way to the station?' he would say, first of all, 'Well', with his hands clasped and thumbs together. After some consideration he would let you know with such a slow and lengthy description, that you would sometimes get the shortest cut but miss the train.

Now I thought, 'We have said good-bye to England, a country of people who make you feel at times a little impatient but are always to be depended upon, and from to-day we are getting into touch with the French people who are the most clever and acute in the world. Travel is indeed interesting'.

CHAPTER VII

SUMMER IN SPAIN

§ I

Velvet and Rubies

IMAGINE Spain as black velvet scattered with rubies. Imagine Spain as a sheet of sandpaper with an ear-shell put upon it. It is a country where barren desolation and gorgeous brilliance are intermingled. It is a country where light and shade, heat and cold, wealth and poverty, love and hatred — where everything exists in an extreme state and jumps from one extremity to the other. All such adjectives as 'lukewarm', 'moderate', 'faint' or 'temperate' are only allowed to exist in a damp country together with mould and mildew.

It is an entirely dried-up country, but you should not come to the hasty conclusion that it is a dry country. There is in this country the enchanting lustre and suffocating smell of greasy oil. 'Oh! How Spanish!' — This simple expression can be applied sometimes as the best praise and sometimes as the worst abuse.

When we were about to leave Paris for Spain, there was a crowd of people in front of an hotel in the Champs-Elysées. They had gathered there to see King Alfonso who had escaped from his country. He had taken refuge in a hurry after the last glorious ceremony of washing beggars' feet, accompanied by the Queen, before all the officials of his court.

Next morning we had already crossed over the frontier.

The waves of the Bay of Biscay were seen from the right window of the train, and passing the port of San Sebastian, which would have been beautifully lighted at night, we turned inland. When the train was crossing the edge of the Pyrénées, the mountains looked aged, and on the craggy rocks mouldering towers, where beacons once shone, were standing solitary. Along the earthen bridge over a ravine that goes round the skirts of the cliff, a peasant on a donkey was going clip-clop. Thus, the scenery in the Basque region was very much like that of China, but near Burgos the landscape gradually became weird. The rusty-red high table-land without even a shrub on it looked like a wrecked ship that had run on the rocks, the upper part being flat, but the precipice overhanging the cliff curved inwards to the ground like the bows of a ship. The lower edge of the beetling precipice stands on a wide barren tract, which for some distance was scattered with pink flowers, but soon only fennel was growing in clumsy masses. Suddenly, however, a conspicuously green patch of land would be seen in the distance sometimes. It is a forest of stone-pines, each tree having an oval mass of clear-cut green at the head of its twining trunk, and the thick belt of those trees somewhat looks like the background of a modernist play. If you go close to them, you will find their trunks are sadly wounded in order to take the resin from them, each having a small cup fastened to it.

Villages were very seldom seen. Both the roof and wall of the houses are made of earth that is plastered and hardened and they are built in tiers as if they were clinging to the grey, sharp slope. In this vast stretch of land, they were gathered in a muddle, like weak animals that flock together huddling to each other in fear of something man knows not what, and because of their protective colouring you would not see the walls, before your eyes are accustomed to the scenery. Only the shutterless windows showed like black dots, and I wondered if they were cave-dwellings. I stared, however, and discerned the outlines of the grey houses with windows like eye-sockets and thought that the cluster of houses looked like a weird pile of skulls.

If you travelled in the deserts of Castile, shaken in a train for more than half a day in the fierce sun of late June, you would feel very much fatigued. I had a nap, and awakening I felt a little uneasy, and I wondered whether I was fully awake from my nap or still half-asleep, because the shapes of the rocks outside the window were so strange and fantastic. Large rocks, all of a somewhat strange roundness, covered the entire area as far as the eye could reach. Some of them were like hardened drops of candle-grease, some stretching themselves flat loosely covered the earth, and some, like kneaded dough, had deep fissures in them. On the back of a rock like a huge tortoise, another big rock in the shape of an egg was placed, which, being split in the middle because of its weight, opened a wide mouth towards the sky.

Referring to my *Baedeker*, I found that this was the plateau of New Castile which was once covered with ice in the glacial period, and I could now gaze at the scenery before me with a little more settled mind. The violent dance of the rocks continued, with threatening shower-clouds hanging very low over them, and through all this ghastly scenery our train climbed up with gasps and pants.

When we turned round a corner of a rock, suddenly, near at hand, a grand palace rose up against a beautiful peak of the mountains. 'Escorial!' The Emperors from Philip II to Philip IV raised this grand structure of both palace and temple with their sovereign power, aided by the religious faith of the people, which put aside all jealousy of the luxury of the sovereigns. Now the railroad came up to the summit of the plateau and Madrid was within hailing distance. The train, suddenly gathering force, rushed down the slope, the smoke flying back like the waving mane of a horse. Over the sky of Madrid there was a rainbow hanging, with its fresh and vivid colours.

§ 2

In Madrid

Madrid in late June was very hot and our hotel was noisy. Until about three o'clock in the morning motor-cars drove about with shrill noises. Bugs lurked in our wooden beds, and when we asked the porter, who spoke broken English fluently, to call us at seven o'clock in the morning, he was quite ready to assure us that he would do so, but when the time came we found he had clean forgotten! The cooking, however, was good enough for us to forget all our discontent. We were served with fried fish. I thought that the cuttle-fish boiled in its own ink would go together perfectly with rice. How rich and sweet the fruit was! I dwelt on the harvest of the impressions of the day every evening, wetting my burning throat with a glass of fragrant wine diluted with cold water poured from an unglazed jar.

Although it was soon after the Revolution, the revolution-ary atmosphere was extremely slight. Mr. C. of the Japanese Legation told us about the first general election in the Republic, which was coming on in a few days, and gave us a lot of information. In short, the common people, having no patience, desired their business conditions to improve at once, so that life would quickly become easier, and politicians, for their part, flattering the showy temperament of the people, excited the populace with the vain prospect of a Republican party which would bring about Paradise after the fall of the Royal party. But this party could not, after all, do as they promised, so the people at once thought this was no use either and decided that Syndicalism might do some good instead. Their mood was just like that of an invalid who changes his medicine time and again, deceived by advertisements, so we could not bring ourselves to try to understand their views seriously. The general election, which took place on the 28th, was also extremely dull, and I could not see any passion in it although all men of about twenty-three years of age had the franchise. As I came from a country where violent campaigns are fought out, the first general election of Spain gave me the impression that the whole town was too indifferent to it, and I thought it frightfully boring. Women, though having a good opportunity in the Revolution which was going to rebuild everything from the root, made no endeavours, in spite of their having no vote while all men over twenty-three years got it, and they took to habitual church-going. I was told that if women had been given the franchise, people would have no end of trouble because of the Catholic party, which would carry matters with a high hand. Their revolution, I was informed, only goes into the flippancy of pageantry at once by choosing, for instance, a 'Miss Republica' with beautiful ornaments such as a high comb and mantilla, or by drawing festival carriages about the town carrying labourers in hunting-caps. On the day when we went to Seville, there was a strike of masons taking place, and I heard a gardener saying, with envy, 'I've heard that Russian Bolsheviks have told them not to work, giving them two pesetas each. What a good job it is!' Yet I had not seen one poster anywhere which would help such a populace trust the present government. The best way to induce the illiterate people into a revolution is by propaganda in the streets, and as I saw evidence of this in the streets of Russia, which has a genius for this sort of thing, I was very much dissatisfied with Spain. The political upheaval in this country was not really a revolution in which the national spirit of rebirth that had been pent up within broke out and blew off the King, but was nothing but a quarrel between the political parties in which the Republican party won the victory and obtained the rule from the Royalist party, while the Alfonso family collapsed of itself like a fruit that falls after rotting. In a book of geography I once read that Spaniards were idle and fond of having a nap in the daytime, but since I experienced the heat of the day in this country, I thought that a short sleep was unavoidable for people who lived in such a climate. Taking a siesta in the daytime, however, they sit up far into the night, and there is idle talking in the streets even at three o'clock in the morning, thus living in a way which is expressed in a Japanese 'haiku' poem, 'There shoots a star, and the topic changes on the summer evening bench'. So they never seem to be able to take to serious and steady study. Spain, the country of heat, therefore, has a very dim prospective light before her except that she may turn out by chance a transient genius leader, and the cry of 'Tanto monta!' (Excelsior) is nothing more than the incoherent utterance of a drunkard. Why was it that the flower of civilization opened, in ancient times, only in hot countries such as Egypt, Greece, Rome and

Spain? Was the heat of the sun a little milder in olden times? Now, anyhow, it was hot, hot, hot!

One day we visited the celebrated art museum. The two portraits of a Maya painted by Goya, one draped, the other nude lying with her legs stretched out in the same posture, penetrated me (though I am as thick-skinned as my heels about pictures) with a clear-cut impression with the smooth charm mixed with electric weirdness which you might feel when you stroked the back of a young leopard. Compared to these pictures, his *genre*-pictures were very light and jolly. A game with ladles in a sort of blindman's buff, a game in stilts, and another in which a man is bounced on a cloth, the four corners of which are held by women — all these things are recollected with pleasure. Another picture to which I took a fancy was a picture of Hell with the old ideas of the fourteenth century. This reminds me somewhat of our *Toba* pictures. Devils in the form of crickets and toads were swallowing up men whose hips and feet were still sticking out of their mouths, and a demon was roasting a man on a skewer. The man depicted hanging down by his ears must have committed the sin of eavesdropping! There was also a man crushed under an enormous strawberry. If it is a sin to eat fruit, both of us shall definitely have to go to Hell! Seeing these pictures gave me an extremely easy and peaceful mood. The holy humour of some bishop who could not think of anything but good things from the bottom of his mind, must have thought of such pictures, when he tried to contrive some terrifying things for the salvation of the common people, and it made me feel more reverent than the ordinary holy pictures.

§ 3

Seeing a Bullfight

As June 28th was the day when Spain was to be re-born, the day of the first general election after the Revolution, we went out into the streets with great expectation to see how it was going on. We had been staying in Madrid, the capital of Spain, and managed to extend our stay to be there on that day, for that purpose. But with much disappointment and dissatisfaction we came back to our hotel, where the porter brought us entrance tickets for a bull fight which was going to take place in the afternoon. I dropped off to sleep while thinking it very interesting that there was a difference of a few shillings in the charge for seats according to the amount of sun and shade on them. I slept like mud during the noon-day hours, as people should do in Rome as the Romans do, and we did not go out until four o'clock. To my surprise there was a great change in the appearance of the streets. They were all hurry and bustle. The way in which the people were making for the bullfight-ring was like that of blood throbbing upward to the head of a man who was going to suffer cerebral haemorrhage. Then we too changed into two of the blood corpuscles, and were pushed along in the stream of humanity.

Climbing up the stone-steps under the seats of the ring, we suddenly came inside, and felt with a shock that Rome was living, it was so much like the Coliseum. In the centre was a wide sandy area surrounded by a fence about four feet high, and along the outer side of the fence there was a space of six feet around it, and rows of stone seats for fifteen thousand spectators spread in the shape of a mortar. Above it was the blue sky, and the afternoon sunshine was dividing the large amphitheatre into two parts, dyeing it light and shade, purple and gold.

People came pouring in and seated themselves on the stone seats, after putting cushions on them. Behind us, there was a throne, and on the seats near it, Spanish beauties with blood-coloured nails were seated, having gorgeous shawls hung on the rails in front of them, and moving their large fans to and fro. Everything was Roman — exactly Roman. Nero was going to appear in the throne.

Were not the people around us shouting noisily, 'Give the Christians to the lions'? *Baedeker* says, 'When ladies are of the party it is advisable to sit in the upper rows in case they should faint'. 'But not I', I thought to myself, and remembered the story of Monte Cristo, who saw the cruel spectacle of hanging a criminal in order to train his heart.

Towards five o'clock there was no room at all in the spectators' seats. On the other side of the arena, fans and white handkerchiefs were fluttering almost hurting my eyes. Looking around, I saw that all eyes had a feverish glitter. One could see even by their dresses that most of the spectators were simply absorbed in the sport, for the admittance fee was as much as ten shillings, while they were most of them poor folk. How many days do they have to work in order to get that sum of money? The population of Madrid is eight hundred thousand, and the ring holds fifteen thousand seats. The fights take place twice a week, and there are two hundred rings in the whole country ... My mind was for a time shaking off the excited feeling of a character in *Quo Vadis*, and looking round with critical eyes. And when the trumpet announcing the opening of the sport sounded at five o'clock to the minute, I thought with a cold smile that the improvement of Spain had gone no further than to open bullfights punctually, and to re-dye the colour of the screen into that of the tri-coloured flag. But soon after I was absorbed in the classical sight of the opening ceremony.

First came officials of the seventeenth century, riding on black and white horses. They wore black wide-brimmed hats, long plumes of ostrich feathers proudly stuck in them, and had finely trimmed pointed waxed moustaches that flattered their superiors and domineered over their inferiors. They led brilliantly, and following them, six toreadors strutted with an heroic air. They had coats of mail closely covered with arabesque designs of golden braid on the red and blue ground. Their pink and yellowish trousers of velvet were skin-tight. Altogether their attire had the gorgeousness of court-dress, and at the same time conveyed the gallant smartness of a Japanese acrobatic fireman's livery. Thrown over their left shoulders were cloaks with gold and silver embroideries, and the scarlet linings showed as they flapped open. They were followed by lancers on horseback, and privates in scarlet tight-sleeved dresses, which you might see in an old Japanese play. Amid the wild applause of the spectators, first they gave a salute to the front seat, and then walked round the ring before they went out.

The gay colours which filled the sandy arena all went away like the ebb of the sea, and there was only a wide stretch of sand left. The sand was light pink in colour — like a sheet of blotting-paper which is waiting to absorb the scarlet blood of wild bulls. It was by no means a peaceful colour. All was vacant, and only the sunshine divided the circle, dyeing one half bright. There was the bloody tenseness of fifteen thousand expectant people around it. All of a sudden the door in front was wide open, and further on was the darkness that leads to hell! In an instant a coal-black bull dashed out like an inky whirlwind and stood in the burning rays of the sun. Oh! that sight! It gave me such a thrill that it was etched on my brain. The three-year old wild bull, which had been fed several nights in the darkness, with plenty of food, was overflowing with his reserve of energy, which seemed to be burning up in purple flames from his back. He stayed still a short while with his hoofs in the sand.

Just at that moment, one of the toreadors came forward with a scarlet cloth in his hand. The bull which had found something on which to vent his anger, excited by the red cloth, rushed violently in a straight line in the face of the red cloth, the sharp horn skimming it with the sound of a match striking. The toreador turned his body so that the bull, striking the air, charged clean past him. He dashed two or three yards in vain, and stopped short with such force that sparks flew from his hoofs. Presently the bull turned his body round and charged again. The toreador jumped round, and sticking out his chest to make him lightly swing forward, again presented the red cloth before the bull's face to irritate him.

There was a great thrill to be had from seeing the fighter behaving nimbly against the wild bull that opposed him with a dash. Let moralists frown, but to me this was an enthralling sport. When we swim against surging waves, and dive swiftly through or over the dashing and jumping force and never recede one point, we feel a high-sounding joy of heart, and that joy I found in this evil scene. Sometimes the fighter drew close to the bull and spread his scarlet cloth just near his horns. The bull advanced, step by step, and scooped it up with his horns and tried to toss it, but each time the toreador turned him aside just a little, and the scarlet, the gold braid, and the blackness of the bull were intertwined in one mass. It was like Robin Hood smartly fighting with Little John. And when the bull's attacks were too fast and ardent, other fighters came in from other sides and spread red cloths before him in order to divert him. The bull, which was about to break down the enemy with another stroke, left him and charged another enemy.

The second stage of the fight is to irritate the bull by sticking his neck with a short-bladed lance from horseback. This is done by the picadors. They ride near to the fence on miserable horses, which would cause them no loss if killed. They turn the horses' heads aside from the bull, so as not to let them see him, and when the bull gores the horses' sides they prod the bull's back from above. So I found no interest in this part, and thought it simply cruel and cowardly. Added to that, the horses fell invariably, and the riders thrown with a thud and being unable to move nimbly, very likely on account of their thick-padded costumes, they crawled on all fours in a very awkward manner.

The third stage begins with the banderillero who appears with one dart in each hand. The handle of the dart is long and slim and in the form of a fire-cracker, twisted round in red and white or blue and white. He ran forward to the bull in one of his unwary moments, and drove the darts quickly in the bull's back and fled away from him like a swallow. Twice and thrice — six darts were now in the bull's back and his anger was at its height.

Now let me admire the bull to my heart's content. How strong he is! He always dashes unswervingly with all his power, and then when his breath fails, everything comes to an end. He has not an inch of fear, of course, and he never doubts nor hesitates. His dauntless behaviour among all the creatures in the ring, among the fifteen thousand spectators, and the fighters, who seemed to be out to make fun of him, gave me the impression that he was the most admirable of them all. It was as if he was a paragon of unswerving life, shown us by God in order to put us to shame who walk hesitatingly on this earth, entangled by shallow cunning.

The bull's anger is now at its height, with the six darts fixed in his back. But he never moves or jumps: he fixes his bloodshot eyes in front of him, excited by boiling anger. From time to time he paws the sand savagely with his hot hoofs as if saying, 'See what I will do', and looks sharply right and left. The scarlet blood is gushing out quickly down his black shiny hair. It is a colour which does not easily excite the eye but pierces to the core of one's brain.

Now the time has come for the matador to begin his work. Let me describe the bloody brilliance when the hero, distinguished among toreadors, stood before the most fierce bull. The bull rushed forward, like a shell shot from a gun, with the tips of his horns whistling through the air. He tried to pierce the fighter who kept his back against the fence, but the momentum of his too forceful charge carried him in a somersault right over the fence which was nearly five feet high. The sound of the breaking planks, and the shouts of spectators now on their legs, mingled together, and then, as if by magic, the bull stood once again right in the centre of the arena.

Just then a man appeared who seemed to be perfectly at his ease. It is the matador with whom at the present day there are none to be compared. He threw off his cap, and revealed his pigtail, dressed in an ancient way. He had a very audacious air about him. On his right arm he had a bright scarlet cloth hiding a slender rapier, which some artisan of Toledo had forged with the pure icy water of the river Tagus. The hilt of the sword was so small that it could only just be held. The silver snake, over two feet long, had a sudden and unnatural curve near its point. And if you were to draw that point towards the hilt, it would softly bend and make a circle; and if you were to let it go, it would spring back to its former position. It was indeed a mysterious sword. It was not a sword of justice, but an incarnation of spite thirsting for blood.

The giant bull, which saw the red cloth, dashed towards it, foaming at the mouth with anger. The matador holding his body aslant, nearly on one knee, made the bull strike the air. The bull, which was a full-blooded animal, checked himself in a moment and again charged with lowered horns. The eyes of the excited spectators sometimes failed to see whether the matador was reeling or whether he was intentionally stepping aside from the bull, and they groaned heavily, their hands clammy with perspiration. But look! The matador, who had jumped aside, turned towards the audience and grinned, as if to say, 'Well, this is nothing to be so serious about'. At this show of calmness, the audience felt a little ashamed of their former weakness, and, roaring like thunder as if to crush out this feeling, they threw about hats, coats, and cushions like rain.

The bull charged again. The matador gracefully sidestepped and twisted round beautifully, and every time these fine forms of the technique were displayed, shrill trumpets called, accompanied by an explosion of applause. At last the matador drew his rapier from out of the cloak, and couched himself for the kill, when he was only three feet away from the fierce beast, which presented at his breast horns that could pierce even through an iron plate. The matador, who had so far kept his legs wide apart, with his knees a little bent, stood grinding his feet into the sand and gradually bringing them together. I thought that, if the art of this movement, not showy, but instinct with the whole power of the body, be understood by some nation other than the Spaniards, it would be only by the Japanese, who know how to take up the preliminary stance of their wrestling.

The matador now stood on his toes. He drew himself up to his full height, and oh! in the next moment — my eyes could not catch what exactly happened. He stepped forward, sprang back, and lo! the rapier was lost from his right hand and there was on the bull's back the small red hilt. When the thought was half sweeping over my brain that it could not be . . . that the rapier was over two feet long . . . scarlet blood was pouring down to the sand like a tape from the bull's mouth, and his black body fell with his legs up in the air.

The matador, the favourite of Hell, the sturdy 'fleur du mal', turned his pale swarthy face towards the audience and grinned again, showing his white teeth.

Three horses came out and dragged the bull's body away. Attendants levelled the bloody sand, and again I felt that they were neatly sweeping Christian blood, and my heart was shaken with disgust. Meanwhile the front door was opened wide again, and another black bull of the same size sprang out. Thus six bulls were killed one after the other, and my heart was shaken six times between intoxication, admiration, disgust, and shame.

The bullfight in Spain! It is too marvellous to be accused by moralists, saying affectedly that it is cruel to enjoy the killing of bulls. Therefore the abuse is not so small as might be expected. It is like opium or cocaine; if it gets a hold on you, it never sets you free. It burns the core of your heart and makes it sore — benumbs it, and stops the spring of everyday passions that make you strive upward. A revolution carried out while seeing the bullfight is nothing more than a political revolution. But if the day should come when Spain throws away the joy of the bullfight, the seriousness of the revolution would be worth noting. And if the bullfight should gradually wane, we should look upon it with congratulation as the barometer of the spread of education, and the improvement of society. But now give up such sober criticism, and allow me to indulge for a while in the intoxication of that sweet poisonous wine. However, when the bull drove the fighters away out of the ring and stood alone in the arena as if to guard it, and the heavy feeling that reminds one of the calm before the storm pressed upon the whole ring — two or three sparrows fluttered from the roof over the seats down to the vacant sand, and began to pick up food innocently. Why is it that I cannot forget that sight which comes to me so vividly above everything else, although it is such a small matter?

§ 4

Antiquities

One day we went to the Escorial. It is the palace which we had seen in the distance on our way to Madrid in the

train. The notable thing there is the Pantheon, where the
kings are buried under the gorgeous altar. Round the walls
of the vault, made of coloured marble blocks, there was a
range of coffins also carved out of marble with various
designs resembling the grain in wood, and both the body
and lid, long and somewhat narrow, were magnificently
ornamented with gold, but they reminded me of sumptuous
celluloid soap-cases. They were piled up in no less than
four rows. Kings ought to sleep each in his own place, stretching himself full length, but for the very reason that they
want to have mass sung every day at the altar above their
heads, these kings, I was told, sleep as in the berths of a
Japanese third-class sleeping-car. For kings' tombs the
grassy barrows of China and Korea are suitable, because they
seem to be sleeping in quilts forever. Christians hope they
will awake with the sound of the trumpet on the Day of
Judgment, so when these kings in their lidded coffins hear
the sound, they will dress hurriedly, with their stockinged
feet hanging over the edge of the upper berth as in the
morning sleeping-car. I thought the sight of them putting
their hands from under the lids, lifting them up, would be
like a clam putting out its tentacle. The vault for the princes
is covered over with white marble whose coldness pierces
to your very marrow. But if you go out, you will find the
dazzling sunlight reflecting on the granite and cicadas
singing as noisily as a sizzling frying-pan. In the avenue of
pine trees, children were picking up pine-cones, and as they
were as large as those in Korea, it was as interesting as nut-
hunting. On the chimney of a factory near the station, some
storks had built their nest, and while waiting for the train,
I was very much interested to see the father crane flying
peacefully in the air and the mother crane feeding the babies.

Owing to the recent business depression the boiler of the factory seems to have been cold for a long time. Before the babies are fully fledged, the smoke would not come out from the chimney.

Just then, a taxi-man came up and began to coax us saying, 'I am returning to Madrid. I'll drive you there cheap. What do you say to ten pesetas?' The distance was more than forty miles, and if you were to travel the same distance in an English train, you would have to pay ten or twelve shillings. My husband and I consulted together, speaking in Japanese. 'It sounds almost too good to be true,' I said. 'He has got a vulgar face,' he said, 'but he doesn't look a bad lot.' 'But remember,' I said, 'we have to cross a wilderness where no people live.' It is a piece of good fortune for strangers to be able to talk like this to each other right before the natives! In the end we took the car with some misgiving, but I fell asleep forgetting the heat in the cool wind over the plateau, and when I opened my eyes, I found myself in front of our hotel in Madrid. My husband told me, however, that all the time we were crossing the desert, he was feeling a little uneasy.

One day we drove to Toledo in a Cook's charabanc. On leaving Madrid we found it was harvest time in the wheat-fields. The fields were poor as in Korea, and the aspect and colour of the earth were very African. Here and there donkeys were turning the wheels that drew water from the wells, going round and round as with grindstones. In this neighbourhood, poor, slender trees were also growing, and the fields were showing green, being distinguished like oases in the desert. In the villages I saw mud walls and roof tiles entirely Oriental, the wooden doors at the gates having metal ornaments, and men in loose coats of blue cotton were driving donkeys. All these things made me feel as if we had returned to China. But the girls who gathered to draw water at the public wells, carrying unglazed pitchers on their heads, were beautiful in a South European way. In the outskirts of every village there was invariably an open place for threshing, scattered all over with ears of wheat, and horses drew rollers along to thresh. And some people, handling fork-shaped rakes made of tree-branches, threw wheat into the air to sift the chaff in the wind, sending up a cloud of yellow powder every time. Huge piles of straw and ox-carts laden with wheat — all these things made the place look busy and occupied, but at the same time, peaceful to the eye. From village to village the same sight and sound was repeated, yet it was not monotonous but soothed my heart pleasantly like a musical refrain. The music, however, is the funeral march seeing off the prosperity of the past of Spain. The tide of Moors that once flooded this land from the East was driven out by the Christian force of the West, and immediately the Moors, the genius of irrigation, left this land, the earth cracked with drought, and the fields became sterile. The creaking of the winch, as the donkeys slowly went round drawing water, sounded sad, and the church bells alone sounded loud, but they too are now becoming gradually fainter in the general trend of the world. The interest that old Spain has for us is in the fact that it was a junction of the East and the West — that it was the beach of the West against which the waves of Eastern customs dashed.

Toledo was once the capital of Spain. The castle wall in the strong Moorish style, plastered with clay mixed with flint stones, the winding alleys — and in the centre of the clay-plastered dwelling-houses squatted an enormous cathedral; the sight was, as somebody described it, like an elephant amidst a flock of sheep. The houses which have a rough grey appearance on the outside, like ear-shells which are rough on the surface but shine with iridescent colours inside, are decorated with beautiful tiles on the floor and with plaster designs on the inside walls, which one never tires of seeing. Specially interesting was Greco's House. The ivy growing from an unglazed pot placed on the unfloored ground and reaching up to the veranda of the second storey surrounding the court, the hanging lantern and the brazier — everything was small, pretty and bright, which made me wonder how it was possible for him to paint all those dark pictures in such surroundings. Greco's pictures have shades full of bitter taste like the colour of the water in Scotland.

It was hot! Going down the dried-up slope where hollyhocks were in bloom against the mud walls of the houses upon which the sun was reflected, we suddenly came to the edge of a cliff, under which, far down in the depths, the rich waters of the Tagus were flowing between two cliffs that stood face to face. Far beneath, a stone bridge in the Moorish style was hanging like a rainbow, but the curve was too substantial to be called a rainbow, and on both ends of the bridge, stone gates were standing with heavy towers. Such a bridge should have some legend about it, and indeed it actually has a very sweet one attached to it. How beautiful the moon would be, seem from this bridge! The water of this river is clear, fit for the making of swords, and swordsmiths who hand down the special methods of the Moors are still living. In the shops, there are three-foot blades, proudly hung up, which, being used for bullfights, pierce through the bulls' hearts from their backs, striking against the backbone yet never breaking but going round it. They are the swords from the edge of which murderous flames rise, so I would never think of having a protecting sword forged here. The swordsmiths also hand down the secret art of Moorish inlaid work of gold; they cut the pitch-black face of iron, inlay gold stripes in it and draw delicate Saracen designs. One who is tired of the angels, lions and kings' crowns of Western art cannot help being attracted by the art of the lines in Saracen designs.

As it was the middle of the day, it was so hot out-doors that my head swam. The traffic was entirely suspended, and I felt as if I was passing among the ruins of Pompeii. The town which once held three hundred thousand inhabitants has now only twenty thousand. The inside of the thick castle-gate is surrounded by stone walls, as in a Japanese castle, and there were clumsy piles of skin-bottles — vessels in which wine or water is kept, and which are prepared by cutting off the heads and the four legs of pigs and hollowing out the inside. The shape of a huge sausage with traces of four legs made me feel extremely hot, reminding me of China. Lunch in the hotel was made up of eggs dressed with arrowroot paste and fish-fritter, and the marzipan cake, a speciality of Toledo, was exactly the same as the Chinese cake 'yüehping' filled with bean paste. Eastern signs were in evidence everywhere.

After lunch we went to the cathedral. The apostles by Greco, in the picture-gallery, were all lean with saintly expressions. Why are the priests of to-day so fat, like skin-bottles filled with the fat of avarice? They perch very shallow kinds of bowler-hats about four inches high on their heads, and when they take them off they reveal their heads shaved on top, all looking highly disgusting. In Japan, Catholic priests sound rather poetical, so I felt rather angry because I had expected to see, in their homeland, graceful priests. Perhaps it is on account of their riches. The treasure-room of the cathedral was indeed extravagant. I wonder if a man who has not seen it can imagine a surplice with eighty thousand pearls sewn to it. The archbishop would sometimes change this pearly surplice for one having designs of flowers made of coral, and sometimes for a surplice scattered with images of angels, Virgin Mary, and Christ. Because of the gorgeous embroideries of gold threads, the surplice looked like the wings of a beetle and its stiffness suggesting the priests' avarice, made me feel extreme disillusion. Whenever I saw such things as a goblet made of gold brought from America by Columbus, I could not but think it fortunate that Iyeyasu, although he was a cunning old statesman, kept Europeans, whom the people of those days called the Southern Barbarians, away from Japan, otherwise by an evil chance the pearls in Ise Bay might have been put among those eighty thousand on the surplice. In the recent Revolution, a considerable number of priests were driven away or had their fortunes confiscated, and I have heard that the Jesuit priests meddled with political affairs worst of all.

Leaving the cathedral, we dropped into the house of Cervantes, the author of *Don Quixote*. It is still used as an inn, looking like a nest of plagues and bugs. Spain is indeed interesting, because in such dirty alleys we sometimes come upon a most enthralling beauty. Toledo, which I looked at on our way back, was very impressive. The Alcazar, like the residence-castle of *The Cid*, squatted in grey upon a hill, and the vertical line of the bridge, built in the Roman period, made the whole landscape strongly impressive. The town of clay colour was not dazzling to the eye, but a deep shadow was thrown into the core of my heart.

Segovia is famous for its Roman aqueduct. The white granite pillars that stood in a range, connecting that line and the depths of the valley, left long narrow gaps between them, from which the blue sky of June in Spain was peeping, and the sight was almost a perfect mixture of lightness and grandeur, there being no troubled disharmony found in it.

When, on approaching it, you realize the grand bulk of the stone pillars, which are more than four yards square, you feel that the impression of grandness is magnified ten times, and looking at the pillars which appear so high that they seem to be gradually narrowing at the top, you feel a shudder, because the pillars are roughly made by piling up blocks of granite one above the other; the large stones, like giants' toy bricks, look as if they were suddenly going to fall about one's ears with the noise of a thousand claps of thunder, and my heart, which never felt uneasiness in an aeroplane or on an overhanging cliff, shrank quite helplessly. Are the people of an earthquake country specially sensitive to being crushed under things? Weren't the Romans also acquainted with earthquake disasters, and yet how did they build such a thing as this? The transparent and audacious confidence which has never been troubled by the shadow of unpleasant uneasiness (which is sometimes expressed in the words 'Make assurance doubly sure!') has offered actual proof in this structure which has weathered two thousand years and is still standing like a stone screen in the mid-air.

Although standing before such a vivid sight as this, I still obstinately thought that the word Roman was an epithet adequate to relics, but I was astonished again to find the aqueduct still flowing with clear water to feed and moisten the inhabitants of Segovia. In the house of the watchman of the aqueduct, his wife was washing things pleasantly with overflowing water, and strong sun-spots, which peeped through the broad leaves of a fig-tree, were dancing on her back. At the splash of the water hens jumped aside nervously, and crossing the entrance where there was no threshold, they quite naturally entered the house picking up stray grains of wheat. On the dark unfloored ground, her husband was soothing and cajoling a peevish child with dominoes.

§ 5

Portugal

Our trip to Portugal was a comical one. As there were only two of us whimsical persons who travelled in mid-summer like this, we must have looked suspicious and the examination at the frontier was extremely severe. I entered a room pointed out to me and found a small, wrinkled old lady standing alone. She said nothing but pointed to my pockets. She opened my purse, shook my case of medicine, and drawing back one of her legs in an old-fashioned way, curtsied and then felt all over my body from outside my dress. Next, she pointed to my hat. When I took it off, she made a curtsy again, went round behind me and felt within my hair, came round in front, made another curtsy and pointed to my shoes. She was very pertinacious. She examined my soles (my stockings, by the way, had no holes!) and sounded the heels of my shoes.

These examinations were so rigorous because refugee

nobles were trying every way to get their valuables out of the country, which partly caused the depreciation of the money exchange in this country. The day before, in Madrid, I was told that a nobleman was stopped in crossing the frontier in his car, and when they split open a spare tyre, bundles of banknotes came scattering out. I also heard that a noble lady was arrested going out of the country with her property changed into diamonds which she put in the heels of her shoes. As I had heard all such stories with the same light mood as when listening to half-romantic tales, I was rather pleased with this physical examination as an interesting experience. She made an old-fashioned curtsy again, which I had seen only in such an antique dance as the quadrille, but which was now actually made use of at a barrier made by the Revolution! I was wondering what she wanted next, when she told me to pull down my stockings, setting the example herself. I had been told that European ladies inserted bank notes under the tops of their stockings, so now I understood it and complied with the request. Her suspicions were cleared, but she still searched for banknotes, crumpling the collar of the overcoat which I had thrown down beside me, and she puckered her eyes as she considered where to look next. As she was so short that her head came only up to my chin, helped by the joy of looking down on a European lady, I held out my umbrella more or less to tease her. But such was her simplicity that she opened it out with a gesture to show that she thought that it was very important, and I put out my hand pleasantly, at which the old lady smiled and shook hands. Although it must have been very unpleasant in ordinary circumstances, as we did not know their language we did not have any severe questions and answers, and everything ended simply in a comical way.

Crossing the frontier, we went through an examination by Portuguese officials. We were made to write the names of our parents in this country and in Italy. They did not ask their family names, so I wrote down in the book of the Portuguese police the names of my parents and that of my mother-in-law, who died some years ago and who perhaps never had heard of such a country as Portugal. What nonsense! If they had asked her address, I would have written, 'Paradise'!

Along the slope of a hill where cork trees are planted in good order, a peasant was coming down. His attire was very countrified with a hood on his head, and his ox-cart was piled up with cork put in net sacks. In the valley, paddy-fields appeared and disappeared from view and soothed my eyes which had seen no moisture at all for some time. There were houses entangled all over with cobalt morning-glory, and houses which had white walls the skirts of which were decorated with tiles. There were also women, each wearing over her head a kerchief and a thing like a wreath, darned with beautiful tapes, on which was placed a shallow but broad winnow. They wore aprons and carried things in the winnows, keeping their balance by moving their arms and hips. I was surprised to find in such an unexpected place the counterpart of the countryside girls of Japan.

Lisbon is a town which was built from the seashore to the hills, so that a long train would not be entirely out of the tunnel though the locomotive was already in the Central station, and in order to go from the lower town to the hilly part, they avail themselves, at any part of the city, of lifts or electric cable-cars. Therefore the panorama from the park on the hill is superb with the piles of white walls and red roofs. It is not entirely unreasonable that they boast of

Lisbon saying, 'Don't say "très bon" before you see Lisbon!'
Lacking the light and shade of Spain, the view with the soft
colours of Japanese pottery would never tire one's eyes, and
the breeze that comes over the sea is also soothing. You feel
comfortable, but it is somewhat too commonplace for the
home of the Southern Barbarians as they were called in
Japan at the time of the Jesuit Mission. The innumerable
southern flowers that are in bloom in the streets and parks
are beautiful to see, like flowers in a porcelain flower bowl,
but they are nothing more than that.

The next day we visited Cintra. In the restaurant where
we had our lunch, an Englishman was making a fuss to
drive the flies away, which made me smile half with envy.
It seemed as if he saw a real fly for the first time in his life,
though he had seen in the museum magnified flies' legs full
of bacilli. His way of making a fuss somewhat resembled
that of a man proud of sedateness being attacked by a whole
nest of hornets. Posters of angels sprinkling insect-powders
and a picture of a Japanese girl holding a tin of 'Katole',
mosquito-powder, had also attracted our attention. Everything was as dirty as in Spain, and they have rain enough for
them to make paddy-fields, so naturally flies are bred. In
both countries a lot of people are pockmarked, and we have
often seen posters for the prevention of tuberculosis. On the
other hand, advertisements of English things such as Oxo
and Bovril showed the English influence in this seaport, and
in our hotel we were served with porridge.

Returning to Lisbon, the cotton uniforms of soldiers and
policemen, sweet vermicelli-cake made from the yolks of
eggs, which is the same thing as the cake special to Fukuoka,
and several other things, made me think that these must be

the origins of the things usually thought to be the specialities of southern Japan, so close was once the relationship between this country and ours. But now there is not even a legation and no treaties are made between the two countries, so we had to pay fifteen shillings or so for our *visas* and had much trouble in getting out of the country.

In the Library, where we were looking for old books published in the early part of the Tokugawa Shogunate, the director of the Library showed us into a sombre old room. He was talking with my husband in English, but suddenly he asked a question in French, then he switched over to German. Although I was sitting with downcast eyes, in my mind I was giving him a good scolding, 'Don't be so showy! You'd do better to make them wind the clock in the hall which isn't working. I saw a man working under you smoking and cleaning his pipe at the edge of the catalogue-shelves, but don't you mind?'

§ 6

Travelling in Severe Heat

It was a trying journey from the plateau of Castile, where Madrid stands, to the plain of Andalusia. We drove for several hours, gasping in the heat which nearly made us dizzy across the arid upland plains. In the fields like a desert, the scanty grass, that barely remained in half-life, was all but scorched a brown colour. The Chinese, who compared anything violent to 'autumn frost and the fierce sun', seemed to have known the burning sun of Spain as well as the violent force of the hoar-frost which adorns the plain of Tokyo with amethyst, and this thought impressed me anew with the genius of the Chinese for coining metaphorical expressions.

Every time our train stopped at a station, little boys came to sell water, carrying unglazed pitchers and shouting, 'Agua! Agua!' I was dying for a drink of water, but, as I was afraid of typhoid fever, I refrained from it. Even in such a small station, lottery ticket sellers were found, perhaps for the purpose of extracting the money which some people had won by playing cards in the train, and a man, who burnt his eyes in the sun and lost his sight, was singing plaintive songs under the windows. If you threw him small coins out of sympathy, he might have laughed at you with eyes wide open after the train started, but it looked romantic, and the train stopped long enough for us to listen to the songs quite leisurely. Soon the beggars went away, and only the shouting of 'Agua! Agua!' sounded like the croaks of weird birds.

What made us miserable was that though we were suffering from indigestion by reason of the heat, we unfortunately had only powdered medicine with us and no water which was fit to drink was obtainable, so we poured upon our parched tongues doses of heaped teaspoonfuls and forced them down our throats. The powder stuck to the roof of the mouth, and it tasted like clay. With great efforts we managed to swallow it, but thanks to this, we soon recovered.

As *Baedeker* says that at the edge of this plateau there are some salt lakes, I eagerly expected to see them, thinking that the sight of water would refresh me a little, but what I actually saw was the shore of dark-green stagnant water baked with salt which was produced by the violent sun heating and evaporating the water — salt, white like the crystallized sugar of old dates. Therefore the sight served only to make our throat more parched than before. The scene around us was that of late autumn. The salt was coagulated near the roots of dead reeds like thin ice, and the sight was suitable for a 'haiku' poet to stand at the water's edge with his hands folded behind him. Only it was surrounded with the intense heat of a hundred and twenty degrees! It was indeed a region of extreme incongruence.

Our train rolled along with the rattling of wheels. The back of the seat before me was covered all over with dust like mould on the leather, and at the left edge of the seat near the left window, my husband leaned languidly, and at the seat near the right window, part of the leather shone brightly. It was the trace left by my husband who took refuge from right to left, languidly getting up, as the burning sun intruded into the right window when the train turned a corner a moment ago. The malicious sun began to peep in again from the left side, and he shifted again unsteadily to this side and took a gulp from the wine bottle, falling into a light sleep. The sunlight again turned to the window on this side. The train seemed to have got to a slope at the edge of the tableland, for it was meandering considerably.

They say that a man frozen to death does not feel the cold, but the same may be said about the person who falls down in a swoon in consequence of the heat. Whenever I felt that the sight and sound before me seemed to recede farther and farther away while I kept my eyes wide open, I put out my hand without a word, and my husband passed me the wine bottle in silence. When the strong drink of this district stimulated my throat, I would suddenly come back to myself as if hit on the back and would find myself drowned in extreme heat, and ridiculing myself with the exaggerated expression, 'gasping for breath', I could think, for a short while, with clear consciousness.

We at last crossed over the divide of the Sierra Morena range, and our train went down steeply into the Andalusian plains. I looked up at the rugged mountains and peeped into the gorge, which is the source of the great majestic river Guadalquivir, to cool my dried-up senses with the song of running water. But as the gorge was so deep, I could not see the bottom, but only half-way down, and when it became a little wider, I involuntarily uttered an exclamation of surprise. At the bottom of the gorge there lay a deep-pink stream. I gazed at it and found that it was the blossoms of oleanders. The oleanders, which were growing thickly, firmly joining their hands together as if to fill the gorge with their own tribe, were in full bloom. They seemed determined not to give an inch of land to others, for they wanted to feed themselves without losing a drop of water. They continued in an unending line, winding with the gorge. The poisonous-pink stream looked as weird as a huge serpent that has had its skin entirely peeled, and it continued interminably, sometimes hiding itself at the bottom of a cliff and reappearing farther on, and now diving from the right, now from the left, under the iron bridge over which our train was dashing down, every time pushing back our desire for the green of water. It was beautiful like a voluptuous courtesan, and I keenly felt that I was in a strange country.

At about six-thirty, when the evening sun was piercing through our train, we arrived at Cordova, and, getting out of the train, we went to our hotel. While we were having a bath, the evening of the southern country had changed into night, and a cool wind floated like water through the veranda under the grape-trellis. The city lights were seen far away and, in the waning moonlight, the shadows of the vine-leaves fluttered upon my wine-glass, and the shadows of the grapes that hung in rich bunches were also waving on the tiled floor. I put my glass of white wine to my eyes and muttered a line from a Chinese poem, 'Come, fill my precious glass, and let it glow in amber!' and thus I fell into a sweet reverie, mellowed with wine. I now had no fear of being annoyed by telephone calls. I was not bothered with the necessity of writing a notice for the newspaper delivery man, telling him not to force us to take papers that we did not want, and I was entirely at ease. The lovely stars seemed to be twinkling at the points of the swaying, rustling palm-leaves. I enjoyed the peaceful rising of those stars up to the highest branches. 'How peaceful and quiet we are now', I said. 'Yes', said my husband, and nothing more. 'How peaceful and quiet!' I repeated. 'Yes', he said again. We spoke in this manner once in every quarter of an hour.

§ 7

In Seville

The Andalusians say, 'Whoever has not seen Sevilla has not seen maravilla' (a wonder). The thick clumsy walls of the Alcazar enwraps the gorgeous, delicate interior like a sweet pomegranate which has a rough outside, but delicate beauty within. The superb beauty of the Saracen art in palaces we saw later at the Alhambra, so what is described here will be only about the beauty of the garden which is also a relic of the Arabs who once ruled over this place. The hero of the *Arabian Nights* also rested in such a garden as this.

A garden of the Arabian style is full of small paths with

the sweet, suffocating fragrance of jasmine, and it is difficult
to see through the intermingling branches of bushes that
have lustrous leaves like southern plants, so every time we
turn a corner, we are sometimes surprised with heaps of
dazzling red flowers, and sometimes with the leaves of ferns
trembling with dewdrops in unexpected gloomy grottoes.
And at the end of such a small path, there is a maze made of
hedges of myrtle, a garden labyrinth. The evergreen myrtle
trees, with small leaves like a box tree, are trimly pruned, and
the thick, dark green hedges, nearly five feet in height, stand
in range, barring our passage, and in the middle of the maze
there is a fountain like liquefied crystal where, I was told, an
ancient queen used to take a bath under blue sky. It is the
custom of the Northern people to confine themselves within
stuffy rooms, but the beauties of the South played with
water, breaking the reflections of white clouds. Was their
skin pale, reflecting the green of the tree leaves, soft and weak
with the fragrance of the white roses, or was it elastic in
energetic chocolate-brown colour like a seal resting on a rock
sharing the healthy blood of the Moors, I don't know which.
But what is sure is that a man who pined for her was irritated
in the maze, seeking for her. When he wanted to peep
through the hedge, putting his face against it, the young
leaves of the myrtle softly yet severely worked as a blind,
and its sweet scent, that seemed to warm the blood, made his
passion all the more violent. When he stood on tiptoe with
yearning to look beyond the five feet of green, a white dove
which was flying, tracing rings above the fountain, suddenly
came down on him and perched on his shoulder in a most
friendly manner. But the shadow of the naked queen which
rested a moment before in the round eyes of the dove, was
not to be found even if he peeped into them.

Drawing such a scene in fancy, and complaining about the prosaicness of the modern bathroom shut up closely by a lock that severs us from the open air, I walked bending my head down a narrow path paved with white marble and noted that the stones were full of small holes. In the centre where the straight paths gathered in the shape of a star, there was a tiled chair. As usual in a hot country, even a little stroll under the trees would cause slight perspiration and fatigue. On such occasions, the king seated himself on this tiled seat, and immediately he sat there, from the holes in the marble stones, innumerable lovely jets of water shot up like silver threads, dancing as the king moved, sometimes low and sometimes high in the air. When the swarthy king of the Moors wandered about the garden developing a stratagem all alone, and sank down into the chair with a sigh for the declining fortunes of his tribe, the jets must have sprung up like frightened fairies. When the king of Spain, boasting of his conquest in occupying the castle, gave a banquet lasting the whole night to his subjects attired in beautiful dress for the occasion, and suddenly sat down in this chair in the garden, the holes in the marble must have shot water forcibly upwards, which splashed the flustered people's feet, while the king was having a hearty laugh.

The narrow path soon comes back below the high palace. There is an iron gate intertwined with jasmine, and two watchmen in black enamel helmets, in seeming ancient style, guarded the entrance to the subway, half asleep. The dark subway, which we entered, is said to be the secret passage to the golden tower which stands on the shore of the river far away from the Alcazar. Going a little farther down, we found an oblong pool. Although this pool is now buried underground, covered with a floor by the prosaic people of

modern times, yet formerly it spread a mirror in the centre
of the gorgeous palace, reflecting the beauties who gathered
round, and when they left, the carvings in the arches re-
doubled the gorgeousness of the palace.

Seville, the town of Carmen, is a fit place for her to have
lived in, the main street being called 'Sierpes' or Serpent
Street. Neither horse nor car are allowed to pass; the cafés
freely intrude upon the roadway with their chairs, and, with
their drinks they take relishes such as snails, tough and sweet
when chewed, or barnacles flavoured with lemon-juice. Most
of these gentlemen, being thick-set, are of the type that I
would call 'Don Jose', with goggle-eyes, looking extremely
near-sighted, and blubbering faces with long-arched eyebrows through pining for girls' favours. Women trailing
mantillas of black silk lace softly behind them and swinging
their long thin black skirts came and went. Their figures,
all in black, are just the reverse of unpretentious. It attracts
men's attention the longer to their proud features. If the
jealous Spanish beauties wore charmingly designed dresses,
and the men would look merely upon those designs, they
might tear off their dresses. Therefore the fans with which
they can gaily attract people's notice whenever they want,
are most fitting for their purpose as ornaments to their persons. They open their large fans, gently fan near their
breasts three or four times, then suddenly shut them and
open them again at once. How capricious they look by that
gesture! Every time the slender ivory bones swish with a
cool sound.

They open and shut their fans so frequently and they walk
so slowly that strangers could forget their nostalgia by competing in guessing how many times this or that woman would

shut her fan before coming up near them. If they were to walk rapidly, their earrings would shake and tear off the lobes of their ears. Their earrings are pure gold in open work and have pear-shaped pearls like tear-drops. The women who wear gold rings no shorter than two inches in diameter are somewhat ungraceful women with a trace of gipsy blood. They wear lovelocks curling in the shape of a '?' and their nails are manicured as red as blood. The ladies who pretend to be graceful in the antique style proudly wear tortoise-shell 'peineta' high above their heads and pay special attention to their lace mantillas. What beautiful expressive eyes they have! Dreamy, wistful, and at times gleaming with passion or with hatred, those eyes are now attracted to jewel-shops and now to fan-shops so gaily-coloured that they suggest the wings of a bird of paradise, and then they float away. There are lottery-shops which are painted in the same red, yellow and purple stripes as the new national flag. They are found at all the prominent corners of the streets, so that strangers take them for post offices!

'Do you remember that bull fighter to-day? He had an ostrich feather in his hat painted in three colours. Did you see it?'

'Yes! I am anxious to take in those three colours in my new dress.'

This was the conversation of girls throwing silver coins in a generous manner to dwarf beggars who are not uncommon in Spain. They were waiting for the opening of the theatre that starts at ten o'clock. At half-past nine in the evening, the tambourine for the Spanish dance in the matinée was still gaily sounding in the theatre.

There is nothing so interesting as a market, especially in southern countries. There were all kinds of melons and pumpkins, and heaps of tomatoes. Olives and lemons were not well treated here; rolling in the passage and trampled on by people, they emit a fragrant smell. Along the pillars, large garlics were hung. Two large bunches of big green grapes that looked as if they were carved out from jewels only cost twopence. Even then it was we alone who paid the price asked and while old women were haggling over their bargain, the lively snails that seemed to have been gathered from the vine-leaves in the morning, taking advantage of the chance, slowly crept out over the edge of a barrel and fled to the cherries that were kept in the next stall. In the seed shops there were pine seeds, pumpkin seeds and sunflower seeds, while the fleshy purslane, which is hated as weed by the suburban residents of Tokyo, was put up for sale as a kind of vegetable. The butchers' quarter, having pigs' heads, legs, trotters and oxen's brains, made me shrink from it with its bloody smell. In the fish shop I found abundance of hair-tail, sea-bream, and horse-mackerel which cannot be seen in northern Europe but which are familiar to us in Japan, and there were shells, cuttlefish and lobsters. 'Hullo! They are selling octopus,' I said, and stopped, when they called me, whistling with their lips, thinking I was a customer. The satisfaction you get when you feel that you are mingling in the life of the natives — to speak with exaggeration, the feeling as if you are embraced by the country, can be obtained more in a market like this than when you are in a pleasant home-like atmosphere, where you are entertained hospitably as a rare guest from a far country, and where you are looked after with kindness because they think that you must feel awkward amongst unfamiliar customs.

§ 8

Granada Gipsies

The narrow, deep ravine which forms a natural moat around the fortress of the Alhambra, and the sharp slope of the hill which forms the opposite bank of the ravine are the abodes of gipsies. The caves made in the rocks by hollowing them out are dotted along the slope one above the other, and, winding footpaths crawl upwards by the side of which there are dry whitish fences of stone with thick clumsy cacti growing above them in riot looking like so many rackets.

The entrance of a gipsies' den was so low that if you were not careful your head would strike against the roof. The inside had a length of eight yards and a width of four yards, and there being no distinction between the ceiling and the walls, they had the hollows and bumps that were made when the rocks were scratched away and only lime was plastered over. On the surface of the rock that was white like the make-up of a prostitute four or five well-polished copper pans and ladles were hung and shone brightly. At the end of the cave there hung a black curtain a yard wide that showed there was a room still farther inside, and when the hanging cloth shook the confusion of gloomy things was glimpsed behind it.

Soon after, we sat side by side pressed against the wall of the den, and some gipsy dancers gathered jabbering at the entrance. In tight yellow coats with big black spots on them, and skirts, which with two or three pleats bulged out at the hips were hemmed with black tapes, they were like fairies or wasps, stooping in at the rock entrance and again busily going out. When they nodded to each other, the stems of the red carnations which they put in their jet-black hair shook like feelers. The youngest girl was most like a wasp. The older ones were plump and sensuous with the wildness and voluptuousness of a camellia, and some of them were even as offensive as an over-ripe persimmon about to fall off from the tree, their dresses being also in red and black. Soon the girls came in all together.

Just as the waves rush into a cave near the seashore, the flood of colours whirled into the den, and as soon as they stood on both sides there arose such an explosive noise that I could hardly keep my eyes open. There were ten dancers and three musicians playing guitars and tambourines. They were indeed terrible notes. The music was struck up desperately as if to drive away such an annoying thing as common sense. Rising to the inciting tune one of the dancers in yellow sprang out from her chair into the middle of the den like one possessed, and, in the space of about the size of an ordinary bed, she began to dance, bending and twisting her body. In her hands, which she held above her head, castanets clicked feverishly like teeth chattering with a chill. To the tune of the musicians she gradually twisted round, taking tiny steps on her toes. In the abundant black hair which was folded about her back a celluloid comb of red and blue was fastened carelessly. Now her backbone began to dance. Every time the wave of muscular movement which started from her shoulders came down to the hips the light pursuing the shade flowed with an undulating movement over the dress of yellow and black. It was the glossy waving of the back of a poisonous caterpillar squirming along in a hurry. It was not hatred but charm, after all, that almost gave me an impulse to crush it underfoot. Suddenly the girl pirouetted so vehemently that it seemed as if her earrings would be shaken off and turning to the front she dropped down into her chair.

The rhapsodic beats of hands and tambourines continued unconcernedly while the trembling note of the guitar linked the beats. Another girl stood and danced on her toes, making by her finger-tips sounds like those of electricity. Sometimes in her obsidian eyes there was a mischievous look, and, stooping, she gesticulated as if to invite one to her, drawing her hands in towards herself, and then suddenly she would straighten herself, raising one of her shoulders, protruding her chin and stamping her feet as if to irritate a man saying, 'Oh no! You can't do that!' And the singers shouted the tune with their shrill voices, 'O-ray-yah!' Her enchanting smile arrogantly expressed how delightful it was to play with the audience's heart like a cat playing with a grasshopper, now catching it and then letting it escape, confident that it was entirely in her hands after all, and her smiles, parting the blood-coloured lips, revealed lurid-white teeth in beautiful array. The dance now seemed to be at its height. The dancer stayed in one place, and sometimes jumping up into the air and sometimes striking the ground with her knees, beating time, she danced, wriggling herself, while her red dress shook and whirled round her body like flames. The rhapsodic gesture seemed to express the agony of a woman who is being boiled in a kettle and suddenly she was seated in a chair.

The irritating gipsy dances continued, showing the strange mixture of confidence and desperation, and after a few such dances were repeated, the 'capitan', a man with a short neck and a ruddy face, where greed found its vent in fat, chanted a song. The dance *ensemble* was nothing more than a violent and wild symphony of dazzling colours, and when the colours were suddenly divided into two, the brilliant sunlight that peeped through the narrow entrance opposite attracted us strongly. When we went out unsteadily into the open air we felt as if nothing had happened, like a man who had gone through a strong attack of an ague. I looked round as if to see for the first time the blue sky that almost looked metallic, and the clumsy wall of the Alhambra, the whitish stone fences, and the cacti laden with dust.

At the foot of the stony zigzag path, two mounted police were standing side by side in antique black helmets in order to guard strangers who went into the unsavoury quarters.

Next to that we visited the cathedral. Never in all my life shall I forget the grandeur of an old Spanish cathedral! Painfully dazzled by the fierce glare of the sun outside, we pushed open the heavy door and entered into the darkness and utter silence. The light that filtered through the stained-glass fell on the paved floor and quivered in masses of rays, and the little choristers who came and went shaking their incense-burners and scarlet robes and white-laced surplices, made me feel that I was born in olden days for just half an hour. The fragrance of the incense and the voices singing a Latin hymn filled the huge cathedral, and now and then the monotonous shrill sing-song of boys of ten or twelve years old mingled in the hymn verse by verse. They were voices that sounded pleasing to our ears only by reason of tradition. A choir-boy yawned with his mouth wide open and a plump priest, who had his head shaved in the shape of a poppy head, boxing his ears, sang 'Ave Maria' with his deep bass voice. It was amusing to see such a sight, but on both sides of the nave there were chapels in small partitions for noted families and it was sickening to see that they had iron lattices like the cages of fierce animals. I have described already the stupendous foolishness of the treasuries, but the main image of the Virgin Mary in this cathedral was studded with sapphires and corals even to her shoes and gloves, and I was told that she had several other best attires in which she was dressed on festival days. I saw the priest's palanquin with an uncanny feeling, thinking that when he visited a death-bed in it he must have prayed beside the dying man, 'May this man's belongings come to the cathedral and his spirit go to heaven!' The crown of Queen Isabella kept in this cathedral is of simple workmanship in silver and looks pleasing compared to those of the priests. It is also interesting that the treasure-box given to Columbus to make the funds for his expedition, still remains, but now of course empty. The Pandora's box that did not disappoint the opener! Out of this Jack-in-the-box all the sky-scrapers have popped out.

In Japan the sun rises higher towards midday, but in this part of the world it was so hot that it seemed as though the sun was coming down directly over our heads. My ears sang and I felt faint. The pressure of the sunlight entered even into my eardrums and I am sure that even Confucius could not have helped having a midday nap. Just as snakes and frogs hibernate to pass the coldness of winter, so the whole town slept in silence under the dog-day heat. When you look down upon the town from the window of your hotel at about one o'clock in the afternoon, there is the burning sun above and thousands of whitewashed houses standing in silence below as if they were petrified, and it is a strange sight. Only in the distance swallows are darting up and down like swarming midges. However, when the evening sun is just setting beyond the Sierra Nevada, ten thousand feet high, bathing the mountain range in purple, there arise again the crowing of cocks, the barking of dogs, the braying of donkeys and the shrieking voices of children — laughter and the noises of the streets are revived far away below our veranda, like the brawling tide, and the day of Granada is made the more lively and attractive for all these changes.

CHAPTER VIII

NORTHERN EUROPE

§ 1

Hamburg

On the way to the north from Spain, we stayed two or three days in Paris, visited the battlefields, and then started for Hamburg. Directly we passed the frontier into Germany, an old woman came to sweep our carriage and began to scour energetically, so that everything became as clean as it could be. The ladies in the same compartment were in low-heeled shoes, and on the covers of the magazines which they were reading with their legs stretched out artlessly, a picture of a young man and woman in shirt sleeves was drawn standing side by side in the ripe cornfields with smiles on their faces sunburnt to a salmon colour. A sightseeing party of schoolgirls from Denmark had small satchels like those used by postmen hanging from their shoulders. They were going back to their homes in this train.

Crossing the lower course of the Rhine, the train ran all the time through a district where factory chimneys were to be seen. The fields were well looked after, and though there was no such scenic beauty dotted with cornflowers and poppies as seen in France, they were trim and clean, being kept more properly. German cleanliness is that of a napkin ironed and folded, while France has the beauty of silk gloves used two or three times, which, though soft and sweet with an aroma of perfume, we would never think of putting near our mouths. Now I remembered partly with yearning and partly with dissatisfaction the simplicity and modesty of the life of the Japanese who express cleanliness and beauty by one and the same word.

Hamburg is a port town. As I dogmatically decided that port towns are sooty, I was surprised at the neatness of the hotel near the moat of clean water. In our travels we stayed at more than sixty hotels, but this was the only one where I found in the lavatory a waterproof bag which could be closed tightly at the mouth, with the notice for ladies: 'Maids will dispose of this bag'. This was the first thing about which, when my trip was decided on, I had asked my friends who had been abroad. Their replies were all complaints, saying for instance, 'asked a maid and gave her a tip'. 'I have heard,' some of them said, 'in England they burn it in the fire, but when central heating was introduced into boarding-houses, the pipes in the lavatories were blocked, causing much trouble.' Thus I, as a woman, was much annoyed by the fact that they do not take into consideration this unavoidable necessity in connection with the equipment of lavatories, so that I was almost led to look upon society in general with distrustful eyes, wondering whether they were not ignoring some inevitable facts in the social system on grounds of dignity and expediency. It may sound very poetical if I say, quoting from a 'haiku' poet in Japan, 'Nowhere can I throw away the bath-water, insects chirping all around', but as a matter of fact I had been very much annoyed, and therefore I was delighted with this Palast Hotel. It was also proper that they provided us with sheets of paper in the shape of a ring, which we could use and throw away. What dull nerves they have got that they sit on the seat one after the other in the lavatory and are never annoyed! If this custom were a

Japanese one, the Japanese themselves would noisily complain that it was a barbarous custom, and I thought it regrettable that Europeans complained only about our system of lavatories without saying anything about their own. In French theatres an old woman wiped the seat nonchalantly after each person as if to clean it by a charm and made a profit out of it by tips. If I were allowed to speak more about such an unsavoury subject as this, what interested me was that the difference of the characteristics of the nations is seen by whether in hotels they had violin-shaped vessels for the use of ladies. I did not see them in Scandinavia or England. In Germany, in the hotels for foreign tourists, they were kept in cupboards. In the Latin countries, in the cheap hotels where there was no w.c. equipment, a jar and a bucket were sometimes provided so that it was known when they were used. The fact that this sort of thing is considered so much a matter of course gives to us Japanese food for thought, as well as the fact that in shop windows in Holland, washing apparatus was so openly arranged for public inspection, and therein we may find some suggestions for solving the relation between climate and birth-rate, and population and the extent of a country. Now let me stop speaking about such a thing.

We saw the great tunnel that runs underneath the Elbe, and the other sights of the city. The astounding stone image of Bismarck looked very much like our Buddhist nationalist priest Nichiren. Facing the difficulties of the country, the people thought passionately of their national heroes and a violent craze for Bismarck arose all over Germany. Even in the dining-room of the Palast Hotel there were portraits of Bismarck and Moltke, and a picture of Bismarck also hung in a well-known café. Mr. F. took us to a restaurant. A bald-headed old man in a white apron, who looked a typical master of a dainty-shop, brought us raw fish in a bowl and said something like this: 'These lobsters from Heligoland were netted only this morning. This turbot has a good lustre behind the gills. Look how fresh this is! What? You can't eat so much? Oh, no! I'll cook them in such a way that they'll melt in your mouth!' A poster of an American Line Shipping Company was hanging quite artlessly on the narrow wall, which was just like Germany. The food was indeed excellent. In Europe, where we had to eat only things which were heavily flavoured, the faint sweetness characteristic of fresh lobsters boiled quickly was specially welcome, and though we were full of lobster, they were so fresh that even my husband, who has a poor digestion, was not affected at all.

What Hamburg is noted for is the Hagenbeck Zoo. I was absolutely fascinated with the sea-elephants, which are like flabby elephant-skin torpedoes with tiny fins and tails. They have smooth domed heads and their eyes are extremely charming. Eagerly waiting for the keeper to give them fish, they crawled like large hairless caterpillars wriggling their huge bodies, and climbing up the bank, they held the upper half of their bodies upright, while their insides seemed to go down to the lower half in a muddle, to an outburst of laughter from the spectators. They opened their small round eyes wide and peeped into the next cage, and then feeling tired, they fell forward suddenly with a flabby shaking of their whole bodies. Now they kept their eyes like slits and sighed deeply, giving an expression of being irritated, and when at last the keeper showed signs of giving them fish, they gurgled in their throats and coaxed him. A big rhinoceros was standing majestically in its thick armour. It is a remnant of the prehistoric age and only on this account is jealously protected from becoming extinct. When will it be that people look upon guns and warships with the same feeling, saying, 'In ancient times they had things like this, with which they killed one another?'

What made us angry was that, while we went along looking at the cages of gorillas and monkeys, we came upon the natives of the South Seas kept in their respective huts within railings and fed just like other animals. Zoologically, of course, there is no difference between them and the white bears or deer kept in water or among rocks just as in their natural surroundings. One of the causes that it was so offensive to me was probably the fact that the shanty of those natives had, at the roof ends, a cross of timber projecting from them as on the roofs of our shrines. If they wanted to exhibit the races of man in order from the gorillas, in the belief that man is an animal in its most advanced form, they had better keep the greatest beauty in Germany and Einstein in the last cage! It can be one outlook anyway, but I hate their way of treating the aboriginal natives as if they had evolved from animals while they themselves had descended from God, taking for granted that the wide difference of the two was not a matter of degree but of quality which made an absolute gulf that could never be crossed by either. It is a positive proof of the fundamental prejudice of the white, that there has arisen no protest that it is an insult to human beings to keep natives like this in this garden. I have heard that they stopped keeping Ainus (of Northern Japan) through the protest of Japan. If countries had no power to protest, there would be no knowing which countrymen they would keep in the Zoological Gardens to be looked at with the same curious eyes that see the sea-elephants, by the people who are proud that they alone have the right to go to heaven.

§ 2

Denmark

We made for Denmark on the next day.

In front of the Central Station of Hamburg we took the airway company's bus. Our bus soon arrived at the aerodrome, and I found it just the same as a railway station. The only difference in the service was that they gave, with the tickets, cottonwool to stuff in the ears, and some pieces of chewing-gum. Going through the turnstile, we found aeroplanes arranged in a row. The eight seats in ours were all taken and my seat was the foremost one. Soon a stout and trusty-looking pilot came to his seat, explosive noises started, and the aeroplane began to taxi along the ground. The aerodrome field was rich in green grass dotted with daisies and buttercups, and the white and yellow of the flowers flashed past like meteors leaving a trail of sparks behind. The aeroplane ran, crushing down the wetted green grass, and sprays of water were splashed about right and left with a swishing noise. While I was looking around, stretching my neck like a crane, the spray which was raised by the wheels suddenly stopped. That marked the moment of the take-off, and the green field immediately began to sink downwards, gradually but steadily.

I had long been waiting to experience 'a wind that takes us for thousands of miles', and the feeling of flying up into the air was indeed fresh and pleasant. The wings of the aeroplane were shining in dull silver, and now it turned round, balancing itself, in the act of pointing its nose in the direction of Denmark. I would like to recommend you to learn ski-ing if you want to taste the sensation of flying with a leisurely mind. The experience of curving round, in which you cannot turn standing straight, sweeps away the uneasiness for you, making you feel it a natural course that the aeroplane banks. Especially the superb experience of air-taxi-ing and of the shock which you feel at the moment the plane lands will not be spoilt by closing your eyes in fear, if you are accustomed to the sample of these experiences on the snow-covered slope.

We flew for some time at an altitude from which red-roofed farmhouses seemed like chocolate-boxes for Christmas presents. Clouds blotted out a meadow, a river, and a canal one after another. When a white cloud passed below us, I felt for the first time that I was actually separated from the ground. We came out over the sea. The channel was so shallow that its bottom could be seen from the sky, yet the border of water and land may have affected the pressure of the air, for our aeroplane was slightly shaken. Our seats suddenly fell sheer downward and a gap was formed between my seat and my bottom, and then my bottom settled, chasing after the seat. Of course, all this happens in a moment, but the analysis of the feeling in an air-pocket would be something like that. The one which I experienced was no more than a miniature version of it, but still it was unpleasant enough to make me feel as if a vacuum was formed near my diaphragm.

The aeroplane entered Denmark and flew above meadows all the time. Cows were fastened at certain intervals to make them feed on the grass gradually from one end, and this could be discerned from our altitude by the light and dark green, and by the cows standing side by side that were eating the edges of the dark part of the green.

Clouds came and went, and each time our aeroplane shifted its height in the cloud and ran through it. It was quite impossible to tell, just by physical feeling, how high we arose or what distance we dropped, so what was most interesting was to come out of the clouds. Sometimes we came down so low that even the horns of the cows were seen clearly, and sometimes, when we flew high up, I would search for cows and find them looking like fleas hiding at the edge of a mat. Then I would feel an acute pain in my forehead. Again we were enveloped in clouds, and soon, when we came out over the coastline of the Baltic Sea, there were rows of tents, and sea-bathing people were waving their caps. Casually I looked about and found the shadow of an aeroplane falling on the waves to the right. I was delighted to see our aeroplane looking so smart.

All at once Copenhagen came under our eyes. The moment I thought, 'Hullo! Is it passing over?' our aeroplane banked steeply, heeling over on its side, and set to going down in rapid spirals. The large town began to move round and round like a gramophone record, and when I imagined that the solid ground pressed forward like a tidal wave with tremendous force, I felt a sudden shock at my feet. Our aeroplane gave two or three sprightly jerks, dashed forward, and then regained its stability and smoothly ran and stopped at the fixed point.

The motor coach of the airway company hurried towards the city of Copenhagen.

Denmark is a country of solidity. It is German solidity, plus the smell of the earth but minus the force of arms. It is quite natural that names of Japanese agricultural economists and gymnasts were found in the register of the Tourist

Hotel. The sturdiness of the Danes as the descendants of the Northmen still remains, but the roughness has now been modified. They are a respectable race that have re-established themselves, through days of trial, to the tenacity, simplicity and productivity of the mother earth, where they have settled down after a life of piracy in which the jaws of hell lay just below the bottom of their ships. But they are generally homely-looking. The women have ruddy faces, the cheeks of which seem to have been made of lumps of flesh into which the cheese or fresh butter they eat had changed. Their bodies are also stout and stiff, and their legs are not watery like a Japanese forked radish but solid and thick like a log. The children look lovelier than those of any other country, but their loveliness is that of a bulldog puppy. They are all the more lovely because they anticipate the sturdiness in their grown-up days. Of course, some of the young girls are extremely pleasant to see, not because their features are artistic, but because their faces are fresh and bright both spiritually and physically. Nearly all the men have snow-tanned tips to their noses and are of the same type as North Pole explorers, having rough skins and ragged hair. If you go to a pleasure-ground such as the Tivoli, you will find some clumsy imitations of Saracen architecture or of a pagoda of the East, and if you compare this with an exhibition in France you will feel the contempt which was expressed in the words, 'earthy peasant', with which the sons of Tokyo in their decadent period used to insult unrefined people. But their good quality is apparent in their very clumsiness in imitating other people.

If you go to the Glyptothek or the Thorvaldsen Museum, you will be impressed with the quantity and quality of the sculptures from the Greek to all later ages, and with the smooth technique of Thorvaldsen, but what is most charming is the visitors. A young couple who seemed to have come from the country were absorbed in appreciation and criticism, both wearing similar large-pocketed coats of waterproof cloth and hats of the same quality. They carried on their backs rucksacks for shopping still deflated, and I thought that there must be a pair of cycles at the entrance. I came across such couples more than once, and it made me pleasantly imagine the highly cultured topics beside the fire in a farmhouse. They are quite different from those who visit the Louvre. A boy of about thirteen, in a boy scout's uniform, was looking up at the image of Apollo entirely fascinated, sometimes approaching it with his eyes on some curve of the flesh and sometimes receding to gaze at it as a whole. His eyes told that he was not forced by homework to write an essay such as, 'Give your impressions of the image of Apollo'. I thought with an envious feeling that this was indeed a country which produced Thorvaldsen. I thought also that the statues of Christ by Thorvaldsen which were to be found in a church here were the most appealing that I had ever seen. The Ethnographical Museum was also amazing. Take the exhibits from Japan, for example. There were, besides such common things as armours and sword-guards, ornamental hairpins that had such designs as steamships, which were in fashion at the time when 'blackships' or steamships first visited the shores of our country. There were also the saddles of horses for brides in the country, which made me blush because in Japan ethnological museums are conspicuous for their absence. Though many other things might claim our first consideration, still I had to feel irritation again, thinking that all specimens of local customs which could now be collected for a mere song would soon be irretrievably lost. As Denmark is a country that has a dolmen on their banknotes, we found a great number of things of the Stone Age. They were arranged educationally, making, for instance, models of shell-mounds in which they were found, and a father was giving explanations to his child. For the first time in Europe I found plenty of couples walking with the real joy of taking their children along with them.

In the evening, walking in a park by the sea, I saw some young men assiduously engaged in putting a boat into a boathouse. I also saw young couples having a walk, and some of them wore coats made of the same waterproof cloth. The psychology of Europeans is inscrutable. Men protect themselves with a shirt-front like a cuttle-bone and a suit of wool even in summer, and women are in full dress when they are half naked, even in winter. This could be borne because it is rare for me to be dressed like that. But as it is women that are the weaker sex, it would be natural for them to attire themselves in such a way as to give them full scope for activity in order to equal men. As it is, they walk on stilts of high-heeled shoes and fashion would have their skirts slender like slender envelopes, though they were broad like a lantern in old days. Now a close-fitting suit is fashionable, so that no pockets are allowed and all one's property is carried in a handbag. It may look smart to carry bright patent-leather bags under the arm, but it seems dangerous to carry them in a town so bustling that one could easily be victimized by the light-fingered gentry. I felt sorry for a Parisian woman when she was choosing a hat in a fidgety way. First of all she puts her bag on a shelf in the shop and, keeping an eye on it, she puts the hat on with both hands, and then putting a hand on the bag, she peeps into the mirror, and the other hand arranges it this way and that, and while she is changing hats her eyes are kept on the bag again because she has to use both hands. A Chinese proverb says, 'Stable in property, stable in mind', but in her case, having no pockets, one gets a suspicious mind. As they put their purses in an unsafe place, all men are to them thieves. The trouble with us is the necessity of serving fashion, thereby compromising our own characters. It seems to me that the generous air, common to the Danes, owed much to their big pockets with buttons.

While I was thinking to myself in such a queer vein, a couple in whitish costumes came towards us. It was a sailor and his sweetheart. The woman had on, at the edge of the short skirt that was in fashion last year, different cloth patched round, and on her breast she wore a ribbon matching the cloth. On the hill near the shore, where the masts of boats at anchor are standing like a forest, is a huge rock on whose side is represented in sculpture a group of stooping explorers drawing a sledge with all their might. But sturdiness is not their only virtue, for on a rock near the sea, where the silvery grey water of the inlet stays in dullness, there is placed a bronze statue of a young, fresh mermaid resting her hand on the ground and keeping her tail in a curve. They are indeed an interesting nation and I now remembered that Andersen was born in this country.

The next day we went out into the country in a charabanc. There were woods and woods of beech trees. They had no extremely big trees nor were there deep forests. But the trees, nearly the same size, continued neatly and cleanly, same as the human society of Denmark. Our guide said with evident pride, though pretending to be perplexed, 'I am sorry, but in this city there are no slums worthy of your

visit', which rather tickled the tourists, because in nearly all·
other cities they were made to inspect the slums. This is
indeed a peaceful country! The country where the difference
between rich and poor is so small shows the same tendency in
its topography which is even, and our guide made us laugh,
saying, 'This place is the highest point on Sjaelland being
4700 ... (Everybody was bewildered for some time) ...
centimetres high!' The castle of Frederiksborg has a beautiful situation with its shadow thrown on the lake beneath.
Inside there is, as usual, plenty of armour and shields, but
what is noteworthy is the presence of the busts of scholars.
Speaking of the busts of scholars, we noticed that of the six
busts that were ranged in front of the University, two were
those of linguists, which recalls to us the fact that this is a
country that even to-day has Jespersen, the veteran scholar
of English philology.

We had our lunch near this castle. It was a tidy restaurant
but all the Danish people opened their lunch-baskets which
they had brought with them and only ordered big glasses of
milk. The young girls' answers, 'Ja, ja!' attracted our attention, which sounded as deep and strong as a man's yell. The
earrings worn by Northern women are big pearls fitting
closely to the lobes like cuff-links and lack the delicate grace
of trembling jewels. Finery which is unfit to their nature is
of no use. Next we visited the old castle of Helsingor
(Elsinore) which is famous as the scene of Hamlet. It is on
the Baltic Sea, surrounded with double banks of grass, and
a row of antique bronze guns pointed towards the sea. The
gloomy citadel, with the dismal waves of the northern country
breaking against the foot of the battlements, is a most suitable scene for the ghost of Hamlet's father to appear. In the
watch-tower, armed sentinels are still mounting guard.

It is only about two and a half miles to Sweden on the opposite side, and the windows of the houses are clearly visible. This is the mouth of the Baltic Sea, which in days gone by the Russian Baltic Fleet passed for the East, and after a long weary voyage, passing round the Cape of Good Hope, they all sunk down to the depths of the distant Eastern Sea, their hulls rotted and covered over with oyster shells, as in the words of the satirical ditty, 'Each wrestler displays in the ring, appearing never to lose'. They passed the straits proudly and majestically, and the people who stood on both shores are said to have looked after them with the belief that the small island country in the Far East would be crushed with one stroke. On our way back we went along the seashore. It looked like rain, and although it was July 12th, the weather was cold with the temperature at fifteen degrees, but they were swimming in the water quite unconcernedly. Although they were poor swimmers, I could not but admire their physical strength which, trained in this manner, would enable them to go on North Pole expeditions. Our touring through Spain and Denmark in two weeks made me realize the fact that the climate of the one makes me only one-tenth as tired as that of the other. After a whole day's sightseeing I still found myself fresh at night, and I went to bed reluctantly. This even made me think that it was natural for the Danes to be so hard-working. But, on the other hand, I had to think of the long dark winter, because even in July it was cold like this, and I felt the greater respect for the people who are fresh and lively under such a depressing climate.

§ 3

Tea with the Jespersens

The next day we visited Dr. Jespersen. His house, close to the wood of Gentofte in the outskirts of Copenhagen, was a simple cottage which had a wicket in the hedge of beech trees that covered his nameplate. In the porch there were a number of cane chairs which tempted one to sit in the sun. The Doctor and my husband sat facing each other, while Mrs. Jespersen invited me to a small table placed in a corner which she called her own nook. She was an old lady who looked like a good housekeeper. She pushed a half-knitted sweater into a big work-basket and treated me to some of her home-made biscuits. She was hospitable in a very homely way, and in answer to my remark of delight that they were just like Japanese biscuits, she fetched the whole tin and told me to take a lot. When I said, 'We came by aeroplane', she suddenly took my hand, saying with emphasis, 'Never fly again'. 'Are your children all right', she asked, 'left at home?' 'My mother', I replied, 'is living near my house, and our maid has been with us for about ten years.' 'That's good,' she said with a look as if to say that she could now talk to me at ease. 'In our house too, there is a maid who has been with us for thirteen years, although I have heard that this is rare in foreign countries', and when that maid came in with the tea, she made her stay with us to join in our talk for some time. Speaking of children, I mentioned that our eldest son was fifteen, and she said with surprise, 'It's only six or seven years younger than what I guessed your age to be!' Learning my age, she turned back to her husband to let him know her interesting discovery, but over there they were now at the height of learned discussion, so she smiled and said in a low voice, 'He's always like that. I expect your husband is just the same. He forgets himself whenever he talks on the subject of his study.' 'Look at this grey hair if you think I am young,' and I turned my back to her. 'How amazing that you don't have your hair cut! My daughter-in-law has just got her hair cut at last.' At the table over there, the learned talk seemed to have come to a temporary pause with Dr. Jespersen smiling as he said, 'My international language "Novial" won't spread through lack of propaganda, unlike Esperanto', so Mrs. Jespersen said, 'Let's join them over there', and stood up to get some more tea.

I now had the opportunity to gaze at the Doctor for the first time. He was seventy-two and had his hair brushed back carelessly from his coarse forehead which was ruddy like the tip of a nose when exposed in a cold wind. His small round twinkling eyes, his strong build, his stooping shoulders, caused by long years of desk-work, his husky voice, like that of a sailor brought up in the salt breeze, showed that there was much of a retired explorer about him. Compared with the refined grace of English scholars, the rough touch of the Danish scholar may be said to be that of a wooden sculpture in peasant art, giving out Nature's own flavour. Therefore, whenever a person like me who has something of the wild in her nature, sees the inimitable sedateness of the English, she cannot help feeling a roguish temptation to shake them up with a great earthquake, but she would never have thought of such a thing before Dr. Jespersen. He said that he had seen several Japanese before, but only separately, so he had never heard a Japanese conversation, and he asked us to let him hear one. But I felt rather shy, talkative as I am, when

I tried it intentionally. Then we were ushered into the house to see his study. The way he hung Shakespeare's portrait on the wall in front of his desk attracted my notice, because it happened to be just the same as in my husband's study. Around the wall books about languages were closely packed together, and there was a picture of him as a young man teaching English to his son. He showed me a picture which he had had taken with his wife when they travelled together in Spain last winter, to avoid the cold, and Mrs. Jespersen was in the same coat of serge as on this day, in the middle of July, a fact which was enough to show the coolness of Denmark, as well as the simplicity of their life. After showing us the rooms of their house, they locked the door and took us for a walk into the wood. The road in front of his gate led directly to the entrance of the wood, and though the road was a quiet one Mrs. Jespersen made a great fuss about the bicycles, being afraid of them. I heard that Dr. Jespersen had an accident with a bicycle and was seriously injured last year so that he had to stay in hospital for a long time. The wood was of beech trees of moderate size which had slender trunks and no lower branches, and high overhead they were intertwining their branches in a perfect pattern. Their leaves were so green and soft that they seemed almost eatable, and the path under the trees looked like an aisle beneath a dome of green stained-glass. There were a small pond and grass fields, where Iceland ponies played, all of which gave slight changes to the scenery, but the monotony of the wood as a whole was fitted for us to walk in conversation in its quiet faint light, and the carpet of dead leaves, soft under our feet, gave us another pleasure. 'Why', Dr. Jespersen asked my husband, 'do you still use Chinese characters in Japan? You had better abolish them.' Following him we walked, talking about things in Japan. 'I shall go home before him,' said I, 'so that I can be home by this winter.' 'Oh!' she said, stopping short, 'it is really splendid to go home to be with your children for the Christmas!' She was delighted, taking it for granted that that was the reason, so I felt a little awkward. After strolling about in the wood, we returned home and entered through a wicket at the back of the house. The hedge was also of beech, and Mrs. Jespersen pointed out a tree stump placed in the open place and said that it was their joy to have afternoon tea there. If it was in Japan, caterpillars would drop into the tea-cup, and I envied them, but then I remembered that where there are no caterpillars there are no silkworms, their relatives, either. After having a short rest we took our leave. The Doctor saw us off, coming with us for about half a mile as far as the terminus of the tramway. The tramcar on our way back carried, as usual in this country, healthy, pleasant and simple people. Nowhere could I find a girl who had the fragile beauty of Ophelia, or a pale-looking pensive young man like Hamlet. They died without issue!

§ 4

East Prussia and Poland

After dark we arrived at Königsberg, the capital of East Prussia. The buildings looked substantial, but rather sombre, and in the street a procession with drums and torches at its head passed quietly yet steadily with the smoke of the torches trailing behind it. It looked as if it were the funeral of some general, and the sound of footsteps beating time, thud, thud, thud, being strong but sad, somehow compelled people to take off their hats. It was just like Germany even in such difficult times, for the next day the plebiscite for or against the present Government was going to take place. The tense and uneasy feeling was all over the street oppressing even travellers, and although our hotel was first-class, we were served with an omelette which left in my mouth fat like paraffin (it was so large that both ends hung over the dish), yet I had not the heart to complain about it. Every other light in the corridor was off.

The next day we went to see the Palace of East Prussia and then visited Kant's tomb. The building near the latter was turned into one of the polling stations for the people's voting on the next day, and on the gate there were posters with such captions as, 'Be ashamed if you do not vote!' And in front of a notice-board on which was written, 'O for "Yes" and X for "No" ' a serious-looking committee were keeping people in order. When they saw us come in, they asked what we wanted. When we asked them where Kant's tomb was, they understood our intention and pointed to the graveyard just on the right. I looked with pity on their tense faces because they seemed to have forgotten the great philosopher who is the honour of the city, being too much engrossed with the great occasion of the day. Kant's tomb was very simple and sombre in taste, but recently they had enclosed it, like the cage of a hippopotamus, with iron bars and sandstone of a red-brick colour, and instead of 'the starry heavens above me' it had a ceiling covering it that bore designs of heavy blue and brick colours, so Kant must be smiling a bitter smile in Hades. In the museum there were relics such as his desk and shoes. Kant looked like a poor uncle with a head swollen with wisdom, but his portrait without his wig, which is the usual appendage to his figure when he is shown us as a great scholar, had something of an infant suffering from under-nourishment, so I thought it would have been better if it had not been exhibited.

After spending some time looking at various specimens of amber, which is the special product of this region, we started for Marienburg, where there were various things worth seeing, but somehow we did not have the leisurely mind to appreciate the stylish taste of the Middle Ages, owing partly to the fact that this place stood on the edge of the Polish Corridor, and my thought was drawn only to the undertone of the strife of this world. The Polish Corridor is the name given to the narrow strip of land that leads from Poland to the sea, cutting Germany into two parts, Germany proper and East Prussia. It was the greatest of wrongs against the principle of self-determination of peoples in order to give to Poland an outlet to the sea and to punish Germany in some way. Therefore everybody looks upon this land as the next source of strife in Europe, and to-day, when the passionate hatred against Germany has decreased, and Poland is not so popular, the outspoken words of Mussolini, 'The Polish Corridor was created upon temporary sentiment, so it cannot be recognized as proper. Therefore we will not be slow to render some help for the revision of the pact at a proper time', are listened to with attention. Of course, these words came out from the intention of Italy to restrain France by flattering Germany; but those who have seen the real state of affairs cannot help thinking that it was a too unnatural persecution of Germany. East Prussia is where Wilhelm I was born, and it might be called, historically speaking, the centre of the German Empire, but it is now isolated; even the whole surface of the frontier river being given to Poland in order to make it inconvenient for East Prussia to transport commodities. Therefore it is natural that Germany should appeal to the world, even in a caricature representing a map of German territory cut into two with a pair of scissors, East and West Prussia, with the words, 'If it were a piece of paper you might cut it as you like ...' Is it only a corridor that is long and narrow? Isn't it also the shape of the fuse for exploding the peace of Europe?

Soon we left for Danzig. In the course of two hours they examined our passports both in Poland and in Danzig. The free city of Danzig has land belonging to it, as large as Tokyo, and special money and stamps are used. This is a town that has prospered since the time of the Hanseatic League, but it is now obliged to let the Poles share special privileges such as citizenship and customs, so as to make it convenient for them to export commodities. The side facing the Baltic Sea seems to be well-equipped but more interesting to travellers is the older part of the town. There were small alleys having very elaborate rails at the steps of the entrances with different carvings well preserving the original state of the Middle Ages. Gates were found now and then in the streets, reminding me of old Yedo where, I am told, each street had its own gate. On the bank of the river there was a large and antique unloading wharf built in the same style as we had seen in Bergen, so it was known at a glance to be one of the Hanseatic towns. From all this medieval reverie my mind was awakened to the oppressive present age, by the shouting of a newspaper man selling extras. When he hurried away after pasting a sheet on a telegraph post on the bank, a painter who was working on the top of a very high ladder came climbing down to look at it. He had been engaged in repainting a prosaic modern building which was next door to a house that belonged to the Hanseatic age. After glancing intently through the rows of figures, he at once turned on his heel and climbed lightly up the ladder, which was still shaking at the top by the vibration caused by his coming down, setting to work immediately. He must be a German! In the street I found a bronze statue of the Kaiser and in the Rathaus there was a wall-painting of the Kaiser standing in a suburb of Danzig. The writing beneath it was given only in German and not in Polish.

We started at two in the afternoon for Posen in Poland. At the frontier station on the Polish side we noticed the network of barbed wire entanglements surrounding the platform, having an entrance of three or four feet wide at only one place. It was past five when we arrived at Posen. Cook's would not change the money of Danzig. As it was only three hours' ride from Danzig which was made an independent city by Poland, we felt dissatisfaction though it had nothing to do with Cook's. Generally speaking, Poland is not very popular on all hands. It is partly due to the gloomy individual temperament of the Poles who had been oppressed for a long time, and partly to their egotism. We had wished them success in their independence out of a poetic chivalry that sympathized with the Polish patriots, but soon after she became a great country by good chance, like a *parvenu*, she selfishly claimed Danzig and the right to extend her land to the Black Sea, encroaching by force of arms upon Czechoslovakia in the south and Lithuania in the north. It seems that I am not alone in thus entertaining a prejudice against this greedy country, because diplomats everywhere told me that she was an unsavoury country.

On the following day, after seeing the Castle of Posen,

we walked in the market. There were cabbages and fruits, and although the quality was inferior, they were more numerous in kind and quantity than in the northern countries. I found an old woman who was selling dried herbs such as camomile, gentian, linden-blossoms, wormwood and cudweed. Her customers must be withered old people. It would be uncanny to see a European boiling herbs for medicine. Mr. Massey, Professor of the University and English Consul at the same time, invited us to the Hotel Bazaar, which is well known as a meeting place of patriots for the independence of the country. The statue of Bismarck in front of the University had been taken down to make room for the monument of a bishop. Their national religion being Roman Catholic like France, and politically, of course, bearing a grudge against Germany just as France, it is quite natural that these two countries bordering Germany from north and south should become friendly; and the first foreign language taught in the schools is French. On the part of France, they are hospitable to immigrants from Poland, which I had felt when I heard a Polish hymn sung in a church on our visit to the battlefields. But, according to Mr. Massey, while French peasants are not accustomed to clearing waste land mingled with pebbles, the Poles make it their daily work in the fields to take away stones from the earth full of moraine carried by the glacier in ancient times, so they are fit to do the work of reclaiming the earth of war sites and are welcomed by the French people. His explanation fully satisfied me, while I shuddered when I imagined the bullets and shells that fell like rain or hail, and at the same time I noticed that the round cobble-stones that annoyed my feet in Moscow, Reval and Kovno, and which again hurt my ankles in this place, were what he called moraine. Posen showed little sign of development after the independence. The Opera was closed, it being financially impossible to carry it on, and the city seemed to have become generally dirty. The only innovation that attracted our attention was such as needed no money, as for instance, changing the names of the streets, one street being named Sienkiewicz, and the only pleasant memory about Poland is that Mr. Denbinsky, a fine old scholar with whom we became acquainted in Paris, came to our hotel to present us with a bouquet of red roses.

§ 5

Second Visit to Berlin

At two-thirty we left Posen for Berlin. The frontier was strictly guarded, each platform being surrounded with barbed wire entanglements so that it could not be crossed over. This network was seen at the two stations before that of the frontier. The officials examined even the inside of the lavatories. In Germany the names of the stations were written in German letters as of old. In Berlin we entered the same hotel as the one at which we had put up in April. Although the room at the corner of the cross-roads was a little too expensive for us, we took it thinking it would be convenient for observing things in the streets. To be sure, in no more than an hour the street became lively, and a troop of five or six hundred uniformed men, clubs in hand, came along with a flag at the head of the procession, and holding aloft their brands proceeded to music. About fifty cars, shining with the silver colour of the helmets of the policemen who filled them, glided along with a troop of mounted police following. It was the memorial day of the promulgation of the German constitution. It was kept so enthusiastically to-day, because two days ago the result of the people's vote for or against the present government had shown that the votes against made thirty per cent of the whole. This showed that the rise of the extreme right nationalists, bent on taking the place of the present government, was not to be despised. Therefore there was not to be seen any bustle which is ordinarily associated with so-called festival days, and as night wore on the traffic decreased even in the Friedrichstrasse, which is the main street of Berlin. On the street, which was as clean as if it had been wiped hard, the bright street lights were reflecting beautifully.

I am told that one should not say that the streets of Berlin were clean in spite of bad times but that they were clean because of bad times. The municipal office increased the number of street-cleaners by way of relieving the flood of unemployment, so in the morning they push their mops forward all at the same time to wipe clean the surface of the streets. It was indeed a sad luxury. Our hotel may be taken as an example for cleanliness and rational equipment. There were two thermometers to a room, one on the inside and the other on the outside of the window, so that it was very convenient when going out from the warmth of the room. There was also a thermometer in the bath to measure the temperature of the water. By the telephone in the room a memorandum-book and a pencil were provided. Beside the letter-paper at the desk there was a small measuring instrument, and on the table German taxes were compared with Swiss taxes in a diagram by way of explaining higher hotel rates. Everything was business-like in a way that spurned trusting to memory and going by rule of thumb. In the streets German women take the quickest and longest strides in the world. When they look at foreigners like us, they stare straight at us with a piercing gaze, but once they have looked at us to their heart's content, they seem not to think any more about us. In France, when I went by *métro* in Japanese dress, they glanced at me stealthily and inter- mittently, and whenever our eyes met, they turned their eyes aside. It may be said that this is more polite, but it is some- what mean and makes me feel uncomfortable. The German way is anyway the best for my nature, but they stare so hard that a Japanese lady who came from Paris, where she learned to dress in the latest fashion, once muttered, 'Are they looking at me with antipathy because I am attired in French style?' A shop-window that specializes in green shows ladies' clothes all in that colour — hats, necklaces, shoes, handker- chiefs, handbags and everything. Yellow things are dis- played in another window, black and white things elsewhere, thus, everything is much too uniform, like a coffee-set, and makes us feel some want of variety. Those who have not the eagerness, however, to enjoy dressing as a kind of creative art but wish to get easily a respectable outfit will find such system highly convenient. In department-stores, I observed that women went directly to the departments where their objects were to be had according to the plan in their mind and were not attracted on the way by some dress, the design of which happened to catch their fancy. I did not see any customers who went shopping in company as if for a picnic. Therefore German women pass over without notice the things which would be unexpected bargains. They seem to enjoy their own hobbies by thus saving time, which is money. I once said, praising French women, that they were good housewives, but admiring German women, I would like to say that they were good economists.

Germany was now at its economic crisis, and the money exchange was practically non-existent, because runs on the important banks continued, and while we were travelling round Northern Europe, it was only the German exchange that was miserably left blank on the foreign exchange notice. As one of the expedients to get over the difficulty, the Government imposed a hundred-mark tax on each German who wanted to go out of the country by way of making it part of the national resources on one hand, and on the other to prevent the Germans from scattering their money abroad. By this they wanted to raise foreign confidence towards the economic power of the country, but while it called forth much criticism, their plan seemed simply to have ended in exposing the exhaustion of the national power all the more because others thought that Germany was in such a bad way as to resort to such drastic expedients. The newspaper which I saw one morning reported that they had blown up the train which was carrying the Minister of Finance, who had gone over to Italy for a conference, and that there were some casualties. Italy and Germany, France and Poland, Yugo-Slavia and Czechoslovakia, the latter two of which we were to visit later on, were all on bad terms with their neighbours and were friendly with each other as being the countries next but one. In our school-days we used to quarrel with the class-one-year senior and be friendly with the class-two-year senior. Countries, though they sound very important, are not after all very different from schoolgirls. In the gossip column of the above-mentioned paper, I saw a news item about starving people in the suburbs who attacked a baker and divided the plunder among them, there being some casualties among the police. It was a reflection of bad times in the country, and this event and that of the explosion of the train were reputed to be outrages perpetrated by the Communists, or instigated by them. This was probably true, so the people's minds were leaning towards Hitler all the more. Among the newspapers, only one employed Roman letters, while others were all printed in the rigid German type as if to insist upon their nationalism.

One day I confined myself in the hotel all day, and packing our things, I was much worried about the plan of our future travel. I had intended to return home by myself, parting from my husband at Moscow in December, after making a trip to the Balkan Peninsula, but now I found it hard to decide whether I should put off my returning till next February in order to satisfy my desire to see America. At last I decided to go home alone, and thanks to that, I was able to be at the death-bed of my mother who died in January of the following year. It was the very first day that I stayed home all day during the whole eight months of travel. Brooding over such things I was entirely downcast with fatigue. In the evening we paid a visit to Herr S., who was a scholar of Japanese, and I found on his book-shelves a number of Japanese books, old and modern. He talked with us in fluent Japanese. In spite of the fact that he was a specialist scholar like this, he was full of patriotism as well as of the sense of duty as a citizen, and he talked about his own people frankly and quietly. When Mr. Ramstedt talked to us in Finland, I listened to him with a smile at his blind love for his country which led him to turn every goose into a swan, and I listened to his talk with the greater good-will because he was a Finn of eastern blood — his way of talking was specially oriental which might be represented by the Confucian saying, 'The son conceals the misconduct of the father. Uprightness is to be found in this'. But I thought it was the attitude of Herr S. that ought to be respected. He was not irritated, although he was deeply troubled about the affairs of his country, and looking steadily at the root of the evil, he tried to inquire into a measure to overcome the difficulty. His way of living was indeed a modest one, living on the sixth floor without a lift, and the electric lights were scanty along the staircase. When we were leaving, I noticed at the back of the door thick iron-bars fixed, and he said, 'People are getting bad. Sneak-thieves break wooden doors without any difficulty'. I thought how dreadful it was that they should break the door so high up in a building.

On August 13th, we went to Potsdam by charabanc, and from the outskirts we took a small steamer and went down the Havel to Potsdam. The Palace of Sans Souci was built according to the designs of Frederick the Great, whose French taste is observed in the French fashion of the buildings and gardens. But the florid gaudiness of the rococo style does not appeal to me. Partly on account of this, I could not help looking askance at the famous water-mill left untouched in the garden, based on the king's idea that even a king cannot break the law of a country, for I thought it was only the clever king's trick to play at being a popular monarch, using as a tool that obstinate master of the mill who refused to move when the king wanted him to. The palace where the Kaiser resided plainly showed his *parvenu* bad taste. The large hall was altogether absurd, being a perfect magnification of shell-work souvenirs sold in a sea-bathing resort in Japan. It was even vulgar; for instance, the decoration of roses was made of scallops, the buds being conch-shells, while several dragons, no less than five or six yards in length, having scales of shells were clinging to the walls. The pillars were a medley of stone samples, inlaid as they were with Russian lapis lazuli, stone from Persia — whatever was rare and valuable, and there was even a lump of sulphur one foot square. This is the result we get when we allow the military to have everything their own way. On our way back our small steamer passed a villa colony called Wannsee, where the citizens of Berlin go swimming. There was no sign of bad times .seen on the surface in that neighbourhood, but as it was very cool because of the rain on this day and the day before, the thermometer standing at fifteen or sixteen degrees, it was not very crowded.

On our way home, near the entrance to the University, we visited the tomb of the Unknown Warrior. Here, too, we saw a flame flickering, never to be extinguished. We had seen the same flames under the Triumphal Arch in Paris and in the Monument Tower in Brussels. They are very good to commemorate the past, but somehow I felt something which made me turn my eyes away. I do not know what they burn, but the undying fire that flickered in a purplish pale colour, like the tongues of snakes, looked weird, symbolizing rather the flame of an undying ire or grudge of the country and the people than the unceasing grief. It is the flame rising up night and day as if waiting for the time to burn the world again with the whirling fire of Destiny. There is nothing so appropriate for representing the lament for the dead as the dots of red light of incense-sticks with fragrant smoke slowly curling up in spirals.

CHAPTER IX

SWITZERLAND

§ I

Climbing the Jungfrau

On August 14th at about two we started for Switzerland. I saw no less than two gentlemen in the dining-car who had the scars of wounds on their faces. One seemed still in his twenties. Scars from duels are seen too often in Germany to attract one's notice. They do not look bravely grim but simply barbarous. They are very much like, and more foolish than, the scars of the natives of the interior of Africa who have them as the marks of their tribes, or the brands on sheep's buttocks which their owners put to distinguish them from those of others. Our train ran through a well-cultivated plain and passed by orchards, meadows and coal-mines, and when we came to vineyards of a hilly district and pine woods, where they were extracting the resin, the sun set. It was in this neighbourhood that the German Minister of Finance was nearly blown up. The perpetrator of that crime was still being tracked and a reward of a hundred thousand marks was set on his head but he still remained at large. The small towns along the railway looked thriving with many factories, but at night I found the electric lights were very weak. Even in the stations, only about one third of the lamps were lighted, and the station employees walked about with lights on their chests. It was very gloomy.

We passed Basle at midnight and entered Switzerland,

where, when we came to the side of Lake Neuchâtel, day broke, but heavy rain fell all day shutting out our distant view. We arrived at Geneva just at noon and in spite of the rain we went out for a trip in a charabanc. I saw in *Punch* afterwards a picture of a charabanc in the pouring rain with the words of a guide saying, 'The waterfall you see out of the window is the biggest in the world'. Our sightseeing in town was something like that. The next day we left our luggage in the hotel and left for Interlaken.

When summer comes all the villagers of Interlaken train themselves for the open-air performance of *William Tell*. Younger folks wear their hair in an old-fashioned style, while even an old man of eighty-seven tries to learn the stage speech by heart, repeating, 'Down with the cruel tyrant!' stroking his white beard. As it was going to be performed on Sunday, we went to see it. The rain, which we were anxious about, cleared up, and about the time when the Jungfrau began to glitter in the fine weather, people began to make preparations for the play.

While we were having our tea in our hotel, there came a clear sound of bells jingling under the window, and looking down, I saw a herd of clean white goats climbing up the path with polished bells on their necks. While I was looking at them, thinking that they were very smart, a shepherd in old-fashioned attire appeared with a crook. The goats were actors to-day. Even the live fish, fresh from the lake, that sprang out from the basket of the fisherman, who was the first to appear on the stage, were acting a part to make the atmosphere suitable to that of a lake, before making a table dainty. Literally the whole village was acting in the play.

The open-air theatre was set among thickly-wooded green hills and into the stage water was drawn at one point to make a small inlet. The path that runs down to its shore from behind a rock on the right passes through the open area in the centre and dies away in the mountain on the left. The simple country cottage in the Swiss style, that has stones upon the roof, and a church deep in the wood were arranged naturally; the only stage settings being the castle of Uri in progress of erection and the house in the centre which is so made that they can have a scene of the inside of a house when a curtain upon which the front door and windows are painted is rolled up. The play began quite naturally with a fisherman who appeared in a small hut beside the creek. While he was mending his net, squatting with his legs crossed, he began to sing a boat-song in a low tone. When he threw away a weed, picking it up from the net in which it was entangled, it fell with a plop into the water and the ripples spread wide. The sound created quite a peaceful atmosphere, making the audience forget that they were sitting in the seats and making them feel as if they were passing by a peaceful village on the lake-side.

Soon a peasant woman came out of a farmhouse with a pail in her hand and stood beside a trickling flume. The water was cold, heralding the arrival of autumn, and she looked up towards the hill shielding her eyes from the sun with her hand; the people who had spent one whole summer driving cows into the mountain to feed them on the grass of the peak were coming back to the foot of the mountain and she shouted loud with a voice like the sound of a horn, 'Heigh-ho, heigh-ho!' The echo filled the whole valley for some time, and just as it was dying away, the answering call from the height of the hill, which had mingled with the echo quite indistinguishably, was left clearly alone after it. The white shadows that now flickered among the trees at the edge of the mountain high above were pointed to by both the actors and the audience saying, 'Look, look! Look at that!'

Joyful voices raised in song were also heard. Intermingled with the sound of the cow-bells that clanged at long intervals, the high-pitched jingling of goats' bells sounded busily, and presently at the corner of the mountain-path a troop of shepherds who had finished the work of the summer appeared. The cow which yielded the most milk of the whole herd led the others with a flower on her horns, and they all came down slowly. While the shepherds were in transports of delight, holding the hands of their wives and children who came to meet them, the herd quietly chewed the grass on the roadside.

Men who disposed of the hay, and women who washed things beside the flume — everything in the play was so near to daily life that even the actors, let alone the audience, might forget that they were acting in a play. Poets might envy them that their daily life could be art; and moralists would also envy them, since, oblivious of the fact that it is a play, they would act with real feeling in the following scene of guarding their native land, which would serve to foster in them the idea of independence and love for their country.

Soon the thunderstorm that suggested the tyranny threatening the peace of the village was to rage, or ought to have raged . . . but this, of course, was not easily to be performed. On the brows of the fishermen who staggered shouting, 'Rage, rage, ye winds! Ye reservoirs of heaven, pour down and flood the earth!' the sun was shining brightly; only the water of the cove was agitated a little with a splashing noise. Evidently the villagers were churning the water with planks at the farther end in a corner.

Otherwise everything displayed the features of an open-air play to perfection, adding freshness to the performance. It would not be possible, except in a pageant, to show an express messenger who ran through the scene flying on a horse with clattering hoofs, or refugees who ran away from one mountain to another. Above all, when the open place, which had been boiling with the noise of the people, was left empty, Tell, having been arrested and the villagers returned to their houses, exchanging looks in silence and despair, the sound of the water that bubbled in the flume was suddenly heard distinctly with great effect.

At the conclusion of the play all the villagers came out, having in the centre Tell and his wife hand in hand with their sons, and sang the Swiss National Anthem in chorus, together with the audience. And while they were on their way back to their houses following the path among the trees, waving their hands all the time, the spectators applauded to the echo and with their admiration for the splendid performance was mingled naturally their congratulation to the Switzerland of the day that she won her independence.

There was no fatigue felt as with the after-effects of drink, which one generally gets after seeing a play, and a refreshing feeling as if one was served by a villager with home-made cider was indeed the real value of this open-air performance.

It was daybreak. The snow of the Jungfrau was inhaling the light from the dawn still lying behind the horizon, and Interlaken at its foot sees the twilight of morning earlier than elsewhere. Notwithstanding that the dark green spur of the mountain was still sunk in dusky darkness, the silver peak of the Jungfrau itself, rising in the sky high above the dimness, was shining bright and clear and seemed to push farther forward every minute. The scenery caused some uneasiness to my sleepy eyes in that it looked top-heavy. But soon, from among the folds of the naked rocks, white clouds rolled out and at last enfolded the whole peak. It was not visible any more. But wait! Among the pearly clouds part of the mountain surface like broken marble appeared and disappeared here and there, now in a diamond shape and now in a triangle, and the whole mountain seemed to be slowly moving.

Urged by my husband who said, 'Hurry up for breakfast, or we will miss the mountain train', I went down into the dining-room. Quickly finishing my breakfast, I ran up to the window again and found that it was already broad daylight. At the farther end of the distant gorge, the Jungfrau stood white facing us, restored to the well-balanced hard beauty which I was accustomed to see in picture cards.

The rack-and-pinion electric car climbed up higher and higher along the edge of the gorge of Lauterbrunnen. In the bottom of the gorge on which we looked down, houses were scattered. They were picturesque and seemed to have been placed there, carved in the round. While I was looking up at the fantastically-shaped rocks, called 'Devil's Fingers', on the opposite mountain, sometimes mild-eyed Swiss cows of a cream colour would draw near to our car with a clanging of bells, and sometimes children picking cranberries or girls carrying rucksacks on their backs would wave their hands towards us. Now and then for a short while our car was wrapped in the green of a slightly gloomy wood, but then our windows suddenly became brighter as we crossed over the traces of avalanches that slipped down sweeping the ground.

When we came out from the wood, the majestic figure of

the Jungfrau suddenly seemed to overwhelm our windows.
From the snow-white peak rising up skywards, a glacier was
forcing its way down aslant to the left, and the front part of
the mountain, making a sheer cliff as if the face of it had been
sliced off, on which snow could not settle, stood upright
exposing the layers of rocks that ran in waving lines. From
Interlaken, we saw yesterday an avalanche of snow slipping
down the wall of these rocks, covering the whole surface.
In the distance it looked like a piece of white cloud flying
down, and we simply gazed at it with an utterance of surprise. But now, looking closely up at this cliff of one thousand
feet, I found it hard to realize that it was the same place
where that great avalanche took place.

We changed cars at the Scheidegg for the Jungfrau
Railway, and climbing another thousand feet, we got to the
Eiger Glacier station. Now, all was glacier before us, and
our car dashed straight into it and was swallowed up by a
tunnel. This tunnel was quite different from the ordinary
run of tunnels, built at the foot of a mountain to avoid the
difficulty of the altitude. Because of the eternal snow and the
layer of ice on the surface, there was no hope of laying a
track to climb the mountain, so, as a worm that gnaws the
core of a tree, they bored a hole inside to climb up it. The
business of climbing is well accomplished in a tunnel that
runs up more than 3000 feet, piercing the mountain from
the entrance at an altitude of 8000 feet above sea-level to the
Jungfraujoch at an altitude of 11,300 feet. There are only
two stations in the tunnel. When I looked down from the
square hole cut open in the stone wall upon the Aletsch
Glacier stretching below, all was white as far as the eye could
reach. I felt as if I were peeping out from the window of an
airship over the Milky Way in heaven.

Our car still ran up the tunnel engraving the degrees of the altitude on the passengers' backbones with each tooth of the geared wheels, and climbing higher up at each jerk, it reached the upper terminus.

We were now at the Jungfraujoch, 11,300 feet high. It is the same height as the summit of Mount Yarigatake of the Japanese Alps, but there was an hotel built in a niche cut out of the upright cliff. It is a fine hotel of four storeys, equipped with a lift. In midsummer, as we sit listening to the rustling sound of snow blown up against the window, and call for cold drinks, perspiring in the heated rooms, we feel satisfied to find that we are not satisfied in such circumstances with too much satisfaction! But when you go out pushing open the double door on to the veranda, over which icicles are hanging down, brushing aside a complicated feeling of incongruity like this, you will find there the ruthless world of ice and snow. The veranda hangs over the Aletsch Glacier, which, being the longest in Europe, ravishes one's soul with the grandeur of a prospect meandering endlessly as far as the eye can reach.

Looking above, I saw black clouds whirling up from the summit of the Jungfrau, and the sky was dark. At the right shoulder of the rugged mountain figure with big patches of deep snow and craggy rocks with acute corners where even snow could not settle, the Silberhorn was standing clear-cut with its pyramid smooth and silvery, true to its name. The clouds of snow were incessantly flying up, eddying in the violent wind that passed over the peak.

Suddenly, from the clefts of the whirling clouds, the sunlight shot out, and a group of weak but clear beams swept the peak and slipped down the cliff, running across the glacier to we knew not where. Will not a person of a saintly soul with an inward eye discern in this a spirit soaring in heaven?

I caught sight of a flying eagle, but it was to be seen for a brief moment. Only a flock of small rooks were flying, like a shoal of small fish rocked in the high waves of the ocean, winnowed in the wind along the cliff below our veranda, and now and then they perched on the rail of the veranda to rest their wings. Some of us placed for them an apple on the snow of the rail. When one of them pecked at it, the apple turned over and fell down on the snow of the glacier and rolled and bounced away without stopping. Even when it became as small as the point of a needle, it was seen clearly still rolling, because of its fresh redness, and I felt an acute ache in my forehead. The man who had apples got interested in the game, and he threw them all over the balcony, one after another, to the extreme delight of the on-lookers. Then we went up by lift to the topmost storey and went out, pushing open the door half buried in the snow against the wind which tried to press it back. The snow was falling heavily, and it was so soft, except for a path that had been trodden hard, that we were buried knee-deep, and so at every dangerous place near the precipice, there were robust guides standing on guard.

We went up to the shoulder of the peak, but no view was to be commanded owing to the snow-storm. Therefore we idly retraced our steps on the way to see a cave which was cut at the side of the glacier. Going along a passage of slippery ice, we found an octagonal chamber of about twelve feet square cut out of the ice, and on the ice-pillar in the centre there was stuck a naked candle. In the world of ice, spotlessly pure but cruel-cold, the brief candle was burning, and the flame with its manifold reflections on the pale-blue wall was wavering as if it were frightened. It had a quite suggestive effect.

From the Joch we went through the tunnel again down to the Scheidegg and turned to the right for Grindelwald. The Jungfrau was now left behind, and the next mountain, the Mönch, stood in front of us. True to its name, it was covered with snow in the shape of a monk's hood and it was a grand peak. Next came the majestic Eiger, of which, although it had a summit like that of Mount Yarigatake, the face on this side was precipitous like a pyramid cut in half, except for small hollows that looked as if made by chopping with a hatchet. But the powdery snow blown against it having accumulated all over the scars, it reminded me of a hawk's wing with white dapples. It was indeed a smart peak with a gallant air.

Our car entered a wood, but our view was not blocked, because the big fir trees had their mossy branches wildly torn and broken by snowy winds and thunderbolts. Notwithstanding that the railroad was descending a slope of nearly forty-five degrees, we did not feel in the car that we were going down ourselves, but the grassy mountains that stretched beyond the wood seemed as if they were swaying up aslant in a rocking movement. When I thought of the summer clouds moving up like that, my husband said to himself, thinking of something, 'Ah, yes!' and he continued with a laugh, 'I have often seen this scenery in my dreams. The impression which I got when I came here a long time ago must have been left in some corner of my brain. I used to wonder, "What a wild dream to see a mountain moving up into the sky".'

We got off at Grindelwald. The Wetterhorn was seen at the end of the highway that runs through the village. The

lower part of the mountain was surrounded by rocky preci-
pices, being splendidly cut off like the lump of ice-cream
which is passed round and sliced at the dinner-table, and at
the upper part a glacier, which looked rather sticky, curled
round and projected over the edge of the cliff, loosely
hanging down. The aspect of the mountain was at once
grand and superb.

On the right two horns, the Eiger and the Schreckhorn,
were standing face to face with a U-shaped gorge between
them, into which the glacier fell dividing those two peaks.
At the farther end of the gorge, the Finsteraarhorn was
glittering in pure white filling the entire gorge. The sight
of the lofty peak of 15,000 feet and so purely snow-white as
makes the teeth ache acutely, standing heavily and stately in
the centre with two mountains over 10,000 feet high as
sentinels, like the deva-kings in front of a Buddhist temple,
indeed gave the impression that it was a holy secluded
mountain. Surrounded by such imposing yet hard and wild
landscape, the quiet peacefulness of the area around us was
still more emphasized. The light green meadows along the
gentle slope, and orchards with trees stretching out their
loaded branches looked all the more pleasing, with their
somewhat familiar and tranquil scenes, to the eyes of those
overpowered by the mountains of surpassing grandeur.
Gnawing sweet plums, we descended a meadow-path to the
gorge where the glacier dropped in, and passing over a
dangerous plank-bridge into a cave, which had been made
out of a rocky mountain scooped out by the torrent of
frozen ice, we found white turbid water dashing out from
within.

After that, we went back to the station, and it was past
eight when we returned to Interlaken.

§ 2

Holy Mountains

On August 18th we left Interlaken and got out of the train at Berne. The Monument to the International Postal Union consisted of the statues of women, that represented the five continents, hovering around the Globe hand in hand. But the figure jumping up in Japanese clothes was slovenly and disgraceful. Europeans would not be much impressed, because it would give them no realistic feeling, but before the figure with flying skirts and with both hands occupied by holding hands, I could not help averting my eyes. In the street in front of the park stalls were spread for the sale of tomatoes, cucumbers and apples, each in small heaps, kept by healthy-looking housewives. They seemed to have been brought there, fresh from their fields or gardens, and the vegetables and fruit, that did not pass through wholesale dealers, were uneven in size, some being big and some small, but they all looked fresh and pleasant to the eye. I learned that elderberries, black when ripe, were put into wine, and it struck me very country-like.

There was a fine white building illuminated with alternate red and white lamps, the base being surrounded by flower-beds. I thought it was an hotel, but I learned that it was the Parliament House. The wall-painting in the House of Commons, representing white clouds trailing over the Lake Lucerne, where Switzerland was originated, and the Goddess of Liberty that was shown vaguely appearing in the clouds, was beautifully painted, not at all funny like a puzzle picture. The city of Berne, having the coat-of-arms of a bear as the name suggests, from ancient times has a place for keeping

Alpine bears, which with faces a little longer than ordinary were seen climbing tree-trunks skilfully. The clock-tower in the centre of the city was so constructed that bears trooped out when a knight struck a bell, and biscuits in the shape of a bear were sold in the shops. The shops in the streets built in such a way that the first floor projected over the ground floor with the sidewalks beneath it, leaving an arcade so that people could walk along it, suggested a snow country, and at each corner of the street there was an old-fashioned monument with a coloured fountain spraying out slender jets of water. It was a quiet old town. In this part of the country, stations and signboards had German letters, betokening the German temperament of the people.

It is one of the pleasures of a tourist to go from one country to another examining the signboards in the streets. Especially interesting are those of barbers' shops. Those in the Scandinavian countries have a brass oval plate, and in the port towns barbers' shops were found so frequently that they are almost said to be standing side by side. They seem to be thriving, because, after a long voyage, seamen want first of all to be tidy and look better. Watchmakers, or rather watch-menders, hang the sign of a cog-wheel outside their small shops, and shoemakers suspend red boots. But the plate which hangs in front of a barber's shop is seen to become gradually round from its oval shape after Latvia. It is the German way, and in Berlin, of course, and even in Posen of Poland, they were round, suggesting that it once belonged to Germany. In Switzerland, Geneva being a town in French style, that kind of plate was not found; but the barbers in Berne all hang up the sign. What was interesting was that in Lucerne, which is an international pleasure town, only the first-class barbers' shops were in the French style, and the small shops frequented by the townsmen had the plate sign. The sign-staff with red and white bands twining round it is in the South European style and it shows that formerly barbers were surgeons as well, inasmuch as it represents the shape of a bandage on a wound. So people who come on a tour to Japan will know that the European culture that first entered our country was South European.

In the afternoon we left Berne for Lucerne. Sometimes we passed between hill-sides upon which apple trees bore plentiful fruit so that the branches were weighed down. The village houses were like those in mountainous districts and the towers of the churches had sharp spires. We got to Lucerne at night. There was a renowned old bridge at the mouth of the lake. The long bridge, surrounded with planks as high as our breasts on both sides and roofed in the ancient style of Switzerland, crossed the river sideways and in irregular zig-zags over the swift water. While we were having our meal in a small hotel on the river, we heard the steps of people crossing the bridge echoing across the water, thud, thud! Somehow it reminded me of Nara rather than Japan. It may have been that the tasteful construction of the bridge had much in common with that of the corridor of the Hase Temple with the irregular angles and the roofs. The reflections of the lights of the bridge shone in the rapid torrent of water and were broken up into beautiful golden fragments which seemed to be pushed forward into the lower course. Standing at the edge of the bridge, I saw small eddies on the surface of the water appearing and disappearing like nymphs' dimples, and the transparent water being invisible to the eye, only the shoal of small fish swimming all over there looked like a swarm of dragon-flies shooting through the air.

We spent the night at Andermatt. The hotel of this village was full up, but we got our supper anyhow. In a place where Italy is reached in one stride, macaroni is always ready to be served. The dining-room was filled with middle-aged ladies of a certain common type. They were plainly dressed in the German way, lacking, however, the German crudeness and suppleness. We soon found out that they were a party of schoolmistresses from Austria, and thankś to them we had to put up in a villager's house near by.

Before going to bed, we made a round of the village. Houses were constructed with balconies in the Italian way. Beside the village-folk who were talking on a bench a splendid St. Bernard dog was squatting. When I beckoned him, saying, 'Come on!', he stood up with a ponderous movement and began walking towards me, at which I could not help feeling a twinge of fear. He was indeed a huge dog, as large as a calf, and he would have been far taller than I, if he had stood on his hind legs. I did not call him expecting that he would come near so steadily, but I could not escape from him now. When he came near, I found that he had indeed a peaceful, mild look. He gazed up at me for a while, but soon put his big, round head heavily on my lap so that I nearly fell on my face. It was so large that it covered the whole of my lap, and its warmth steadily oozed through the soft coat of the throat. It was a warmth that could not be simply called the temperature of a dog's body, but which could be accepted with joy and respect as something spiritual, radiating as it did from an animal which knew no fear because it had a noble mind. The fact that I was trusted by the St. Bernard dog slightly tickled me and I turned my heel with joy in my heart. The lodging which was offered to us was one of the old-style village houses with a creaking ladder running up from the road to the first floor; but our bedroom was a neat one, the pillow-case having been stitched with a design of edelweiss. At midnight I was awakened by a heavy fall of rain, but I felt myself perfectly satisfied. It was a long time since I had heard the sound of raindrops on the eaves round the house. Next morning I found that the plain, the mountains, the village, everything were drenched as if they had just been drawn out of the water, and there was a heavy cloud hanging over the mountains that rimmed the plain and into the mountains our train climbed up again. This road, that leads to the Furka Pass, being cut among the ghastly, desolate, rocky mountains, represents one of the aspects of the scenery of Switzerland, which is generally too beautiful, like a coloured picture-card of a superior quality. The Spanish mountains, mouldering in small bits, made me think that the height of misery would be mouldering; but the loneliness of this ravine was that there was nothing even to moulder. In ancient times the peak was composed of a single mass of rock, but a glacier cut into it slowly and steadily till there appeared a defile. It would not be enough to say that its cutting was like the grinding of the rocky stone, because the sides of the cliff were so fantastically smooth that they looked as if they had been licked by a devil's tongue. The occasional dull light that was filtering through the cloud was at once caught by the smooth rocky face. I was waiting for the cloud to be pierced by the sun in the hope that it would moderate the dismal scenery, but the desolate sight could not be lightened so easily as that. The part of the rock-face that received the weak sunlight had the lustre of a scar which made the landscape still more weird. I felt as if I had stepped into a scene of Dante's *Inferno*. It is quite natural that the neighbourhood was noted for avalanches, and I saw small images of Christ standing obliquely in such places as an entrance to a gorge, or the end of a bridge. Indeed, I almost felt like crossing myself in front of them.

Going to Gorner Grat, I waited at the hotel till dusk for the head of the Matterhorn to clear, with my chair pressed against the window of our room; but all to no purpose. The curtain of night was closed at last. There being only one guest besides us, the night in the hotel, at an altitude of ten thousand feet, was in utter silence. Beside the stove I told the daughter of the landlord stories about our volcanoes. 'Wait a minute,' she said, 'such a story is too good for me to hear alone. I'll go and call my aunt here.'

To an old woman repairing socks, with big spectacles on her nose, the daughter was translating my story into German, but suddenly she jumped up from her chair and burst into laughter. 'I told Auntie', she said, 'that a volcano had a hole at the top, and that eggs were boiled by the heat of the mountain. "Good heavens!" she says, "a rope as long as a thousand metres is necessary in order to lower an egg down so that it reaches a place so hot!".'

With the dawning of the next day, I watched again for the Matterhorn top to clear. The clouds were scudding across. A white cloud was trailing over the upper portion where the hood-shape top slightly projected forward. But it persistently covered the summit, simply tantalizing me who wanted to see it. I waited with the pleasant hope that I should be able to see it, if the gap of the blue sky moved forward, but the cloud loitered only at the part where the summit was, waiting for the next cloud to come. As soon as the next cloud did come, it went without hesitation. How irritating! I stuck to my aim still more earnestly, wiping the window glass which was blurred with my breath, and looked intently.

In spite of the fact that I waited with such patience, I started back with a muttered imprecation, when at last the pitch-black head stood out in a bulk, so weird and over-whelming was the presence of the mountain. If a man were to train his mind, staring at the Matterhorn every morning and evening, he would be able to become a man of iron will like Napoleon. The words of Confucius, who said, 'The benevolent find pleasure in mountains', should be dashed to pieces. No! The Matterhorn is not a mountain. It is a large hatchet made of obsidian that cuts the blue sky, standing upright in its height of fifteen thousand feet.

Although it was the middle of August, there was on the ground a thin layer of snow, which had fallen during the night, and my footsteps crunched with a refreshing sound. Breathing out white vapour that was wafted behind us, we climbed the peak at the back of our hotel and found a most remarkable person. His shins were like those of mummies, dried up and hardened, and the toes of each foot faced each other on account of his extreme bow-leggedness. It seemed to me that it was precarious for him even to stand still. But, he was carrying a coil of rope on his shoulders and made for the Stockhorn in rapid strides as if flying along the ridge, growing smaller and smaller while we were gazing at him. We followed him as long as time permitted us. It was a promenade above the cloud at ten thousand feet, where one could command a view of the mountains of four thousand metres on both sides. Of course, there was no path. You have to jump from rock to rock, but the rocks were all steady and firm, and there was no danger at all. Every place where we would have been at a loss to find a safe footing, the footprints of the bandy-legged mountaineer left in the snow made a good pointer for our way. They were a size smaller than my footprints and pointing acutely sideways. I would never have dreamed of the existence of such a person.

This Gorner Grat is a ridge surrounded by snow-white mountains and glaciers, and is in the shape of a rock boat which is pure black and long and narrow. Looking down, I did not see the mountain side which formed a cliff, but far below my feet there was a glacier that ran round the foot of the mountain with scaly triangular waves. It was the wide breadth of the Gorner Glacier that poured down between the Stockhorn and Monte Rosa. The sight was very much like that of the wide waves looked down upon from a very high deck while they washed the side of the boat, and it gave me a hallucination as if the glacier was moving with a speed visible to the eye. While I was enjoying the feeling of dizziness caused by looking down upon those things I heard a muffled sound, brrr-rrr! It was the noise of a snow-slide down the mountain side. As the slope was so stiff, the avalanche was invisible, and I only felt the vibration in my body through the corner of the rock which I had firmly held in my hand. I felt a strange eerie feeling and drew back my body which was leaning over. Brrrr-grrr-rr! The noise became faint and distant and was — I am afraid I am blaspheming the god of the mountain — something like flatulence in the stomach. When it became strong and high-pitched, shaking the mountain like an electric shock, it compelled us to be silent, and when the noise died away, there reigned supreme a cold piercing stillness.

Feeling as if I was drawn back by the back hair, we left Gorner Grat and went down to Zermatt. What attracted my notice were the huts with timber-sides in the log-cabin style, the posts at the foundation being laid on a huge round slate exactly the shape of a Japanese sword hilt. In front of a barn in this antique style, old guides were intent in talk, leisurely smoking their pipes, some standing and some sitting. It was indeed a peaceful sight. But I could not accept the peacefulness as it was, and I gazed at the scenery in the mood that expected a person, just as in the cinema, to come up from the depths of an alley to report an accident and the relief party to be organized at once to march into the mountains in troops. I am not a cinema fan, but I now realized the influence of the cinema on our lives. We had our meal at an inn where my husband put up eighteen years ago, and after that we visited the museum, where we saw the broken rope which caused the death of two men at the time when Whymper made the conquest of the Matterhorn. It was really with a feeling of regret that we left the valley of Zermatt behind. The Matterhorn hid its head coldly, only Weisshorn and Breithorn were seen again and again even after I thought I had seen the last of them. The sight of a pure white peak rising up ponderously between the top of the black rock of the front mountain and the cobalt sky behind it was indeed unspeakably impressive.

§ 3

Chamonix

We travelled along the main railway line from the Visp to Martigny, where we stayed a night. As I had torn myself away from the mountains, which I never tired of seeing, I felt a little cross, so the impression of Martigny was unfavourable. This was already the district where French was used. After seeing the mountains, I could not help wondering why the people are made so prosaic. The people of northern Europe smell of wood, and in southern Europe, the Spaniards and Italians having their temperatures heated by the strong sun have something of the wild smells of the fields like a strong and rank smell of wild grass, but the French people, who live between the two, are the most artificial of all. Thus, the people of this town did not possess the quiet, honest nature of the people of mountainous districts, but what was distinctly felt about them was the smell of the rusticity left behind by the new fashion. The following day we left Martigny for Chamonix.

The village of Chamonix is situated in a valley at the foot of Mont Blanc. This is a summer resort that belongs to France, and music as well as café-tables overflowed into the narrow streets of the village. The gay main street soon fell off into the lonely suburbs of the village, where blacksmiths were making cow-bells, the clanking of the hammer echoing to the mountains and mingling with the murmuring sound of the river Arve.

Everybody was attracted to the centre of the village, and there were crowds of people in the halls of the hotels. In the cool moist atmosphere that streamed into rooms through the windows, ladies attired in various colours walked round fluttering their thin silk clothes, like colourful fish in the southern seas, while young men and women in mountaineering outfit pushed the revolving door forcibly and entered with their coils of rope carried sideways on their shoulders and ice-axes under their arms. The reason why they reminded me of a cinema-picture was not only that I had often seen such a sight on the films but it appeared that they desired to conquer the mountains for the sake of conquest, or rather I should say that they gave a strong impression that they were imitating the smart manners of conquerors instead of showing their love for the mountains. I now recollected, with all the greater feeling of esteem, those men and women whom I had come across at each station amongst the mountains of Norway. They went out of the third-class carriages of the train in an unaffected manner in order to enjoy the pleasure of going into the bosoms of the mountains, which showed that mountaineering had become part of their nature.

We walked towards the centre of the town, where souvenir shops and cafés were standing pell-mell, and came directly to a small open place near the Arve. In the main street there was a bustle of people, but here in the open place just behind it there was entire emptiness, so we were able to appreciate with leisure the bronze statue of Saussure, which stood just in the middle of the place. This geologist, who was the first to climb the top of Mont Blanc, wore the old-fashioned plaited hair down his back, and stood looking up to Mont Blanc for ever with a telescope in his hand. The statue of Balmat, the famous guide, stood close on his left. He was a small man, who looked as nimble as a goat, and he was pointing upward as if to say, 'To the right of the ridge over there . . .'

While we were looking up at them intently, a Catholic priest, who had just come there unknown to us, began to pray in silence looking towards Mont Blanc. The pale young priest was in a loose black cassock and a white surplice with lace on it, and the red colour of the edge of the prayer-book in his hand was so conspicuously seen that it looked rather enchanting. The acolyte who accompanied him was in a scarlet robe and a white surplice, and he slowly shook to

right and left an incense-burner hanging down by a thin
chain from his hand. They were praying for the safety of
those who climbed the mountain, or perhaps for the souls of
those who never came back from it. But the incense rose
up in a waving line and twined round the gaitered legs of
Saussure, being swayed by the winds from the mountain as
if to suggest the vanity of man's desire; and the whiteness
of the mountain seemed to me strangely cold and hard.

Among the numbers of glaciers that stream down into the
valley of Chamonix, the largest is called the Mer de Glace
('Sea of Ice'), and there is a mountain railroad as far as the
verge of the snow. There I tramped on a glacier for the first
time in my life. The glacier, which was seen from the top
of the cliff of the shore, resembled a violently rippled river,
except that it had large stones on its surface instead of leaves;
but if you come down to the water's edge — correctly speaking 'ice's edge' — you will find that what you thought were
ripples are actually huge undulations of ice. The tops of the
ridges of ice, with deep crevices on both sides, are narrow like
the back of a hack-horse. Following our guide, we walked
up along the surface towards the upper course. The surface
of the ice was grey-white, but in the crevices it was shining
weirdly blue.

By the light, like lapis lazuli, we could dimly look down
to a certain depth, but not to the bottom, only the muffled
sound of liquefied ice being heard out of the depths. The
slope gradually became sharper. Our guide cut out footholds
for us with his ice-axe, and guided us step by step.

With the sharp chopping sounds of the ice-axe, chips of
ice were flung up. They jumped about with a transparent
light in the sun, as if the whitish grey ice had suddenly

returned to its natural state the moment it was broken, and they dropped into the crevices. What a sound! How they crackled with an infinitely lonesome sound!

Before this I had only once heard a sound which rivalled this one in its sheer loneliness. It was the sound of the breaking of the earth-crevices that opened and beat against each other at the time of the Great Earthquake. I heard them while squatting in a sandy garden at a seaside resort not far from Tokyo. The ground before my eyes opened up into cracks and the crevices one foot wide shot up muddy water every time the walls hit against each other with a shaking of the earth. That noise contained such an infinite lonesomeness as to rob me of a feeling of surprise and fear, and in the innermost recesses of my ears it sounded like the deep dull thuds of the beheading of a man. The sound of the chips of ice was like that of a high-pitched soprano that lingered a long time as if reluctant to die away, and engraved on us the thought of the cold ice-layer which was nearly one thousand feet deep. The sound continued all the time, crunching and cracking. Thus crossing over the ridges of the sea of ice, the guide making our footholds, we ran across a huge stone washed away from afar.

'This stone moves sixty metres downwards every year,' said our guide, taking out a pipe and lighting it, and he continued, telling a tragi-comical story to us: 'A long time ago, a man on his honeymoon trip came to see this glacier and fell into a crevasse. As it was difficult to take his body out of it, we consulted a scholar, and he affirmed that after forty years the body would be pushed out from the very end of the glacier, so his wife came up to Chamonix every summer to wait for it. After forty years the body was found as had been expected, in the same condition as when he dropped in. Of course, she must have been completely grey-haired by that time!' Our guide was a ruddy-faced old man, who seemed to have done much mountaineering in his time.

We stood enjoying the sight of the waves of ice and of the groups of rock-needles that pointed to the sky, shooting up to the right and left, when the rolling fog rose up and hid the whole view, the sound of a concertina, that was played to show the landing-place to the mountain-path cut into the cliff of the shore, was faintly audible. Returning with the guidance of the music, I found about my feet a blue paint tube left by somebody. An artist had thrown it away probably after having used it up in painting the blue of the inside of a crevice, or perhaps resigning himself to the incapability of his brush. Whichever it may have been, it was better than throwing away an empty candy box.

When we came to a safer place, it occurred to me to try to cut a foothold for myself, so I borrowed the ice-axe. The edge of the ice-axe, which I swung down, rebounded from the ice with a hard sound. When I wielded all my strength, the edge cut into the ice, but the effort to draw it out was dangerous to my slipping feet. I was struck, as if for the first time, with the solidity of ice. I said casually to myself, 'You ought to have known how solid it is from your own experience when you chipped ice with a gimlet to put into an ice-bag for your sick child'. But I shook my head to shake off such an ominous association. 'Far be that omen from us! My children must be all in perfect health, drinking the iced water with syrup or something.' It is the weakness of a parent travelling, with her children at home, to think the same thought over again, saying to herself, 'You should have known the solidity of ice by the response of your plane that shaved it.'

The next day the drizzling rain shut us up at Chamonix. This was the second day that we had not driven round during our journey. Our hotel was filled with happy-looking people who laughed, saying nearly every three minutes, 'Très bien!' or 'Très jolie!' But how was it that I could not help thinking that I should not be surprised, as in the natural course of things, if some man or woman amongst them were to be reported in the next day's paper to have committed suicide? The technique of women, out of the necessity of attracting men's attention, in displaying the helplessness of lacking independence, or the appearance of having some secret within, to provoke men's chivalrous heart to support them by putting out their hands, or their curiosity to look into their heart, seemed to have expelled the calm and warm atmosphere away from these pleasure-seekers. While seeing these people who had too little to do with Nature, I had a strange desire to snatch away one of them suddenly and put him or her into the position of Robinson Crusoe to see how they would fare. Escaping from the noise, I entered the reading-room and had a little chat with an old French lady. Pointing to a French paper on the table, I asked, 'Is there anything interesting in that?' 'It is an organ of the opposite party,' she replied without so much as picking it up. 'Everything in it is a lie.'

§ 4

Linguists in Geneva

The second International Congress of Linguists was held for five days, and, as my husband attended it every day, I went out with a map in my hand to see the sights of the city quite aimlessly. Sometimes I crossed over the Mont Blanc Bridge to Rousseau's Island to spend some time at my ease. In the Art Gallery I saw a clock in every room, which made me think that, even if it is a country of watches and clocks, they ought to be more or less above the idea of time in a temple for the appreciation of fine arts. While I was thinking in that vein during my inspection, an attendant came up to me, saying, 'Go out! Go out!' On coming to the exit with a feeling of displeasure, I found a Zeppelin flying low just overhead, and I realized that he had shown me a kindness in telling me about it.

One day I looked in at a meeting of the Linguistic Congress. Various scholars were reporting the results of their studies in various rooms at the same time, so the audience chose whichever one of them they wished to hear. I chose Sir Richard Paget's 'The Gestural Origin of Language'. He elucidated his theory by giving examples, for instance, he showed that the word 'blow' was originated by the shape of the mouth in blowing out breath, and the word 'sip' arose in a similar way. His lecture was accompanied by very amusing experiments. He used a rubber hose, which is usually fixed to a water-tap, the one end of which was fixed to a pair of old-fashioned bellows, and the other end he held in his hand covered with glycerine all over. Every time he held it tight, or twisted it, sending out air through it by stepping on the bellows, the rubber tube uttered words, 'Hallo, London! Where are you?' it spoke with a yawning voice. 'Mamma, I love you!' The faint dying away of the 'you-uuu' was drowned by the cheers of the audience. It was indeed a sight to see Sir Richard, an English peer, who probably had a country estate for game-hunting, making the tube speak with his sticky hand. The

Chairman was the Rev. Ginneken. He was a delightful person, being fat and lovely like a baby magnified thirty times. Both his neck and his hands were creased with deep furrows, and the backs of his hands also had hollows like dimples at the base of each finger. He folded those hands in a tiny bundle upon his protruding paunch and leaned back in his chair. He looked sideways up the stage, and whenever the hose talked, he made his round eyes still rounder and looked from the audience to Sir Richard as if to say, 'Look, how interesting!' When Sir Richard was covered with glycerine, he frowned amiably as much as to say, 'Well, well! I'm awfully sorry for all your trouble'. The sight of him would be enough to disperse both the sadness and worry of one's mind. Still, he had the inviolate gracefulness coming from a dignity which is natural to an infant. The fact that he is the author of a very difficult book made me respect him still more, and I was entirely fascinated by this priest. After his lecture, Dr. Tanakadate made a speech. He said that in Japanese also there were some instances of the same kind, for instance, some words beginning with a 'k' sound, such as 'kiru' ('cut'), 'kowasu' ('break'), etc., meant breaking, and the words beginning with 'n', such as 'naderu' ('stroke'), 'nurunuru' ('slimy'), 'neru' ('sleep') and 'nobiru' ('stretch'), etc., were words relating to peacefulness and calmness. Mr. Palmer displayed his 'stunt' by whistling the English national anthem, accompanying it by the vibration of his vocal chords. The meeting was altogether flavoured strongly with the familiarity of a social gathering, rather than a meeting for learned discussion. There were also teas and excursions. The reception by the city authorities was given in a theatre. On such occasions it was my hobby to guess the nationalities of those present. The gentleman who had a scar on his cheek was a professor from Munich. The scholar who was distinguishedly swarthy was from Sicily. At first I wondered who it was with whiskers like a Chinese scholar, but as the conversation became more lively, his gesticulation told me that he was French. It is a typically French gesture to open the hands, shrugging the shoulders and bending the head on one side. After some light complaint or something like that, they never fail to use that gesture, suggesting, 'Well, it can't be helped!' When their feeling is still stronger and is accompanied by some sort of resignation, they purse their lips, turning their blue eyes upwards. Prof. S. of Denmark attended in a lounge suit in conformity to the express indication on the invitation card, but he did not appear by any means shabby, because he was sturdy and brawny as if trained in gymnastics. There was a gentleman who looked rather crude with his hair closely cut. I thought him German, but I was told he was a professor of Zürich. When I had met the manager of Nardin, the watch and clock company, he kissed my hand, which made me feel that Geneva was a district under French influence, so it was very interesting to compare these gentlemen with each other. Among the gathering, there was a singularly elegant couple. Their freely developed physique and white, silk-like hair made me judge that they were English. While I was attracted towards them, the benevolent-looking old lady beckoned me with a smile, so I approached her with pleasure and learned that they were Prof. B., the Norwegian linguist, and his wife. As they were people of a country I liked so well, after talking about fjords, I said casually, 'Of all the beautiful women that I have ever seen, the one who was the most lovely and unforgettable is the daughter of the Norwegian delegate at the quatercentenary of the Collège de

France'. At this remark of mine, the face of Mrs. B. suddenly brightened up and she said, 'Oh! You mean the daughter of T.! She is a cousin of Mr. B. Her family are all handsome!' This innocent admiration of her husband made me smile. Pointing to Dr. T., she went on to say, 'Is that gentleman with white hair over there your father? His cheerful smile is like yours'. Pleased at her remark, I walked round again, when I was approached by a middle-aged lady who wore her grey hair in an out-of-date coiffure. She smiled oilily and accosted me in French, but I parried her thrust with the only French I knew, 'Je ne comprends pas!' Then she spoke a few words to me in extremely poor English. While I thought it an unexpected by-profit in travelling abroad to come across a blue-eyed person speaking worse English than I, she found it rather bothering to speak in English, and she must have thought it preferable for her to go away after satisfying her curiosity without further ado, for she suddenly asked me, 'How many wives does a Japanese have?' At this I must have shown a blank face, as if shot by a pop-gun. 'One, of course', I replied, and turned on my heel. I felt like swearing in Japanese. I have heard that, when a Japanese soldier was once insulted in America, he ground his teeth and shouted, 'Remember me!' which would mean in Japanese, 'It will cost you dear!' I think there are very few Japanese who can swear in English.

We saw Prof. Chamberlain in Geneva. He was the first Professor of Japanese philology in the Imperial University of Tokyó, but he has been living in retirement in a hotel here for these twenty years. While we were waiting for him seated in the lounge, the lift came down and the door opened to reveal Mr. Chamberlain. He was as lean as could be, and his hands were so extremely skinny that it seemed that they might crack at a touch. With indomitable will he forced his body, physically worn out, into an appearance of perfect gentlemanly gracefulness. I was worried to think that what little energy was left in him was being dissipated as he spoke — though he always spoke quietly. His conversation was more worldly than scholarly, talking about things in general. He said in very fluent Japanese, 'I am eighty-two according to Japanese reckoning', and his Japanese was very good notwithstanding that it was nearly thirty years since he left Japan, and his memory was so clear as to say, 'Mr. O.'s address in Naka Arai is . . .' I could not help praying for him that he should not have a sleepless night, as it must be hard for him to reconcile himself to his body's decay when he had such a clear head After some time, he entered the lift again, leaving his quiet 'sayonara' behind. Even after the door slid to, he was seen through the bars, and, standing looking at us, he smoothly went upwards, nodding at us, and leaving the impression of 'ascension' heavily in our hearts.

CHAPTER X

ITALY

§ 1

The Land of Fascism

On September 2nd we left for Italy. The Simplon Tunnel is the longest in the world, and it was sultry and suffocating. Into the roaring carriage came the customs officials. Switzerland and Italy insisted upon their boundaries even to the depth of several thousand feet underground, and the round globe was as it were divided from the centre, like a water melon.

After staying twenty-two minutes in the dark, we came out into the open air, and in less than half an hour after passing through four or five more tunnels, we saw things decidedly suggestive of the fact that we had come to a southern country, the land of Fascism: gardens planted with paulownias, banana trees, palms, sunflowers and oleanders; and even in small stations, there were gendarmes with plumes in their helmets, while on the country roads lorries were running loaded with Blackshirts. When our train descended to the plain of Lombardy, where big mulberry trees were ranged among maize fields, we found it very dusty and hot.

Soon we arrived at Milan. The outskirts were dusty and dirty, but among the groups of rusty tin roofs decked with dirty linen, there was a splendid station as if to serve as an example of the reconstruction of Italy, which was begun with this building. On either side of the entrance were stone 'fasces' about twenty feet high to remind the people that this magnificent edifice owed its existence to them. We got out of the train, looking askance at the Blackshirts bending down to peep under our seats and a gendarme who was taking away a third class passenger as if for something very important, and we entered an hotel that faced the square in front of the cathedral.

The cathedral here is the third largest in the world, but it is in such a trim shape that you do not feel its bulkiness if you look at it at a distance, and it is entirely of white marble. The close-grained surface of the stone has turned yellowish with time, even to the tips of the spires, nearly one hundred in number, and the whole looks like a neat sculpture carved out of ivory. The big crowd stirring in the open place before the cathedral, however, as well as the rickety tramcars, which ran along narrow winding streets uttering creaking sounds at every corner that set your teeth on edge, and the blazing hot autumn sun, made me short-tempered, and stimulated my feelings so as to be angry about trifles. The thing which I found to vent my anger upon was the skeleton of the saint who founded this cathedral, which was reverently placed in the vault. According to the amount of the money offered, the bas-relief silver sideboard of the coffin is lifted, revealing, in a glass-plated vessel like a tank in an aquarium, a brown-coloured skeleton lying within, and this skeleton is in a robe woven with gold threads and in a bishop's mitre, of the same material. This by itself could have been borne, but both hands, folded together in a saintly(?) way, were in white gloves, bearing three rings on each hand, and on its feet were a pair of slippers decorated with beautiful pearls. Near the ears of me, a fool from the East, who had thought up to that very moment that the expression 'Dressing the bones . . .' existed only as a metaphorical one in this world, a priest recited in a chanting monotone, 'The topaz on the crown is the offering of the king of —— . . . is the offering of Maria Theresa'. The word 'berabo!' (Well, I'll be blowed!) must have been coined by the sons of Yedo to be employed in such a case.

When we were going out from the Cathedral, we were at once stopped by a Fascist. The square was crowded with people, and the noise and the whole air of the place was out of the ordinary. Following the eyes of the crowd to the sky in the south, we saw aeroplanes flying by groups of ten and twenty, each organizing different formations, and they were drawing near in good order. Fortunately enough we were here on the day of the demonstration of the Italian air force. Instantly the aeroplanes came directly over our heads, and, making the cathedral the centre, they flew round in a circle. Forty . . . fifty . . . sixty. Suddenly the ghastly sound of bombs dropping arose, and smoke-screens were spread in a flash. Then each formation displayed its own special tricks. One aeroplane flew close to the rising tower of the Cathedral, and, leaving a streak of white smoke like a thin white silk cloth behind, it darted high up into the sky again to lose itself in the smoke screen, and paper flakes in five colours came fluttering down from the sky. The pride of the cathedral is the range of saints' statues on the tops of the pinnacles, each being carved by a famous sculptor. If I say that those figures were bathing in the snowstorm of five-coloured blossoms, it may sound as if it was a beautiful sight, but there were the fierce smoke-screens in the sky, and the explosive sounds nearly deafened our ears. One of the paper flakes that I picked up read, 'If this were an enemy air-force, they would not scatter coloured paper flakes, but instead . . .!'

The large cathedral towering into the sky, as the embodiment of the faith of the people who yearn after the kingdom of heaven, and the aeroplanes flying about in the sky, making even the sky into a battlefield, as the crystallization of the pertinacious enmity of the countries that are not satisfied with fighting on the earth alone! The contrast is far too interesting to be disposed of only by one word, 'shameful'. Cynically enough, it was indeed a grand and beautiful sight to see the light and smart aeroplanes, that are the result of the extreme limit of human intellect, flying around the huge cathedral that was fixed there immovable for all time, which is also the result of the extreme limit of human power! If I said that it was the bliss of the people of the present world to see them together, just before us, it might also sound cynical, but it was really a sight worth gazing at, irrespective of the idea of good and evil. It was good sport at first, but sad in the end, as a Japanese 'haiku' poet sang, 'I felt gay, but presently sad, in the cormorant-fishing boat'. When the smoke-screen filled the open place and blew against the windows of the mosaic and tapestry shops, people turned their steps homewards, coughing terribly at the acrid smell, wishing to be ahead of each other; and soon afterwards the rain began to fall quietly to cleanse everything from the sky that had been disturbed by that air raid.

When I awoke at about two in the morning, I found the cathedral clean and quiet, as if it had just been completed, shining white in the darkness, even to the black-and-white mosaic work of the pavement in front. The grand edifice, which looked in the daytime so yellow that, if in an ill-temper I should have abused it saying that the towers looked like horses' teeth, was now revealing to us its true aspect secretly at night, and I looked at it with much wistfulness and longing.

The next night we passed in Genoa, and went to see the Campo Santo. It is an art exhibition of tombs, so I can say shortly that we went for a tomb-viewing instead of for a 'bloom-viewing' party. As Italy is noted for marble, even tombs competed in smartness by elaborating the design of sculptures in various ways, as if to show us the samples of the latest style of expression of sorrow. A widow was stooping down, crying. Another was looking upwards, following with her eyes her husband's soul soaring to heaven. Still another was up on the top of a flight of steps, running after her husband, and, finding the door of Hades mercilessly closed, her smooth white arms were vainly knocking at it in despair. While I was looking at her back with admiration, the guide said, explaining to us, 'The original of this design is seen over there. Although this is an imitation, just look at the folds of this flying skirt.' He went on to please the Americans, saying, 'This old man resembles President Hoover!' or 'That is exactly like Lincoln!' The art of the sculptors and the lustre of the Carrara marble were so fine that the draperies looked all the more beautiful and satin-like for the dust accumulated, and although I felt some loathing, yet I was compelled to admire them against my will. But this way of keeping tombs seemed to impose a duty on husbands to die before their wives become old and wrinkled! It is not a good thing to play with mourning like this.

The drive from Genoa along the Côte d'Azur is famous; but the scenery is not of such a nature as to impress Japanese who are acquainted with the drive to the hot springs of Atami. In contrast to the policemen on the Italian side of the frontier who are full of official stiffness, those on the French side looked very smart in navy blue coats, the buttonholes of which are jointed with a streak of red ribbon about half an inch wide. The carnation fields were pretty, and with southern plants such as loquat, mimosa and olive trees the district seemed to be an excellent winter resort. We drove all day and arrived at Monte Carlo in the evening.

Monaco is the smallest independent country in the world, being one and a half square kilometres, and is kept on the gambling taxes. Therefore, the gambling place, the Casino, was as gorgeous as a palace. Since it was not the season, I had not expected to see any luxurious-looking people, but I was surprised when I entered. The people, who sat close together at the long, narrow table, were indifferent about their dress, and with their fearful tenseness and pale faces held their breath, like those who surrounded the deathbed of one of their near relatives. Official croupiers of the Casino, who were seated on both sides of the table in chairs a little higher than the others, twirled the roulette wheel. Each time the croupiers gather in the silver coins on the table with a small rake. Only the jingling noise is heard, and if you carelessly speak they will turn round and glare at you, so you have to remain dumb!

Going out, I found a woman who was naked in the upper half of the body and who wore long blue silk trousers, and an old woman in a pyjama of black crêpe-de-Chine bearing patterns of maple-leaves, resting on a bench in the garden. The large leaves of the coco-nut trees were rustling in the sea breeze, and the reflections of the port lights were magnified in length on the face of the water.

Our train that ran through the boot-shaped Italy, i.e. from the knee-pan downwards, went along the top of the cliff over the seashore from Genoa to Spezia, but the tunnels, no less than eighty in number, shut out our view. On the blue sea, where Shelley was drowned, yachts were sailing pleasantly. The train was crammed with people, and there were a troop of boys of about fifteen years of age in black shirts overflowing even to the corridors of the second-class carriages. They were drinking wine, but this is because a small bottle is wrapped up with the lunch which they sell to passengers and it does not show that they are specially given to wine.

In Europe, Italy is about the only country where lunch-baskets are served. Besides her, they are sold only very rarely in England and in Spain. If you unfold the paper, you will find, together with bread and cheese, some macaroni (which is very Italian) dressed with ketchup in an unglazed pot, a small bottle of chianti and a bunch of large, green grapes to give joy to the tiresome railway journey.

Stations vied with each other in keeping in the gardens 'fasces' made of flowers planted together, or a miniature hill in the shape of the Italian peninsula protruding into a small pond, and at every station, there were two gendarmes and some Fascists in very important-looking attire, each with a pistol, a dagger and a cartridge-belt hanging from his shoulder. In the train also, Blackshirts came in and asked whose coat it was which was placed in the compartment we two occupied, and examined passengers' luggage whenever it seemed heavy and hard. As they were called 'Blackshirts' or 'Fascists', I expected from their names that I would see much more equality and co-operative feeling amongst them, but the same shirts bore sometimes a blue line or silver braid, and they wore medals on their breasts. Even among the comrades, some of them showed an attitude of class-difference, showing it important to be a captain.

There are two kinds of unpleasantness in travelling.

Troubles of such a kind as, for instance, the annoyance of having lost your way, will change afterwards into pleasant remembrance, just as a small portion of pickles enhances the taste of beer. But the disgust which I felt against Fascists, who are in vain pride, or at least in vain tension, will remain for ever in my memory as disagreeable as bones that stick in the teeth, when I chew the cud of all those splendid monuments of fine art.

We got off at Pisa and went up the famous leaning tower. This is a tower that belongs to the cathedral of this town, just as a five-storeyed pagoda belongs to a Japanese temple, and the base of the cylinder of eight storeys sagged into the earth on one side, making it strangely aslant. Inside, you feel unstable, as if you were lame, rather than that the rooms are sloping on one side. Going up the spiral steps, we came to the top of the tower. Remembering that I was told that Galileo made an experiment in gravity, dropping things from here, I stooped down and found a shade under the tower, and the people having a nap there, spreading themselves in the shade, looked very small. On our way home, we looked back. Part of the sky in an acute angle was peeping between the perpendicular line of the cathedral and the slanting line of the tower, and it seemed as if a portion of the cathedral was cleft down to the base and was just falling down. Only the soft blue light of the Italian autumn sky, that shone in the breach between the buildings in a smooth cream colour, softened the impression, which ought to have been dreadful; and I found to my delight that it looked as if a tower of ivory was falling down silently in a daydream. Otherwise it would have been the same object for curiosity as a show of monstrosities in a circus, because I should have come to see

a deformed temple which had been kept more than five
hundred years in its ill-constructed state.

Our train turned to the left from the seashore and arrived
at Florence in the evening. The Blackshirts, who were
threateningly armed with pistols and stood on both sides of
the entrances on the platform, stared suspiciously even at the
group of travellers who came yearning after the town of art.
I cannot say that I enjoyed the four days that I spent in
Florence. There were too many great pictures — pictures,
explained in books of the history of fine art as being very
important and talked about with great excitement, were exhibited in an imposing array; but it was borne in upon me
that I lacked the ability of appreciating pictures. It was not
easy for me to move from one picture to another if I was
engrossed with the first. If I tried to walk along, simply
giving casual glances at them, I was annoyed by the thought
that in Japan there were a lot of students who were almost
sick with longing to see this gallery. If I could have changed
places with them, I would have done so, but I had to walk
aimlessly, looking from one to another, only to get the satisfaction of having finished walking round the place as I ought
to, just as punctilious persons pay New Year's calls aimlessly
from door to door. During this walk round, an interesting
thing happened. It was in the Uffizi Gallery. An old
American lady asked an attendant, 'Where is the picture of
Christ, and the Three Wise Men offering their presents?'
Now among the several thousand pictures there, one in
thirty had a theme of that kind, so he was annoyed and hesitated before answering. Then she asked the same question
of a painter who was copying one of the holy pictures.
'What painter?' he asked quietly, as if to say that he could
let her know at once if she knew the name, because this

gallery was as it were his own house. 'Well,' she said, 'I know nothing about it, but as I heard that it was the most expensive picture in this place, I wanted to see it.' Her innocence gave me no disgust at all, but rather a keen refreshing pleasure. It made me change my mind and set me to appreciating only those pictures which were attractive to me, giving up the attitude of greedily collecting information from the sense of duty. Thus what is vividly remembered now is the 'Annunciation' by Fra Angelico, and a small holy painting on the wall of an ancient monastery which met my eye in the dim religious light as I walked up a dark flight of stairs. It was full of touches of love and beautiful colours.

What is still more clearly remembered than those pictures is the colour of a water melon, which was sold cut in slices in front of the castle gate. The old castle gate, with thick walls and a stately round tower on top, guarded well the entrance to the city with the arch constructed specially narrow. Darkness came on sooner every day in autumn, and over the castle walls the colour of night fell heavily, making people restless as they still felt they were in summer because of the midday heat. The traffic through the castle gate becoming more and more busy, both colour and sound melted in a greyish tint of twilight; and the red crescents and the green skins of the slices of water melons in the stalls floated freshly in the light of acetylene lamps. The workmen eating them, throwing down coppers on the counter, were dark as silhouettes, a fit study for a picture in colour-print.

Florence, on the river Arno, resembles Kyoto, and an ancient Roman town called Fiesole is on the hill north of the city. There, on the stone steps of the small Roman theatre, vines were swaying in the wind, even the bottom of the Roman bath being buried in grass, and only the round marble pillars of a temple in ruins showed white in the twilight. We walked along a half-demolished castle wall. The wall was made of a pile of large rough rocks in the lower part, which was built by the Etruscans, who lived before the Romans, and the culture of this rude tribe, making the foundation, is now buried in the soil. The Etruscans behind the Romans . . . ! Just as in the Alps one line of mountaintop rises behind another, until almost beyond our range of vision still another mountain is descried in a faint blue mingling with the blue of the sky, so the different periods in history continue one behind another until they vanish into obscurity.

We turned on our heel and came to the edge of the hill where the plain of Tuscany spread beneath our eyes like a dusky ocean. The twinkling lights of Florence were winking at the sky.

§ 2

Rome

I did most of the sights of Rome by myself. Although I did not understand even 'one, two, three . . .' in Italian, I could go round without trouble, joining Cook's tourist party. The charabanc was to start near the Piazza Barberini; therefore, coming out of the Minerva Hotel, I took a No. 14 bus. I was careful not to offend the conductor by rolling the ticket printed with 'fasces' between my fingers, as was my usual habit. I got up when I caught sight of the fountain of Triton which marks the square. Notwithstanding that the water that spurted out from the trumpet-shell blown by Triton was overflowing down the shells of the pedestal, the work of art in the Baroque style seemed somewhat sultry. As this place is described beautifully on the first page of *The Improvisatore* by Andersen, I felt as if I was one of the characters in the story, and I turned the corner at the 'Fountain of Wasps' and came to the foot of the Church of Cappuccini. Cook's office is there, and I went there a little earlier every morning, so as not to miss the charabanc, and passed the time in the church. This is also a place where the Improvisatore Antonio served as a young novice, and the image of St. Michael slaying a fiend is described as having come even into his daydreams. But I looked up to this image thinking it was too handsome. Sometimes, in order to kill time, I listened to the morning service of the priests in brown robes and pointed hoods hanging down behind their backs.

This church is also famous as a church of skeletons, and the underground chapels and passages are ornamented with the skeletons of Capuchin priests. Here and there, some of the skeletons were standing in robes which they had worn in life, but skulls were collected in one room and hip-bones, jointed together somewhat like a screw, in the next room. On the ceiling were hanging lamps of ribs in an arabesque design jointed with backbones. The whole number of skeletons is roughly said to be four thousand. I think I have read, in Mark Twain's book of travel, something like this: 'Imagine the disturbance when the trumpet of the Last Judgment is sounded. Some priest will take somebody else's ribs in the confusion, and others will cause trouble by not being able to find their own legs!' It is indeed a good remark, and I felt amused to think that the Capuchin brethren ought to have a good training for the dressing race in their lifetime.

Soon our charabanc started, taking tourists of all countries.

the fact that it was the greatest in the world and unparalleled
in its exquisite gorgeousness — or rather on this very account.
Who that is naive enough would not be surprised at this
gorgeousness, this abundance of sculptures, and this vastness
of the nave, where people walking at the far end appeared
no bigger than children? But that surprise is a lower kind of
surprise and is usually accompanied by the exclamation,
'Good Lor'!' and simply ends in making people gape and
stare. Even apart from such a Puritanical idea as, 'The
glittering gorgeousness is not what Christ was pleased in . . .'
it seemed to me as if the Popes, whose tombs were niched in
the walls, were keeping their shops each with his own
peculiar design. (It is indeed impertinent to say, 'keeping
shops', but really those tombs gave me this impression.)
Thus the whole did not produce a harmonious beauty as a
large cathedral, and even the gorgeous ceiling gave, like that
of a market-house, only a straggling impression that it was
nothing more than a lid to cover each separate exhibit.
Therefore visitors could boldly walk into the place without
caring about the people in worship. Our guide took us
round saying, 'This is the tomb of the Pope So-and-so. It
is all made of stone produced in ——, Africa', and 'This
is Pope ——'s tomb. Although the stone is common, don't
you think that this globe design is fitting for him? The
picture of the Ascension of the Virgin Mary on the next
wall shouldn't be passed over because it is mosaic, not
oil-painting.'

I gazed with curiosity at the seated image of St. Peter,
placed just in front of the altar, because its lines were somewhat Oriental, like those of the Japanese sculptor Toribusshi,
but I noticed that the tip of its bronze big toe was worn out
by the continual kissing of the visitors who came here one

after another. It is an unhealthy custom, whatever you may say! There were also confessional boxes. They are somewhat like public telephone boxes. A priest within listens to the confession of the person kneeling outside; but it was abominable. Those in the Capuchin church were so made that a priest appeared whenever the bell at the entrance was rung. I thought it was ridiculous, as it looked like an automatic chocolate machine, but in another church he was within beforehand, waiting for his customers. Only the upper part of his body was to be seen in the box, and with one hand stretching out, it was just like a hermit-crab. Unless I looked upon it as ridiculous, I should have been incited to useless anger, for I should have thought that this would lead to the selling of indulgences. In this Mother Church, on the outside of the boxes, 'English', 'French', 'Rumanian', or 'Spanish' was written in order to show that that language was understood there, but fortunately I did not find a box upon which 'Japanese' was written. Another thing I did not like was that a line was drawn along the middle of the floor from the altar, and it was marked in gold letters that thus far comes the Cathedral of Milan, which is the second largest, thus far St. Paul's in London, the third largest, and so on. Visitors might be pleased to know that it was indeed a prodigious structure, but I am sure St. Peter himself would not be pleased with it.

Just at the moment I felt something softly soothing my ruffled mind, and I noticed that the pipe-organ began pealing, filling the whole air of the nave that holds forty thousand people. The sound was grand and simple like the swell of the vast ocean, or the noise of the wind that passes over lofty mountains. In the interval of the music, the sonorous chanting of melancholy Latin hymns clearly floated up, and again the music of the organ rose up in harmony with it, like a sigh of admiration of heaven and earth that praised God the Almighty in unison. It was indeed superb. There was revived in my mind the feeling of a girl of eighteen years old, who, being dissatisfied with Protestantism, wished to be converted to Catholicism. St. Peter's is a church which I would like to visit in blindness.

I do not wish, however, all the sects of Christianity to become as practical as the Salvation Army, but I loathe the pettiness of the Christianity of Rome. See the monuments in the streets, for instance, the Column of Marcus Aurelius, and the Obelisk in the Piazza del Popolo which speaks of the great deeds of Roman generals. On top of these they put a cross, and the king's statue is taken down from the column, whose side is embellished from top to bottom with reliefs of the scenes of his victory over the barbarians and a statue of St. Paul is substituted instead. At the tomb of the Emperor Hadrian near the Tiber, they erected Michael's image, forcing the connection by the tradition that the angel appeared to Gregory VI on the spot. If they would like to be so proud, they had better construct what they like from the very foundation, to make it look down upon all around it. The attitude that shows they are proud of their height, standing on the shoulders of the ancients, not only injures those monuments in their purity as objects of artistic appreciation but also makes people frown with disgust.

Directly from St. Peter's we entered the Vatican. Travellers who were transported by the works of Raphael and the wall-painting of Michelangelo's 'Last Judgment' will have written in their diaries or books of travel, how they had seen the objects of long years of yearning. But as unfortunately pictures were not in my way, I was impressed

323

only by the grand gorgeousness of the Palace which possessed those pictures as an instrument to display the power of the Pope. This Palace, composed of twenty rooms for ceremony, twelve thousand halls, galleries and museums, and many other rooms and buildings, has its own stamps and money, assuming the nature of a small independent state, and the Pope rules over it politically and diplomatically, gathering about him priests and envoys from all countries. Though it is now a time when the influence of religion has declined so much, its potential power must be said to be still great; and if we think of that fact and that the world-powers never forget to make use of it, we cannot help considering that Italy has a strange, unwelcome ornament inlaid in the core of her heart. Therefore, when Mussolini suppressed the demonstrative fête at the time of the funeral of the late Pope and ruthlessly deprived the Pope of his privileges, the Pope was very angry and declared that he would not go even one step out of this Palace, and he stayed for a long time in this sumptuous palace as a prisoner of his own accord.

It may have been necessary for the Fascists to assume such a stiff, demonstrative attitude, seeing that they had, on one hand, to lead a convention-ridden, low-cultured nation, not long after the unification of the country which had long been divided against itself, and to re-establish the troubled land which had been stirred up by superficial socialism after the War, while, on the other hand, encumbered with such a sister-in-law who had long belonged to the family. With this thought in my mind, I walked along the main street back towards the Memorial of Emmanuel II.

In Europe, only England, Sweden, and Czechoslovakia keep to the rule of walking on the left, and the rest of the countries are quite the opposite. I was walking on the right because I thought in Italy, too, the rule must be keeping to the right. As I went along, a gendarme in a plumed helmet called to me, 'Walk on the opposite side'. I looked and found all the people were given the same order. During the ten minutes that I intentionally timed on my watch, twenty-four policemen were counted keeping the pedestrians in order. When I came before the Emmanuel Memorial, there were crowds of people in front of Mussolini's house, a simple and tasteless building, and it seemed that the Duce was about to come out. I wanted to see him, but, as I had not the time, I went back to our hotel where I asked a boy:

'What is the rule of the road in Italy?' but he could not answer. Then I asked the manager. 'Well, whichever you like,' he replied. 'It's only in that main street that walking on the left side is the rule.' 'Why?' I asked. 'Well!' He paused and said, 'Only there policemen say, "Walk on the left side!"' 'People don't seem to know that rule, do they?' 'No, it doesn't matter. A policeman will tell you when necessary.' Indeed, to-day was the first time I was given that warning, although I went to Cook's office every day. As Mussolini was going out on that day, it must have been 'necessary'.

I went out on another Cook's excursion by myself. We were to visit the ruins of the Villa of Hadrian on the Sabine Hills, crossing the Campagna. The avenue of cypresses has a special beauty. The slenderness of the trees stretching long like the shadows of things bathing in the evening sun, and their black colour! The long rows of the spindle-shaped trees left no interval between them to the eye, and the bright southern sky was confined between the two rows like a wide ribbon, the avenue becoming narrower towards the end, where the marble foundation of the Palace was reflecting the sunlight as if there existed a bright world. Walking towards that made me feel as if I was going back to the old world from the present through the passage that connected the two, and the avenue was indeed a fitting entrance to the old ruins.

The dwelling-place of the Emperor Hadrian was charming. For a king or a guest, whichever it may be, a southern country is good for luxury. The Romans and the Arabians knew how to live in luxury. People in northern climes do not know how to enjoy a sumptuous life within the house. Their palaces are no more than instruments to display their power. In the large halls of the castles of northern Europe, towering proudly into the sky, I often wondered if such noble personages as Elizabeth and Maria Theresa urinated at all, and what distant places they had to go to for that, drawing those long trains behind them. But here in this palace, just behind the dining-rooms, there were furnished not only such negative necessities as lavatories but also side by side with them small rooms where they could vomit so that they could cram with more delicacies their stomachs emptied both upward and downward. These dining-rooms were only used in winter, and in the summer the balcony overhanging a river was spread with tables with perfect equipment in case of a shower. There was a pond where fish for dinner were fed, and the slaves were made to bathe in a large bath-house so that they might not smell. Tubes, that do the work of a telephone, led to the slaves' room from every hall. A Roman theatre, a Greek theatre, and a swimming-pool — everything was perfect; and smart rooms to accommodate courtiers and generals who came back from expeditions were made in rows as in modern apartment houses. In the dining-room, where philosophers were fed, fine mosaics depicting food-stuffs were still remaining. Although the more important part of the mosaics had been taken away to the Vatican, I found a picture of bananas among them, which made me imagine that the Romans of two thousand years ago must have slipped on banana skins left on the stone floor. As everything was like this, although it was luxurious, I did not naturally get the impression that their way of living was so indifferent and remote to us, as you might feel in the ordinary palaces, which are often spoken of in a Japanese expression as being 'above the clouds'. This palace really made me look back upon the past with a familiar feeling that came from the impression that I was looking at a simple dwelling-house of Hadrian, and it seemed to be the fittest place where to recite Browning's 'Love Among the Ruins'. Beside the temple of Vesta, which commands a splendid view standing on a cliff, there was a café spread with tables under the shadow of a vine trellis. The meal which I had there was spaghetti, as usual in this country. It is eaten with a dressing of tomato-sauce and grated cheese, winding it on a fork. Italian girls, who painted their lips so thick with rouge that it looked as if a piece of red paper was pasted on them, wound it ingeniously. Up to that stage they had managed very smartly with their little fingers daintily raised, but when they tried to carry it into their mouths opened wide so as to protect their rouge, the sight of them might have been counted among the 'dreary things' by our ancient diarist. Sei Shōnagon. The members of our party were all unaccustomed to eating it and made a merry fuss, shouting, 'Ooh-oh!' as it slipped off their forks. An American, who had once been in Japan, asked me, 'Why didn't you take your chopsticks with you? It is all right for Japanese to throw away two swords, but they ought not to discard a pair of chopsticks.'

When I remarked that the great waterfalls of Tivoli were

not attractive owing to the poor colour of the water, a Swedish gentleman began to boast of the scenery of Scandinavia and said, 'If you don't believe me, ask Mrs. Japan who has just been there!'

As everybody's mind was filled with such great names as Tiberius, Julius II or Bernini, taking it for granted that there was no room left in the mind to learn each other's names from the sense of formality, according to the motion of Mr. California, we called each other all through our tour by the names of countries taking advantage of the absence of the stiff English. The sunlight that was filtered through the leaves of the vine danced on the table in round patterns, and part of the wine-glass shone like ruby. The weather was fine, and soft breezes blew up from the gorge towards us. On the crown of the exquisite Corinthian pillars, the autumn sun was shining aslant, and as I looked up entranced at the reliefs of acanthus, imprisoning a purple shadow at each hollow, I felt as if my body and all was melting into the midday air. The village musicians were singing, as usual, the songs of 'O Sole Mio' and 'Santa Lucia' which sounded strangely afar, mingling with the noisy talk.

'To cut a long story short . . .' Mr. Sweden never stopped boasting of his country. 'Even these matches were made in our country. Look at the label! Without my country you can't even smoke like that, can you?' Although he looked a mild person, he seemed to have drunk too much the wine which he had not been used to drinking in his country!

That night we were taken to the club of railway workers which had been built quite recently by Mussolini. It was equipped with a fencing-room, a boxing-ring, a billiards-room and a library, and the theatre was all that could be desired as regards lighting and everything. The dome was so constructed that it could be split in two like the roof of an observatory, and on a fine night the audience could enjoy the play under the starry sky. It was pleasing to see that they were making use of the advantages of the climate, always keeping the character of the land in mind. The equipment was very good and substantial, being free from showiness. A young Fascist guided us and explained in Italian. What I did not understand very well was that there was nobody in charge of the club during the summer vacation. Are the workmen not specially in need of resting in summer? As I was told that the club was closed till October, I asked, 'Then the club is placed somewhere near the seashore during the summer months?' but the Japanese diplomat who took us there did not see fit to interpret my remark, saying: 'Well, that question is rather too cynical!'

Then I had to look over it again, saying to myself, 'Well, then, this might be a thing made up more for propaganda, as I might have expected, than for practical purposes. They are simply trying to show how well they are treating their labourers'. The hotel that belonged to the club was kept clean, looked convenient, and I was very pleased to find that it was not closed even in summer time.

In Rome we were given a false coin as change. It was a silver coin that had a design of a god holding 'fasces'. When our charabanc stopped near a fountain and our guide said, 'Now, ladies and gentlemen, if you throw your money into this fountain, your wish will be at once fulfilled', everybody threw coppers out of the fun of the thing, so I said from a fit of roguishness, 'Dear! That false coin!' As the silver colour sank flickering into the water, the lady sitting next to me said wonderingly, 'Good gracious! You must have a pretty big wish!' So far, so good, but I noticed that children and beggars seemed to consider it their perquisite to go into the water to fetch those coins. The silver coin would come out into the world again. I had often seen tram-conductors jingling two coins together to test them. It was a sound that I had often heard in China. It is a sound of shame for a country.

The disῖance between Rome and Naples is done in three hours and twenty minutes by the new road, and it is half the time that it used to take. There were desolate wastes where wild buffaloes played and bald hills where nothing but occasional cork-oaks grew. As we approached the seashore, the green of olives, oranges and vines twining round big trees, increased. The houses, very much like the Spanish in that they had windows like holes, nestled together in groups here and there, and motor-cars ran along the dried-up white highway raising the dust like a smoke-screen. The hedges of cacti were laden with dust as though covered with ash. Soon we came in sight of Mount Vesuvius and Naples was near at hand.

§ 3

Naples

Vesuvius is an exact replica of Mount Asama in Japan. The mountain surface, that heaved as if full of elasticity, is the colour of a bluebell in the dawn, and soon, when the sun begins to shine, it assumes the lustre of purplish silver-grey which reminds us of the fur of a mole. And in the evening, when it burns red for a short time, it vanishes into the twilight as a flower withers, and the colour during this time also resembles that of Mount Asama. The round mountain-top

slowly spread downward and had on the left side Mount
Somma, just as Mount Asama has Mount Gippa on the left
side, sharply carved out on the inner side as is characteristic of
volcanic mountains, and the outer side cut the blue sky with
a slow curve that descended to the plain at the skirt of the
mountains. To-day the mountain seemed to be in too good
a humour, and soft white smoke was rising peacefully into
the sky. It filled my bosom with joy rather than with fear
while I was looking at it. If forced to analyse what kind of
joy it was, I could say that the suggestion which the mountains of glaciers, stiffening my heart with wonder, one after
the other in Norway and Switzerland, had given to my mind
that the earth would soon be frozen seemed to melt away at
the sight of the lively manner of a youthful volcano, and my
heart seemed to dance with joy, the stiff mind being loosened
in hope and cheerfulness.

What a silly idea, for nobody knew that the volcano would
not bury me the next day! But the rage of a mountain that
blows out fire is a fault committed by the earth with its
overflowing vitality. It made me smile in the same way as
when I was hit by a ball that came from young people playing
catch-ball. If I should be buried under the rocks of a sliding
mountain in a gorge in Switzerland, where they are simply
crumbling with age, my soul would not be able to rest in
peace.

I was gazing and gazing up at the mountain, resting my
chin on my hand on the veranda of our hotel. The wind that
went along the Bay of Naples came blowing pleasantly into
the rooms of the hotel, and the waves splashed against the
skirt of the concrete bank that was constructed to protect
the promenade below my eyes, and now and then white
spray tried to jump over the low cemented wall. A boy in

rags was eating a prickly pear, sitting on the bank. The lean boy with large black eyes was eagerly gnawing it, with his feet hanging down loosely. The peeled fruit looked just like our persimmon. At the back of the boy, who looked as if he had stepped out of one of the pictures by Murillo, there protruded into the blue sea the old mole of the Castel Nuovo. A fishing-boat was passing. The standing figures of two or three people, pushing their oars forward at the same time, reminded me of an Egyptian galley rowed by slaves. While I was looking at it, thinking it was an unaccustomed sight for me, the boy jumped lightly on to the wall, ran airily along the narrow railing in his bare feet, and disappeared from my sight. He may have been of unknown parentage, but no doubt he was a son of Naples.

We went out and visited the Museum. They treated us there like thieves by making us write down even our passport numbers. There were many wall-paintings of Pompeii, among which some were extremely obscene, which caused some people to call the catastrophe 'Heaven's punishment'. The pictures, however, had no vividness at all. It seems to have been their convention to have such paintings in their bedrooms, as it used to be a convention in Japan to have a miniature shrine in the kitchen. If a thing becomes a convention, it is fossilized and loses its vividness.

Next to that we climbed up to the monastery of San Martino. The view of Vesuvius from this place, with the city of Naples and the sea between, is the usual view of Naples, familiar on the postcards of Naples — the one with a stone-pine in the left foreground. Often it is not a good thing to see too much of a famous scene or painting in photographs. The purity of first impressions will be marred by the useless thought, 'Ah! this is that', which comes into your mind first of all. Whenever such a thing happened, I could not help muttering with an exclamation of annoyance that I should not have seen anything beforehand, but at the same time I remembered that I used to see pictures avariciously, little expecting that the day would come when I should see the actual things, and joy and gratitude suddenly filled my heart. And, all the more for that, my appreciation was disturbed. On our way back we went down some stone steps in a narrow lane towards the sea. In a corner of the steps, there was a small shrine of the Virgin Mary, and the sight of the lighted candles and offerings was very much like that of our fox-shrines. The byways in the evening were very noisy. Housewives all took out the pots with boiling macaroni into the streets and chattered. Except for the jumping notes of the striking Italian endings '-tino' and '-tento', the noise of indistinguishable sounds was whirling in the air. They looked very happy holding their gossipy meeting out in the street. Before they went to bed at night they might most probably cry two or three times! The next morning they might be groaning, suffering from typhoid fever! For all that, I felt it would be a pity to give them would-be education and enlightenment. What I had felt when I saw the Chinese was now revived in my mind after a long time.

As I walked along, taking care not to slip on the skins of paprica thrown away, I saw some prickly pears at a green-grocer's. The fruit that grows clumsily on the edges of the stems linked together in the shape of rackets is very much like a fig both in shape and size. My husband, who picked up one of them, shouted with a frown on his face, 'Ouch! It hurts terribly. Just try this'. As I wanted to experience all things new to me, I took it and was stung sharply. It was full of transparent prickles. As it was impossible to carry them home, we had them peeled in the shop. The flesh was a persimmon colour, as I said before, and both flavour and smell resembled that of over-ripe persimmons. As it was full of pips I found it very difficult to manage it and hesitated. Then the housewife in the next shop cried to me, from behind a screen of macaroni, 'Mangea tutto!' (Eat all!), which I could not. Coming down to the seashore, we found the reflection of the lights already floating on the sea along the promenade, and the ridges of the softly undulating waves glittered. On the stalls catering for the people coming out to enjoy the cool evening air, pomegranates and the peeled cacti were spread glistening, and although the dishes of shellfish stripped of their shells with slices of lemon on them were sure to disagree, they made my mouth water, suggesting the cold feeling when they slipped down the throat. My husband being unable to get along with his fingers stung with the prickly pear, said, 'Let's go home'. My fingers also smarted slightly, as a reminder of an overdone act of curiosity. The tweezers that we took with us from Japan saw a time when they came in useful anyway.

The next day we climbed Vesuvius. Going along the seashore till we came to the base of the mountain, we took the Vesuvius railway that belonged to Cook's, to go up to the top. The lava-stream which flowed out in 1872 had for the most part disintegrated, and some part of it is turned into vineyards made in terraces. Along the eaves of desolate-looking farmhouses were hung small tomatoes, like red strings of beads. They were probably going to be made into ketchup to go with macaroni all the year round. The hand of human artifice, that was climbing up little by little without growing wiser from disasters, is as persistent as the stems of climbers that can never be suppressed by repeated cutting. Soon we came to the part of the mountain where no plants except small brooms and acacias grew, and at last we came to a sharp slope where only lava was to be found. Suddenly a mist rose up to hide everything from our sight. A man who hired out raincoats went round the car, as if he had been waiting for the mist. The weather seems always to get cloudy from this part as if conspiring with this man. Somebody has written that he found a little relief when he remembered that Goethe, writing about his regret, said, 'I did not even see my own shoes', but what is regrettable is regrettable, whether or not we share the experience with a greater man. We have not come all the way simply to go through this experience, like that of an ant walking on a large mound of chocolate in front of an inhaler. Cook's guide apologized as if it were his own fault. On the way, there is a rest-house where is sold 'Lacrimae Christi', the famous wine of this place. It means, 'The Tears of Christ'. In some cases such names may be called poetical, but think of a name which is given to thin vermicelli—'The Hair of an Angel'. What a silly, stolid, Europeanish name it sounds! All names are not gratifying which sound religious.

While people were all having a meal there, a German couple, who came by the same car, opened their lunch-baskets on a projecting rock near by. They had not to pay any liras to the raincoat hirer and sat down in the mist quite comfortably because of their thick, greenish-brown overcoats, like those worn by soldiers, which even I would not have the courage to wear, though I am so careless about clothes. Northern people are indeed steady and sound.

Our train went down the mountain again and past the ruins of the fire caused by the eruption of 1906. The lava-flow annihilated the houses of Torre Annunciata, a town near the seashore which is famous for the manufacture of macaroni.

Soon we arrived at Pompeii. The town which was planned out in chequer-board style, there being not an inch of unoccupied space, and the streets and alleys being arranged in good order, had houses all remaining with their pillars and walls to a height of two-thirds of the original. On both sides of the main streets, tiny shops stood in rows, in sauce-shops pots and pitchers remaining, in butchers' shops marble tables on which to chop the meat, in bakers' shops large stone grinders and ovens. We had seen in the Museum large beams to weigh chopped meat, round loaves of bread having hollowed lines in a star shape, olives and eggshells which had been excavated from these shops. Skeletons of a family who were killed together are left in one place, but what makes us imagine most vividly the life and noise which was experienced here, were the traces of the wheels left in deep ruts in the roadways. A miniature temple shelf in a pawnshop had a picture in relief of a large temple leaning on one side and houses falling down. We were told that this commemorated the ruin caused by the great earthquake sixteen years before the enormous eruption. Our guide explained, 'The people of Pompeii thought, in those days, that Vesuvius was already an extinct volcano. They constructed one after another temples, amphitheatres, courts, prisons, and, at the corners of the streets, fountains; they rebuilt an ideal modern city of those days, without knowing that the last earthquake was but the shaking of the mountain at its waking. Seeing the completion of the restoration work, Vesuvius suddenly . . .' Our party listened to his words with a nonchalant air. Only we citizens of Tokyo, with Mount Fuji near them, secretly counted on our fingers, thinking how many years had elapsed since that earthquake disaster, and we were feeling a little uneasy.

Sometimes he would say, 'Well, only gentlemen, please!' Is there any suffragette who will shout here for the equal rights of men and women?

When we came out into an open place, the sky cleared and Vesuvius showed itself. It looked farther off than I had expected, but it was about the same distance as Mt. Asama seen from the plain of North Karuizawa. As we thought of having a summer cottage there, where we could look upon Mount Asama, this similarity of distance and the fact that this great earthquake took place on August 24th was a little disconcerting. When I read *The Last Days of Pompeii*, I was wild enough to cry out that the eruption that crushed only evil people was not incisive enough. It could be called a grand burst of rage of the great earth only when good and evil, beauty and ugliness were alike blown up in one swoop. I can bear to be buried somehow, but it would not be very pleasant to become part of a show excavated after two thousand years. But what will the village of schoolmasters over there have left after two thousand years? Are not the houses roofed with tin-plate or thatch? When I thought of this, I suddenly burst out into bitter laughter. Oh, yes! There is the lavatory porcelain. I earnestly hope that the day will never come when archaeologists discourse upon it with serious looks.

The next day we went over to Capri to see the famous Blue Grotto. As soon as we went out into the sea from the breakwaters of Naples, the waves became unexpectedly rough, and people began to suffer from seasickness. A priest in a cassock was also looking downcast, holding his head in a posture of prayer. It is rather pleasant to look unruffled among crestfallen Europeans. Mr. America said, trying to be amiable to me, 'Yes, Japan is a country of the sea!' Near the Isle of Capri, the colour of the water being glistening sapphire, it made me imagine the beauty of the Blue Grotto, but the sea was rough and the entrance of the cave was extremely narrow, being about three feet high, so that the part where the mouth of the cave was only glistened for a moment among the waves now and then, and there was nothing for it but we had to land on the island and take a rest. 'If it were in our country,' said Mr. America with a sigh, 'they would naturally have dug out a hole from the top of the island mountain down to the cave so that they could go down by elevator.' In Italy, if you are having a rest in a café, a couple of beggar-musicians will often come, and if they find a Japanese, they will try to get tips by playing his national anthem with the high trembling note of the guitar.

§ 4

A Town like Amethyst

The next day we went northward to Assisi passing through Rome without stopping there. The church by the station, where St. Francis died, had been demolished by the earth-quake and had only just been restored. A rose-tree no bigger than a little finger is specially kept with a fence round it and is called 'The Rose without a Thorn through the Virtue of the Saint'. I smiled to see the similarity of this to, say, a bamboo in some temple in the countryside of Japan shooting up leaves from 'A Stick used by the Priest Shinran'. The town of Assisi is built on a hill about two miles farther from this place. Both this and Perugia, the next town, are built on small hills, and the plains below are either cultivated for vineyards, or in some places there are wastes of lime with the earth washed away. It is very much like Spain. It seemed to me as if they had fled up to heights, driven by the Flood. In Assisi, we found all the hotels full, and, spending some time in looking out for a *pension*, it became so dark when we got to San Francesco that we only got a faint glimpse of Giotto's wall-paintings. The lower church, where St. Francis's tomb is placed, was dimly lighted, and though it was crowded with people who might be taken as pilgrims there was a somewhat calm and quiet sombreness all around in the church. Franciscan friars were in long loose robes of a dark-brown colour with white cords, and their bare feet in leather sandals. The ends of the cords hung down to their feet, and the silver crosses dangling at the ends of the rosaries glittered for a moment now and then. While bishops of other Catholic churches wear gorgeous surplices, sometimes scattered with jewels, sometimes woven with gold threads, and sometimes having the life of Christ represented in embroidery (so that the pictures may come out in strong relief, Christ's body is often stuffed with cotton and looks very much swollen, like a wrestler in a Japanese play or a drowned person), the priests of this brotherhood are attired in a very tasteful way betokening self-denying poverty. Santa Chiara's had been closed already, but the sight of the sunset in the Umbrian plain viewed in front of the gate was one which I shall never be able to forget. It was one of those windy days in autumn, and clouds were moving very low, threateningly, and only the mountain edges in the west were crimson red, and the rest of the mountains seemed to be vanishing in blue and

the fields in faint grey. Those fields and mountains were
once gazed at by St. Francis and St. Clara, with merciful eyes,
with a prayer for their bliss. We went back to our lodging,
sometimes thinking that I would like to read the life of
St. Francis once again, which in my youth I had read through
at one sitting, but forgot all, except for the thrill of excitement
I felt, and sometimes thinking that I had better keep the
impression of his life quietly in the mist of old remembrances.
In a medieval town like this, and even in the isolated Capri,
we noticed Fascist clubs, and young men were seen playing
chess inside. Yet the equipment in primary schools
remained unimproved, so those clubs only gave me the
impression that they were simply currying favour with the
people who could work, and my nerves as a woman seemed
to be sharpened at the idea that they were going to reform the
society of such a low level by the hand of men alone. When
I saw in Denmark young couples from the countryside
enjoying a walk round among the sculptures by Thor-
waldsen with rucksacks on their backs and criticizing them
with each other, I could imagine their fireside talks enriched
by what they had seen and I could not help blessing them.
But in Italy, where only Fascist youths are allowed to go up
and see Rome and talk about the reform of everything with
the pride that comes from the feudal idea that women have
nothing to do with the affairs of the state, I could not help
imagining families deformed and maimed.

It was another full day's trip by train from Assisi to
Venice. I saw from the train peasants coming and going,
driving donkeys that drew carts with wheels painted red,
bodies in blue, and the side-planks painted with pictures.
The fields of Umbria now looked alive with the harvest of

early grapes. The oxen used for ploughing were white, and their long horns were also conspicuous. After Florence, our train crossed over the backbone of the Apennines before it went down to the low-lying land of Lombardy near the Adriatic Sea. The mountains were not very high, but they overlapped one another like folds. The greater part of them had a surface which easily moulders, and the bare river-beds which are flooded in the rain and dry up quickly gave them a wild appearance. Between tunnels, a locomotive engine which had been derailed and turned over lay like the dead body of a quadruped, and the noise of the wind that came rustling through the mountains covered with chestnut-trees made our hearts somehow restless. Yet the compartment of the train, having eight seats, was always filled up, and the passengers were the kind of people who throw things away out of the window quite indifferently. Crash! I was awakened from my nap again and again by the noise of an empty bottle thrown on to the rails from the next compartment. Now we approached the level region after a long time. They were mending the wild fields which had just been reclaimed from the waste land by gathering the rough stones in one place and burning the grass. The marshy district, which was once given over to malaria between Florence and Rome, and the dried-up desert south of Rome, showing the trace of exploitation that never ceased to stop, made me appreciate the vigorous efforts of the people, and I could sympathize with them, comparing the topography and the population with those of our own country. Mussolini spake unto his people: 'Be fruitful and multiply! I will find you a place for living'. From a desire for expansion, are the countries of the world going to quarrel again? It is not at all what I felt afresh in Italy, but what I specially feared in this country which is under the rule of men-kind was that the decree might sooner or later be issued, 'As it is now a time of emergency, one-third of the women and weak men shall kill themselves'.

While I was thinking in this vein, I fell into a nap again for some time. The train seemed to breathe a sigh of relief after going down to Bologna, and ran towards the north passing among vineyards. Now and again the wheels of the train roared as it crossed over a steel bridge. Each time we must have been crossing over tributaries of the river Po. The village houses hung maize along the eaves, and autumn had arrived in this plain too. Again and again our train met with goods-trains heaped up with succulent beetroots, which made me imagine that it was late autumn in the northern districts. While I was being shaken in a dark, dreary and dry mood, the train arrived at Venice at last at some time past seven o'clock in the evening. The exit of the station opened directly to the bank of a canal, and gondolas were waiting for customers just as taxis do, and small river boats came and went like buses. Our boat passed along, dividing the water where the lights were reflected on the surface of the water. We went underneath the Rialto bridge, and as it proceeded winding along the Grand Canal, I felt my stiff heart gradually softening and the dryness going away at the same time.

The Cathedral of San Marco looked sweet. Although it seems strange to call a grand and gorgeous cathedral 'sweet', it was really a full, rich church as the name San Marco sounds to the Japanese ear. It is probably because it has curves of several round domes overlapping each other and round arches in a row, instead of having the acute lines in the Gothic style that point to heaven as an expression of their

earnest prayer, and these curves and arches remind us of the
rich, warm curves of, for instance, women's breasts or a
bunch of grapes. The gold mosaic work of the ceiling,
representing such figures as an antique and innocent Christ,
stimulated our smile and was looked upon in simple admiration. The dark marble walls that had stripes in the shape of
the grain in wood were also good. I could not appreciate
the reddish-brown marble with white lines that decorate
Florence and Rome, because it looked like corned beef.

San Marco is good because we can simply steep ourselves
in the innate beauty of the church itself, for after it was once
built up elaborately, it became antiquated as time went on
without any artificial additions, and it contains no precious
treasures which we are obliged to see, blinking our eyes each
time, for instance a masterpiece of So-and-so at such-and-
such an age, or an artistic tomb of the such-and-such century.
Good men and women were at prayers, in the faint light
dimmed by the smoke of incense, and San Marco seemed
familiar to us like the Buddhist goddess Kwannon to whom
we can pray for even silly, useless wishes without reserve.
The reason why this church appeals to me so much seems
to be that the Oriental taste of the Byzantine art is secretly
pleasing to my blood. The design of a bird in mosaics on
the floor and the glistening pieces of mother-of-pearl inlaid
in the cross, again reminded me of the historical fact that in
the distant past the same fine art, which originated in Asia
Minor, branched off far into the East and West, because
they looked exactly the same as the *rōkechi* dyeing and the
lute which I saw in the Shōsoin Treasury at Nara. When I
went out of the Cathedral, I found a mark on the pavement
a few steps from the entrance, beside which was written 'The
trace of an Austrian bomb'. As it was so sudden, I felt a

shudder running down my spine, which I did not feel even when I saw the ruins of the Cathedral of Rheims. To an old woman who was coming to worship in the church, with a look as if to say that it was San Marco that diverted the bomb from the Cathedral I felt like telling the story of Japanese Buddhists who said that the large gingko-tree in the grounds of the temple of Asakusa checked the fire by spurting out water at the time of the great earthquake. Exactly as in Asakusa, numbers of pigeons were flocking together. Vendors who sell beans for them attract people's attention by rattling bamboo-tubes. When I came to the edge of the open place, I turned back, saying to myself, 'Wait a moment! Was it actually a bamboo-tube? It might be bamboo because this is a port that communicates with the Oriental countries'. Then I heard a strange sound near my ears. Somebody was speaking in Japanese. 'Hullo! A glass-factory. Just have a look. Cheap, cheap! Come in!' Those words of my mother tongue sounded more weird, like the words of a parrot, than ridiculous.

There stands the Palace of the Doges next to the San Marco Cathedral. The stately Council Hall looked fitting in which to move the audacious resolution which the Doges had decided on to fetter thousands of people and to make the enemies shudder, living thousands of miles away. Out of the round pillars of marble that stand in rows in the corridor upstairs, only two are in red colour. The sentence of death was passed by the judge looking down between those pillars, and on the small bridge that leads to the prison, called 'The Bridge of Sighs', the victims who were driven away threw their last look to this world. The street that runs in front of that makes an outlet of the Grand Canal to the sea. There were gondolas all over the face of the water,

and the boatmen who were calling to their customers were
very noisy. Gondolas look very smart in shape especially
when they glide into narrow waterways. But when they are
rocked up and down by the waves of a small steamer as they
are moored in long rows, the spell is broken. As their bodies,
as well as the hood like that of a rickshaw, are all pitch-black,
they look too dismal, giving the impression that coffins are
kept in them; but when beautifully-attired ladies are in them,
they probably seem still more beautiful from the contrast.
Unfortunately I did not see such a sight myself, but the
gondola that seemed to be owned by a family of name had
a boatman decorated with a wide red ribbon hanging from
his shoulder like a cordon of an order, and even that seemed
very beautiful to me.

We went over in a small steamer to the Lido, a long
narrow island across the Lagoon. Looking back I found the
Palace of the Doges standing with its row of marble arches
in the shape of a pattern of lace, and the high tower in the
square, which had made me frown because of its prosaic
bulkiness when near at hand, was now viewed with a kindly
feeling as a landmark of Venice which was gradually vanishing into the haze. But on the right of the scene like a water-
colour painting, torpedo-boats and destroyers were lying
together in ghastly, dismal, grey colour, displaying the
force with which they had wrested Trieste and Fiume from
Austria. Soon we returned to the mainland again and visited
the Art Gallery and the Museum of Marco Polo. The city
of water was indeed quiet without having any motor-cars or
bicycles at all, and the shadow of Fascism was also faint
here. The waves that were caused by river-boats smoothly
washed the foundations of the houses, and the reflections of
the mooring-stakes dyed red and white like the signs of

barbers' shops were stirred at the same time. In order to visit the house where Browning died, we passed through small alleys between houses and crossed small squares in front of churches several times. In the narrow canals cabbage leaves were floating upon grey stagnant water, and all the bridges were shaped like arches with staircases that they might not hinder the passage of boats. The house which we sought was found vacant and looked dreary, but at least it was not useless that we rambled round the city of Venice.

Our hotel served us with macaroni as usual. Even to advertise the menu in the lift, they had to put a stamp on it. It may be hard of us to think that they are raising a fund for Fascist salaries by collecting taxes from the stamps put on all advertisements for sightseeing and even from the notice in the lavatory which tells us not to throw away fruit skins into the w.c., but blackshirts are doing the office of severely supervising adherence to Fascist rules, so they are kept at a respectable distance by the people. In all hotels, just behind the manager's chair, a photograph of Mussolini is hung with his forehead shining brightly.

Italy, the country of Mussolini and macaroni, from which we were going to part to-night! Directly you come from Naples to Venice, you feel the atmosphere of Northern Europe in the quiet attitude of the people. It is of a colour of antique beauty, the colour of faint purple that floats in the transition stage from the burning red of the Latin race and the pellucid blue of the Teutons. Venice is a town like amethyst which breath has clouded.

That night we took our train for Vienna.

CHAPTER XI

CENTRAL EUROPE

§ 1

Vienna

AT dawn, peeping between the curtains in the sleeping-car, I found that our train was passing by a lake like a fjord. I thought that we had already come to a northern country where the sunlight is weak, because I saw, as in Scandinavia, sticks standing with a little amount of hay bound up at the heads of them like bulrushes. To-day again we had to continue to ride till the evening. Travelling as we did, we did not like very much to see again a derailed locomotive being pulled up. Yesterday's paper reported that the railroad between Vienna and Budapest, which we were to pass along, had been blown up, thirteen passengers being killed. We talked together with laughter, 'Aeroplanes are now much safer, if things are like this!' Our train threaded through mountains similar to those in Switzerland and stopped only in those poor villages where timber factories alone were remarkable. In the train, as in the Vesuvius railway, I saw a lot of people in thick overcoats and in hats with a thing like a small feather duster attached to them. I was told that it was a custom near the Tyrol, but their attire was on the whole distinguishedly simple and modest, and there were people who carried rucksacks for practical purposes instead of for mountaineering, and others with their hair cut short in German style.

On the platform, too, they sold glasses of fresh water drawn from a fountain in front of the station, instead of wine-bottles wrapped up in straw, and people drank them, eating sausages at the same time. The country of chianti, the country of macaroni, was already left behind. We arrived at Vienna soon after we crossed over Semmering, where trees were beginning to turn red.

Vienna is a city which is decaying through age. The buildings are imposing, and the grace of the streets does not diminish even if you walk and walk, while the windows of the shops in the main streets seemed to be full of more luxurious things than in Paris, all the more because they were not showy and cheap. But along such streets there were walking people simple and modest, who were not quite in keeping with the dignity of the streets.

The splendid Opera House, monuments of musicians, advertisements of piano factories, cathedrals and hospitals! But faintly covering all those things was a shadow of sad emaciation. If a town had an arm and you could put a thermometer under the armpit, it would stand at only a little more than 35° Centigrade, in the case of Vienna; it is a town somehow so low in spirits. It was unexpected that in Austria, which in consequence of the war was cut decidedly small, I did not feel the slightest suspicion of the restlessness and irritation of the people's minds. Is it because the citizens of Vienna are naturally quiet, like the people of Kyoto, rather than that they had been too violently cast down by the blow? The very fact that their way of taking seats in a bus was so gentle and slow was the more note-worthy because their appearance is very much like Germans. I had expected that I should be able to compare Germany and Austria, who wait for the chance of revenging themselves,

to the Soga brothers, the heroes of a Japanese vendetta
story; but this younger brother seemed to be not very
reliable, and I was given an impression that it was rather
unnatural that a large country was formed in ancient times,
having such a city as this at its centre. Now that I came to
this country, my sympathy was decreased because I realized
that things united will be separated again. But, instead, the
deep misery of the end of the Habsburgs reminded me
feelingly of the Oriental expression, 'They were indeed
ill-starred'.

The Palace of Schönbrunn is full of rooms where,
probably in accordance with Maria Theresa's taste, Chinese
pictures in gorgeous embroidery, and other similar things are
displayed; but the room of the poor old Emperor Francis
Joseph was in a quiet taste because he was, I was told, a
person fond of light brown colours. He lived to be eighty-
seven, old enough to see and remember the sad days when
the Empress was assassinated in Geneva and the Archduke
and Archduchess in Bosnia, and the country itself broken
down. I saw his death-bed with a sad heart. The clothes in
which the Archduke was killed are kept in the Museum of
Weapons. The large, black stain on the trousers of his gay
uniform of light blue is the stain of the blood when the
Princess fell down upon his lap. The coat, having the
traces of knife slashes at the collar decorated with beautiful
gold braid and at the part over his heart, speaks of the
oppressive scene when doctors sought for the fragments of
the shell without being able to wait to have the buttons
loosened. One of the cathedrals in Vienna is said to have
been erected to commemorate the Emperor's gratitude to
God on the spot where the Emperor Francis Joseph was
shot at the age of twenty, but as good luck would have it, he

was quite safe because the bullet hit the collar-buttons. As the Archduke was assassinated on his way to the grand manœuvre, with Serbia as the imaginary enemy, he must have worn a lot of orders upon him, but all those things seemed this time to have been no protection at all. The pistol of assassination, which is the spark of an unhealthy world, never ceases to sound even to-day. Even a few days ago, an attempt was made by a Serbian on the life of the King of Albania in the Opera House of this city. 'After the second Balkan War, Germany and Austria established the kingdom of Albania by cutting away part of Turkish provinces in order to keep away Serbia, one of the Slav races, from intruding upon the Adriatic Sea. This was the second victory of the Pan-Germanic principle over the Pan-Slavian, and the grudge of the Serbians was now still more greatly stimulated . . .' This was just what I had read in the train to Vienna in a pocket-book of European History compiled for the competitors for entrance examinations. Although this dry-as-dust description was meant for the torture of the middle-school boys, I always read it with the same interest as I did the sub-titles in a cinema, followed always by the scenes and events that perfectly fitted the description.

Vienna, the city of historic interest, abounds in things worth seeing. We saw in the Treasury of the Royal Family the beautiful perambulator of the son of Napoleon, the King of Rome. When I saw the room where he spent his troubled life at the side of his grandmother, Maria Theresa, whom I do not like at all, I remembered my days as a child. When I was thrilled, listening to the story of 'Aiglon', which my brother who had come back from France told me, my hatred against Metternich seemed to have sunk deep into my mind at that time. But my nurse, an old woman by now, used to say to me, mispronouncing 'Metternich' in a funny way, 'The enemy who is called *Nickel Mekki* (which in Japanese means "nickel-plated") . . .' This remembrance made me yearn strongly after the people at home.

In the Museum of Weapons I saw a lot of relics of the days when Turkey stretched out her arms as far as to this place, and in the streets they were selling rolled bread in the shape of the crescent moon, made, as they say, to commemorate their driving back the Turkish army. While we were doing the sights, it was necessary for us to prepare for entering the Balkan Peninsula. In the Rumanian Legation, however, we had a very unpleasant experience. We had heard that the Rumanians were great sticklers for red-tapism, so we visited the Japanese Legation to make sure of things, and went to the Rumanian Legation after making certain that any introduction was unnecessary. Most of the people who were waiting to get visas were such people as housewives who were hooded with a cloth, and they seemed to be obliged to come and go on business. Presently my husband was called into another room with some other people who moved in confusion, and I stayed in the waiting-room because I was told that I was not wanted, but he did not come back although I waited and waited. I stayed from nine-thirty until twelve-thirty. As it was Saturday our plans would be upset unless we went to the bank before noon. My husband, who came out after the long lapse of time, said, 'They examined papers very carefully, saying something about "spy"!' After all, they said his height which is mentioned in the passport was different from his real height, so he was told to get a personal voucher at the Japanese Legation. Our heights had first been taken by the

Japanese standard of measurement and then was changed into metres, hence the miscalculation! The official insisted that, if this measurement was true, my husband ought to stand one centimetre taller, and so found fault with the imperfection of the passport. As we could not very well say that we must have worn off a bit because of our long journey, we came away and went back again with an introduction from the Japanese Legation, but, when they saw us enter, they went out for a meal and gave us the visa after making us wait till two o'clock. The consul was a short-sighted Rumanian of Latin type, and the top of his head was smoothly bald. His hair around it was stiffened with glistening pomade, and from about one-fifth of an inch from one ear, all the hair was brushed across to the other side to hide his baldness. I thought that a bald head should be bared fair and square. Owing to this we could not go to the bank, and we were unable to enter the Balkan Peninsula, so we decided to have a trip to Czechoslovakia where we had intended to look in on our way to Russia. We found the Russian Intourist Bureau and asked them to look after the preparations for my return journey to Japan, and after that, when we came back to our hotel, we found Mr. and Mrs. K. waiting for us. They told us that they had heard a rumour of a war between Japan and China. This astonished me because I was thinking of returning through Siberia, but anxiety was of no use, so, thinking it better to go to Cobenzl Park in the suburbs than to eat out my heart confined in my room, I went out. The leaves of the *marronnier* had already turned yellow, and the nuts were dropping off. The outer skin was divided into two in the shape of a small round boat and scattered here and there. Among the children, who were picking up the nuts, there were grown-up people also. One of them said to me, 'Before the Great War they were only given to pigs'.

So to Austria, a suffering country, autumn had come when vines bear grapes, and before the wine-shops could be seen the bush which is a bundle of pine or cedar twigs to show that new wine had been brewed. Probably because I was worrying about the war in the depths of my heart, I wanted to find out things that were similar in some way to those in Japan, such as the rule of walking on the left in the street, and people carrying big bundles wrapped up in light-green cloths. If I had had the usual roguish mind, I would have asked an old man who was digging out beetroots in the fields, and I would have tried whether they were as sweet as sugar-cane or not, but I did not have the chance. On the following day we went and spent two days in Prague, the capital of Czechoslovakia. Our train ran along the bank of the Danube for some time, and after passing villages busy with the harvest of beetroots, with preparations for the harvest festival, it crossed over the height at the edge of the wide basin of Bohemia. There were beautiful forests on either side of the railway, which were protected as hunting-grounds for the Austrian princes in the olden days, and they are now the resources of Czechoslovakia. The sight of hares at a station which were pierced in sixes on a stick, like fish on a skewer, and of the deer left on the ground, was in keeping with the nature of the place.

§ 2

The Capital of Bohemia

We arrived at Prague at two o'clock in the afternoon. The first thing that attracted our notice was that Czechish was written on all signboards without exception, for if German was used, I was told, the patriotic mobs tore them down with shouts of indignation. The antiquity of this capital of Bohemia, which is so full of old churches that it is called 'The Town of a Hundred Towers', is hidden in the darkness at night, and modern neon-signs shine, which are erected on the stone-eaves sombre with age; and we nearly passed by the hotel which we had left in the daytime. The fact that they are full of the spirit of a rising nation in the industrial field is known at once by the coins on which a forest of chimneys is represented. The building of the 'International Sample Fair' looked like a large department-store. We found there a shop selling imitations of Japanese goods made in Czechoslovakia. Under the paper-lanterns upon which were inscribed some Japanese characters, a Chinese salesman was standing in an ordinary European suit, over which he wore a Japanese gown that reached nearly to the floor, and was sedulously arranging cheap gimcrack tea-wares. When I thought that things of this kind are in great demand in Northern European countries, I began to feel a grudge against Czechoslovakia which makes imitations and exports them in large quantities taking advantage of the little cost of transportation. At every street-corner there were advertisements for Bata shoes, which are as famous as Ford cars. As well as the privilege of using the

Danube, Oder and Elbe for their transportation, even a free quarter in Hamburg was allowed to them, and the impression of Prague as an industrial city was so strong that Prague as a town of historic interest did not make a very strong impression on my mind notwithstanding that it had many sights to see. Seeing such things as an antique clock, which had Christ and the twelve apostles, who came out from a little window every hour, and a skeleton pulling a bell-rope, and the hall where the tournaments of knights used to be held, I wanted to imagine ancient times. But the procession of women with head-bands in the Sokoll movement passed by with a loud brass-band, and there was a big statue of Moses, which was by no means fitted to the hall, presented on the occasion of the anniversary of President Masaryk's eightieth birthday by the King of Serbia as they were of the same Slav race which have as their enemies Austria and Hungary between them, giving me the impression that there was an intercourse between the kings with a tacit understanding to help each other in case of emergency; and thinking of those things took my mind from ancient things to those of the present day. Speaking about the faces of the Slav race, I had expected to find the same big round type as I had seen in Russia, but my expectation was wrong. Looking out from the hotel window, I saw different faces and figures, coming and going, one after another. Most of them were of German type, but putting these aside, the rest were people who had big noses full of pimples and effeminate-looking men with white delicate skin; and sometimes my eyes met with faces with protruding cheek-bones of the Mongolian type, or the various mixtures of these different types, such as well-developed cheek-bones and white skin, delicate yellow skin, and rough yellow skin.

While I was thus looking out, I suddenly turned back and asked, 'Wasn't Mendel born here?' so great was the variety. Although I had known that the people of this part of the world were complicated racially, and therefore I had expected that I would see something like a middle type, just as blue and yellow are mixed together forming green, yet in reality all the faces I saw here were only like flour of various colours kneaded roughly. They struck me as not being well mixed, and when it was borne in upon me that the characteristics of human blood are not easily fusible, it gave me furiously to think. As with the people, so in architecture, one church combined in itself Romanesque, Gothic, Renaissance and Baroque, for which it was famous, while on the other hand there was an ultra-modern church which attracted the notice of travellers looking out from the windows of the train. They said, 'Hullo! What's that? Is it a cinema-palace?' It was entirely composed of geometrical lines, and in colour scheme the pulpit had a piece of velvet cloth in dark scarlet, and pink stained-glass and an arrangement of black and gold gave the impression that it was for all the world like a stage for a Russian ballet. Old women who seemed to be very old-fashioned came into this church, and herein is found another complication. One more characteristic of Prague is that the influence of Jews is seen even on the surface of things. We went to see their synagogue. Even for the letters of the clock Hebrew was used, and though the Jews go without hats, they put them on inside the synagogue. The hands of the clock also turned in the opposite way. I was told that the Jews had been fasting two days before. Behind the synagogue there was an old churchyard; the designs on the tombs, such as grapes in relief and a pigeon with a twig in its mouth, telling the class of the family.

356

Jewish tombstones are generally laid flat, but in this place, as there was little room, they were standing upright close to one another.

According to the newspapers, the clash between China and Japan seemed to have very little to do with these countries, but as they were neighbouring countries to Russia, the attitude of the Soviet Government towards this event was most noteworthy for their consideration, so Japan's sending soldiers to Siberia was reported in large letters, and it seemed to be getting difficult for us to go into Russia for some time. At the time of the Russo-Japanese War, Japan instigated Poland into restless stirring, and supported the riots near Odessa, in order to keep Russian soldiers in check from gathering in Siberia, so Rumania seemed to have begun nervously to take care not to have such Japanese rambling about in the country in this emergency. After asking the advice of the Japanese Legation, I decided to go back to my country by boat after seeing Egypt instead of Russia. Added to this, the pound suddenly fell off twenty per cent. Great accidents happened one after the other, and I felt a little uneasy.

On September 23rd we came back to Vienna and spent some time preparing for travel by sea, going to Cook's office to reserve a cabin for me.

§ 3

A Country Grinding her Teeth

On September 25th we entered Hungary. At the frontier we were made to write down in the passport the whole

357

amount of money we had. The Korean banknotes and Japanese money, which I carried with me without changing into foreign money, because I thought I should use it on the way home, appealed to the curiosity of the person next to me, and he asked me to let him see them. This country is called a country of Magyars. Some of the people are actually reddish-yellow, with faces like those of the Great Russians who have plenty of the blood of the Huns. They were driving in rugged, black Mongolian caps and dirty leather overcoats with curled fur collars, which we saw in Siberia.

The soil gradually came to bear a black colour, and wheat sprouted up in green; and beside farmhouses with fences made of twigs there stood sweep-wells. Our train came to the bank of the Danube, the opposite side of which is Slovakia. I remembered that the Czechs, who were to incorporate the district where the influence of Hungarian culture was strong, were so nervous that they required 'Czechoslovakia' to be written without any hyphen.

About thirty minutes before Budapest we came to the place where, a week before, Communists had exploded a train. As high explosive gunpowder was put on an iron bridge which crossed a ravine, both the engine and carriages were hurled down fifty or sixty feet below and broken to pieces in a miserable state. They were already rusted red. Thirty people were killed, and on the spot was found a note with the words 'Once a month!'

At four o'clock in the afternoon we arrived at Budapest and called on a Japanese gentleman who had been settled for ten years in that city, and who was doing his best in introducing Japan to the people of this country. During our two days' stay, I was fortunate enough to listen to him explaining to us about the things of this country so that I could understand them easily. He talked about the history of Hungary on the first day, and about the present social conditions on the second day. So I gained much benefit from his talks both in the museums and in the streets, because I got a good basis for my observation, and I was very grateful to him. The history of Hungary begins with the invasion of the Huns, who were led by Attila, about the middle of the fifth century. After his death there was trouble between brothers, as usually happens; the younger one settled in the mountains of Transylvania, and his tribe live there still. Four hundred years after this, Arpad, the first chief of the Magyars, came into this land with his tribe. The scene of his intrusion is now represented in a panorama, in which the king on a white horse conquering the people dwelling in caves, the original inhabitants, is followed by nomadic immigrants driving cows and sheep. I thought that this panorama which made the people of this country look back on the time of the foundation of the country, was a sort of appeal made by the government in these troublous times to the patriotic feelings of the people. It was in the thirteenth century that Jenghiz Khan and Batu Khan whirled into this country like a storm and devastated everything before them. Villages were burnt down and the population decreased, so immigrants were welcomed, and German villages rose up everywhere. They are said even to-day not to be assimilated linguistically. The 'Jenghiz Khan' pot which we had tasted in Peiping, was also carried into this district under the name 'faniel' (wood dish), which interested me because the table plate attached to the saddles of those horses driving like the wind, could not be earthenware. The food prepared in a nomadic way by roasting meat in a pan, we had tasted in the distant Peiping and here again. It made me imagine the sound of hoofs that crossed the desert day after day, month after month, for I experienced myself the long journey in the train through Siberia, passing the Jenghiz Khan station on the way.

Sipping the delicious wine, which is called Tokay, we listened to the history of Hungary. It is indeed a miserable country. They had only experienced a short time of prosperity, and they had to submit now to the Turkish intrusion and then to the yoke laid by Austria. Their history was a continuity of trouble just as a man experiences when he wants to take away bird-lime from one hand and gets the other hand stuck to it. Rakoczy, Kossuth, Déak — they stood up for independence one after the other, but they were miserably crushed down, and they have lost for all their pains exactly two-thirds of the territory in the Great War. To crown all, there rose the riot of Communists, and the country was thrown into a turmoil for about four months; and after all this they are for the present seeing a time of peace under the regency of Vice-Admiral Horthy. Being a little puzzled by the idea of a kingdom without a king, we went back to our hotel. It is noteworthy that, under the trend of the modern world of throwing away kings from their thrones, this country of Magyars, who have something of the Oriental bravado in them, is now under the trouble of choosing a king in spite of their country being a kingdom. It is no use quoting the fable of the frogs from Æsop to show that there is every danger of getting the wrong king. The instance of a people being troubled by adopting a son from Germany or somewhere near there is seen just before our noses. Unless a braggart like Tichborne, who calls himself a relation of Arpad, suddenly turns up, they will find no answer to their problem. Otto, the son of Francis Joseph, who was the king of Austria-Hungary, had been driven away from Austria, studied in Paris, and is now a grown-up man there. I have heard that there are many people who want to have Otto as their king; some from a utilitarian point of view that they ought to accomplish the task of re-expanding the frontier by receiving Otto before he dies, taking advantage of the feeling of the ignorant peasants in the rural districts that have been divided into several countries, who still long for the old Hungary from the fact that she is a kingdom having the Habsburgs at her head; and some from the theoretical point of view that Hungary is still a kingdom having the Habsburgs at her head, and that there has been no change at all of the national constitution. This was also shared by the Catholics who had been greatly protected by the royal family. But the young blood will not consent to the idea of having the Habsburgs again so easily when the main streets along which we were now walking were renamed Kossuth Street and Rakoczy Street and so forth. Was it because we are of the same Oriental blood that I felt anxious about these things? Their language, too, like Japanese, is Ural-Altaic and the structure is nearer to Japanese than Chinese, nouns, prepositions and verbs being arranged in the same way, for instance, 'Budapest to go' or 'Woman of hat', instead of 'go to Budapest' or 'hat of woman'. So explained to us our friend.

Yesterday we did the sights of Budapest all day. The Parliament House is said to be the most beautiful in Europe, and indeed it gave me an impression of a mouth which has a little too many gold teeth, but it was gorgeous, and all the muddled colouring did not look heavy at all, because it had no designs such as figures of men and beasts. Here also there was observed the history of misery clinging to it, for the plank of the platform bore a trace of the shooting of the Premier, who strongly held that they ought not to go into war with Serbia at the time of the Great War. Yet this Premier did not agree to go into peace until the very end after once entering it, and he was killed at last by the pacifists. The history of Hungary has repeated itself as history often does. At the time when they gave shelter to Maria Theresa, they experienced great trouble because of their loyalty. I could not but wish for them that they would have a fit object for their loyal service, for the temperament of the Magyars has something in common with the people of our country, who cannot do anything at all from calculating motives, whose spirit is sung in a song: 'My mind shall not waver; like the inking-line which a Hida craftsman draws, straight is my love for you.'

On a post card which is sold in the Parliament House, there is drawn a map of the old territory. When you turn down a paper handle at the side of it, those districts which were divided among the four countries are suddenly moved apart, leaving sad gaps between the territory left and those districts, and in the gaps appear the words, 'Nem! Nem! Soha!' which mean, 'No! No! How can we bear this?' If you move back the paper handle again, the territory divided will be closely joined to the mainland, regaining the former state. It is easy to do that on a piece of paper, but . . . To-day, if you play with this sad postcard standing on one of the stairs where much blood was shed, when the Communists governed the country, the breaches between the lost territory and the mainland look like white teeth shown between the lips curled in the snarl of a burning grudge.

Again, standing in the 'Liberty Square', on the platform

in front there is a flag drooping at half-mast that is in mourning for the national misfortune, waiting for the time when it will be hoisted to fly high up on the top of the pole. On the platform are engraved Mussolini's words, 'The treaty of peace is not eternal', and the holy bird of this country, 'tur', which led Arpad, the first king of Hungary, from the foot of the Ural Mountains like the golden kite that led our first Emperor at his conquest, is staring up at the flag with fierce eyes like those of an eagle. Again, in the corners of the square, there are four monuments representing cruel generals overthrowing and crushing the young men that represent Hungary, and tormenting them. The north one represents Czechoslovakia, which was given a part of the territory of Hungary for her betrayal of her master country. The south one represents Yugo-Slavia. She fought fair and square with Hungary, and as the name Slavia shows, Hungary had taken possession of the land of the Slavs, so the statue was made not so cruel-looking, showing their generosity in their grudge. But what they can never forgive is that Austria, represented in the west monument, for whose sake they were thrown into the Great War, though they were defeated because of their weakness, behaved so cunningly in diplomacy that, on the ground that she was a white people, she robbed Hungary of part of the territory. In the south, Rumania joined the Great War after sitting on the fence watching for an opportune moment, and she robbed Hungary of Transylvania, where their ancestors lived — how could this be called the principle of self-determination of peoples? Their anger against the racial prejudice of those peoples who ignore the Magyars as a race quite apart from themselves resulted in their entertaining a warm feeling towards Japan, which is strongly independent among all the Ural-Altaic races. In the old days, when the revolution of Kossuth broke out, Metternich moved Russia, making use of the Holy Alliance, and the great forces of Russia pressed down to the south and crushed the independent movement, which was nearly established. Then, just when they harboured a smouldering grudge against the Russians, Japan trampled down that great country, and the Hungarians, who were exhilarated by the result of the Russo-Japanese War, expressed their joy by holding lantern processions or by naming their boys after Togo or Nogi. As they had such admiration for Japan at that time, there have recently appeared scholars who insist upon the similarity between Hungarians and Japanese linguistically and even physiologically as a result of the study of blood. Also from policy, that trend of thought is encouraged, so the longing for Japan is now a current idea in Hungary, and the Turanian Society is now vigorously working for the movement of shaking off Europeanization, aiming at returning to the old spirit which they had at the time of the foundation of their country.

On the other hand the persecution of Jews is partly founded on the fact that they are a white people, and when I was told of this, I realized that I was nearly forgetting that the Jews are a white race, so great has been the hatred against Jews which I saw and heard of in the countries so far. The Hungarians, who had much in common, with the sons of Yedo, who think it a good thing never to keep what they have earned overnight, are naturally being controlled financially by Jews, who have a genius in money matters. And the antipathy that had been of so long standing was still more stimulated by the attitude of Jews between the time of the Great War and the Communist movement, and the severe movement of ousting Jewish influence has now entered even into the world of scholars. But I learned that even this movement had come to a deadlock, because those who were driven away, going into the same tribe abroad, spread evil propaganda and placed obstacles in the way of their money market. Their forests being taken away by Slovakia and the land yielding rock-salt by Rumania, the country left as pure agricultural land is divided amongst the peasants, after confiscating it from the hands of large land-owners. Thus the country ought to approach a better state, ideally speaking, but the product is seen to decrease. This, I was told, was the result of a large-scale farming system being changed into private farming by ignorant and untrained people.

All the stories of Hungary are explained after all by the word, 'Deadlock'. Unlike the German spirit, which brings out still more force by being suppressed, like an engine, the Hungarians are a people who are Orientally brave but not pertinacious. Therefore, isn't it necessary for the Government to inoculate them constantly with the camphor of the sense of a grudge to keep them always in high spirits? The sight of the 'Liberty Square' made me feel sad for it seemed to me that it bespoke the hard trouble of the Government, as much as the grudge that was burning within the hearts of the people. At the top of the pole of the half-mast flag, a golden palm was pointing towards heaven. Hungary, ignored on this earth by white peoples, was appealing to the justice of heaven, and it made a very strong impression on our minds.

Budapest ought not to have made me feel so down-hearted. The Danube was washing the foot of the heights of Buda on the opposite side and reflecting the lights of Pest, the business quarter. Both the middle island and the river banks were rich in mineral water. As it was just the time of the full moon, the promenade along the famous 'blue Danube' ought to have made our hearts gayer, but the heart of the man who told us, pointing to an hotel gay with lights, that it was painted red when the Communists used it for their headquarters, was still sticking to the things of the world.

In a café, where the air was filled with the fragrant smell of Turkish coffee and the sound of gipsy music, for which Hungary is famous, our friend, touching on the policy of making gipsies settle, instead of devastating this country, was still talking in a reasoning vein and the night advanced amid stiff talk.

On the next day we left Hungary behind and entered Yugo-Slavia. In this neighbourhood the countrywomen walked in shaking skirts that spread like a wide lamp-shade. The sight had something in common with that of a turkey, rustic and at the same time a little proud.

When we were going out of Hungary, they never even asked us about our money. This made me think that it was useless trouble that they examined us when we entered the country, and such inconsistency only serves to advertise the lack of discipline, just as in Russia and Spain.

CHAPTER XII

RETURNING HOME

§ 1

In a Deck Chair

On October 20th we made for Port Said. The next morning appeared the *Suwa Maru*, the boat by which I was to go home, in the harbour. She was quite an old boat, so the passengers were naturally an unpretentious sort; which was a circumstance to be thankful for, and I was able to feel quite at home, although I had all my luggage sent home from Hamburg, as I had intended to travel through Siberia. An Egyptian juggler came on board, and uttering an incantation 'Gilly, gilly, gilly!' produced a little chicken from his hand and tore it in two. The trick was done very cleverly indeed. If I had seen the performance before going inland, I should have hesitated with the fear that both my purse and letter-of-credit would be whisked away by that 'Gilly, gilly!' Soon the gong went, and my husband went down the ladder with other people. Our boat began to steam slowly down the canal. That night I went out on deck and found that the sandy deserts stretched on both sides of the canal, and all was in a vague black colour. Only the moon was shining brightly in the sky. Soon, on the right bank, a night train for Cairo roared past like a serpent of light. The figures of the persons in the windows were each clearly silhouetted in black, and the train ran so close to our middle deck that it seemed as if nearly touching it.

That was the train in which my husband was going back to Cairo.

I wanted very much to jump into the train from our deck, and if it had been possible I might have done it. The beauty of a passing train was brought home to me for the first time.

The next day, after seeing on the left the proud summit of Mount Sinai, which looked like a grave old man of a ruddy face, the dull, monotonous voyage continued. It was hot and hot! The severe heat of the Red Sea boiled up my nerves which had been on the full stretch and made me helplessly soft. Our boat came out into the Indian Sea, and on the deck where breezes softly blew through the ocean, I sat in a deck-chair all day to cure me from the fatigue. I found pleasure in quietly recollecting what I had seen and heard during my journey which was so strenuous that I felt almost dizzy. I thought this, and I remembered that. Sometimes I compared impressions of countries individually, and sometimes I disentangled my impressions and assorted them into groups. Thus, I picked out the rivers — Danube, Rhine, Volga and Nile — and the mountains — the Alps and the Pyrénées — and I did the same with lakes, cathedrals, trees and plants, hotels, food, absurd things, and what not.

One day I was counting the tombs — pyramids, tombs of the Egyptian kings, Greek tombs with beautiful reliefs, catacombs, Campo Santo, and the tomb of Lenin. The tomb of Marx was found near Hampstead Heath in London. The tombstone was laid flat, as usual with that of a Jew, in a cemetery situated at the side of a gentle slope, from which the roofs of the houses in London were looked upon in the distance. It had a simple epitaph carved on it, and his grandson and his faithful maid were interred together in that plain tomb. One tomb in this neighbourhood was adorned with pearlworts planted all over. They are one of the most common weeds that grow in the gardens of Japan, having slender leaves growing in groups and small five-petalled white flowers, and they grow to a height of one or two inches. There may be some who see in them the lesson that weeds, which are generally supposed to be of no use, and looked upon with ill-feeling with the idea that they ought to be uprooted and thrown away, might be used to good purpose if they were cultivated in good order. Others may well moralize that as the plants which in Europe are well cultivated for ornament are doing only harm in Japan as ill weeds, so to a still greater extent must ideas and thoughts be modified by different national conditions. Finding the weeds near the grave of Marx, I felt it a little cynical. The tomb of Whymper, who was the first to climb the Matterhorn, lies in the suburbs of Chamonix. The tombstone in the shape of the Matterhorn did not strike me as quite felicitous, because it was too elaborate in design, but it was in a secluded and retired spot, where the incessant sound of a waterfall was enough to banish worldly noise. The Finnish tombs in the old style have little birds perched on the wooden tablet which serves for tombstone. There are as many birds as members of the family left behind. If too many orphans were left behind and the birds rubbed shoulders with one another, it might seem sadly comical, but one or two of these figures add a charm to the tomb. Of all foreign tombs the one that gave the feeling most of the Japanese grave-visiting was Keats's tomb in Rome. Like the Yanaka Cemetery full of cryptomerias, the cemetery had straight cypresses standing in groups, and it was cool. The white marble tomb of Keats, which is suitable to a poet, with a bas-relief of a harp with broken strings, was standing with an old pine-tree at the back of it, and it stood side by side with that of the painter who was his intimate friend and which bore the design of a pallette. They were surrounded by low fences, and, their front being buried by sweet violets, they inspired in me a desire to visit them, as we do in Japan, with a bundle of incense-sticks and a water-bucket in hand.

Once I enjoyed myself by examining in my mind the expression for 'Thank you!' of each country. In order to compensate for my inability to speak satisfactorily in any one foreign language, I intended at least to gather a sample word of every country where we travelled. If I gathered names of things, they might be the same, because those things could easily be transported from one country to another with their names — but thinking it proper to endeavour to use the language of a country where I travelled at least for expressing my gratitude, I learned the word for 'Thank you!' in each country. Of course, it was nothing more than a faint memory which I took down in Japanese letters, but even that was enough to express my gratitude and would be sufficient to show to some extent how various are the languages of the world.

Collecting the expressions for 'Thank you' like this brought me another harvest among my store of things that I have seen and heard. It attracted my attention to the attitude of Japanese diplomats who are sent to small countries. At first I quite carelessly asked them, 'What do they say in this country to express thanks?' 'I don't know,' was the reply! The people of our legations in three small countries all answered in this way. In the first case I innocently felt very sorry, but soon I was made aware by their attitude that they did not seem to be ashamed at all of their ignorance, and after that I repeated in other places the same question quite casually just to see their reaction. It is not an important matter whether they know the word for 'Thank you' or not, but what made me feel gloomy was their attitude shown to it. They seemed to have no time for such a thing. There were even some who seemed to say that to mingle among the people of a weak small country and to know their way of thinking affected the dignity of the smart profession of a diplomat, and that they thought it a shame to do that before the diplomats of other powers. This made me clearly understand that their mission, as diplomats to countries, which have come into being only to balance the influence of the powers, is not to associate with the people of the country, but to sneak among the powers which are pressing each other in the ring, and to get a third party's benefit if chance allowed them.

I was surprised to find in a country where an ambassador is sent that there was not one in the staff of the Embassy who could even count one, two, three . . . up to ten in the language of that country. It is not only that they lack assiduity, but they are transferred so often that it would be wasting energy if they paid attention to the details of the circumstances of each country. It is just as you feel dizzy in a merry-go-round when you try to look steadily at things that come round in front of you. So they seem to leave things alone except what is necessary for the moment. This could not be helped for those who stand at the head, but would it not be desirable to have a man, at least one for each country, who studies the affairs of the country, mingling among the people to sniff the trend of the people's minds directly and help the staff, in order to make the people of that country understand Japan much better and make them feel on intimate terms

371

with us? Would it not be largely our own fault if it was voted unfavourably to Japan in the League of Nations, when such things were neglected? Mr. I.'s endeavour to make Japan better known to Hungary during his ten years' stay may be a special case. Also in Alexandria, where Mr. T., an Arabic scholar, was staying, we saw him earnestly explaining, when we dropped in a café, to a college student who asked, 'What is the cause of the Manchurian affair?' As a hospital has separate departments for medicine and surgery, it might be good for a legation in a small country to have two departments, a bureau for the powers and a bureau for the people.

Another word which I learned from necessity was 'lavatory'. In China it is called 'maofang', but this was almost a mere name. The Russian for it is 'ubornaya', and the Greek, 'apopatos'. In other countries, too, it was necessary for us to distinguish gentlemen's from ladies'. In Spain 'gentlemen' had 'caballeros' which sounded very classic. In Scandinavia 'kvinnor' was written for 'ladies'. It is not so called because the queen entered it ceremoniously with her long skirt carried by her pages, but in England as well a woman was formerly sometimes called a 'queen'. What was amusing was the inscription 'WOMANS' in a public lavatory in Oxford, the town of learning.

At one time, when I was fed up with curried rice at lunch, I felt I was dropping off into a doze buried in a deck-chair, using my toothpick, and I compared the teeth of the people of the south and north. The people of the northern countries including England have good teeth and toothpicks are not used. In the countries of the Latin races they are provided because they have poor teeth. In Seville, in the Alfonso XIII Hotel, they supplied us with toothpicks which faintly smelled of jasmine, and those given in the Alhambra Palace Hotel had a faint aroma of mint. Since the Hungarians, who are an Oriental race, say, 'The Hungarian riders can pick up a toothpick from the ground, leaning down from the saddle while galloping', to signify how skilful they are in riding, they seem to be of the same stock as the Japanese, who chew toothpicks in their mouths.

After I toyed with my various remembrances, I always dropped into a light nap. Once, a couple of whales floated near our boat surprising the afternoon dreams of the people dozing on deck. Those creatures with small eyes, which are incongruous in their large heads, brought home to us the vastness of the ocean, and they swam away. As they were not big for whales, I saw them go off with a smile as when we see two puppies romping playfully with each other. It was rather the large whirls on the starboard side which stirred the face of the water in perfect calm, that made me expect some large powerful creature hiding underneath, and I was gazing at them breathlessly, but I could see nothing after all. For the rest it was nothing but the blue sea and sky that I saw whenever I raised my eyes. Far away there was shining above the horizon a massive cumulus, dropping its white reflection on the smooth sea face. From near the side of the boat, flying-fish fled in troops, sometimes leaving their traces on the waves like a seaplane that alights on the water, and sometimes shining like rolling balls of quick-silver, and our boat quietly made for home, kicking and scattering flying-fish on both sides.

§ 2

Irritation in the Indian Ocean

On November 3rd, as I had recovered from the fatigue of my travel by lolling about day after day, I began to write in a deck-chair thinking to put my diary in order.

'Europe is the face of the earth. The countries in Scandinavia look like the eyebrows of a young man in some mental anguish. They are dark in gloom at the best of times, but when they clear up they are extremely refreshing. England, like a broad forehead which is the sign of great wisdom, has a few wrinkles of age, which some admire as graceful, but others sneer as the sign of decay. The enchanting Spain is the lips painted in thick rouge. I saw such countries as Esthonia and Lithuania, which are like a stubble of bristles, untidy in spite of their having just come out. Germany is a country of will, resembling the lines of a jaw, that is firmly set. Will not Danzig and the Polish Corridor, troublesome intruders like things stuck in molars, be some day crushed down by being chewed forcefully between East Prussia, the upper jaw, and Germany proper, the lower jaw? Hungary is irritated like the blue veins that stand out at the temples, indignant but showing lack of power. Each feature was worth admiration, but seemed drawn up and tense, probably partly because Europe was wearing a kerchief suffering from the chronic dyspepsia of financial depression after the operation of the Great War which they went through, and it appeared that tumours were retroceding unable to find a vent. When I travelled by train for seven days on end through Siberia and Russia, which

374

continues vastly back from the border of the hair, I felt I
had stroked round the head of the Earth, for it was extremely
monotonous, and when I wondered if the thought that
governs the whole behaviour of a person is hiding itself
under the skin of this close-cropped head, I felt fears which
warned me not to touch it carelessly . . .'

When I had written up to this point, I heard the gong for
dinner, and I walked towards the dining-room. Still thinking that it was a pity that I could not stay in Russia much
longer, I came in front of the dining-room and looked up at
the notice-board quite casually. The news that Viscount
Eiichi Shibusawa was critically ill hit my eyes all of a
sudden. Was my grandfather going to die? With a deep
sigh I thought of Japan far away. His house must be in a
terrible confusion. Famous doctors, visitors, cakes and
gifts, surrounded by newspaper reporters. Was not my
mother greatly upset? Oh!

Walking alone along the deck at night, I recalled my
grandfather with a heavy mind. I used to enjoy the
impression of him whenever I accompanied my mother,
when she visited him asking after his illness. I would call
on him usually at the time when he was having his meal and
listen to his talks, such as the stories of the great Saigo with
whom he ate pork-gravy and of Hijikata with whom he
went to arrest a criminal, while he was eating in a white
apron, the strings of which he tied under the hair of the
nape of his neck still black at the age of ninety. I asked him
to soothe my mother's mind about the matter of travelling
abroad leaving my children at home.

I said, 'I will be back by the winter before my husband'.

'But my dear,' said my grandfather, 'could you come

back leaving your husband behind you although you talk so bravely? Could you return leaving him alone with foreigners all around him? I wonder. You had better not be positive that you will come back.'

At these words of human considerateness, for the first time in my life I sat before him like a fondled child.

Viscount Shibusawa was one of the first Japanese to go abroad. In the second year of Keio (1866) he accompanied Prince Mimbu Tokugawa, who went over to France, and his diary 'The Journal of My Western Voyage' is highly interesting. He was full of ambition and had a clear intellect, but he was a lad of only twenty-seven, quite a blank page about Western things, so that in the diary he says, 'They serve us a thing called "café" after a meal, which is made of hot water infused with beans'. Although he was twenty-seven he was a *samurai* who had been mentally trained by coming and going between life and death more than once, and his supple mind, having no dry husks as was often found among men of his time, welcomed anything new which helped to nourish it. Describing Shanghai, he writes: 'It is equipped with gas-lights (lights which are taken through the tube from coal burnt underground) and telegraph (a thing by which messages are transported to distant places by the power of electricity by spreading out wires)'. At Suez the canal was under construction, so he went as far as Alexandria by train, and he was very much impressed by the work of excavation. A comical thing happened in this train. Tsunakichi, a Yedo hairdresser, began to fight with a foreigner who was sitting beside him. My grandfather stopped them and asked Tsunakichi the reason.

'This foreigner,' he said with anger, 'tried to snatch away the orange which I was eating.'

So he asked the foreigner his story.

'This fellow,' he answered, 'threw the orange-skin at me. He was very cunning and threw it in such a way that it rebounded from the window.'

So he scolded Tsunakichi, who calmly answered saying: 'Oh, no! I threw all the peels out of the window.'

At length everybody understood that it was a mistake arising from Tsunakichi's ignorance of a thing called 'glass', and it ended in laughter. So it was written.

My grandfather told me that story again when I went to bid him good-bye. He was accompanied by a hairdresser, and he had his top-knot cut in France. He told me among other things his impressions of Napoleon III, and the story of crossing the Alps in a horse-carriage. He told me another episode which occurred in Paris. Colonel Ch., who was coaching Prince Tokugawa by the order of Napoleon III, was very arrogant under the shelter of the Emperor's influence. One day when he said, 'The bayonet is far superior as a weapon to the Japanese sword', my grandfather took umbrage and challenged him to a duel. When he told me such stories, he still kept the ardent spirits of his younger days ... but he was now closing the curtain of his crowded career after living his long, long life to the full extent.

Since the day that wireless news reached us, the quietude of my sea-voyage has been broken. I had a quiet mood only for a few moments in the evening when, looking at the sun quietly setting into the ocean, I felt I was seeing off my grandfather, but for the rest of the time my mind was occupied by a strange irritation. It may sound natural if I say that I felt irritation in my journey towards home where my grandfather was on his death-bed, but I was amazed at myself to find that the worry of the irritation was actually due to the peevish mind that did not like going home. My mother, who was the eldest daughter of my grandfather, had shared humble circumstances with him, so she was especially loyal to her father. For five years after my father died, she has lived finding life worth living by being helpful to her father, but she was now going to be a widow in the full sense of the word. At this thought reason urged me to go back all the quicker, because the obligation of making her life pleasant for the rest of her days was going to rest heavily upon the shoulders of us her children. But to a person who has been travelling from place to place, the feeling of love and the sense of duty, which were going to stick fast again around me, seemed suffocatingly troublesome. The reluctance which you feel when you try to steep your body in sticky molasses annoyed me, and when I walked along the deck regularly up and down, a thought that I was like a panther that rambled up and down in a cage in which it was going to be carried away after being caught, gnawed my heart. My grandfather's condition seemed to be getting worse and worse every minute. Feeling it unbearable to send my grandfather off to another world in such a vein, I dropped my tears on the railing of the deck. While I was staring hard at the stain with a vacant mind, the number of similar spots rapidly increased, and rain began to fall. As I held up my hand, I found half of the sky darkened as if ink had been poured over it, and one part of the black cloud hung down to the sea in a long line. It was a water-spout, which I would better call the navel-string of the cloud that connected Earth and Heaven. The air became instantly cooler and my mind was soothed.

The irritation caught hold not only of me but of every other passenger in the boat. It must be the strange influence of the Indian Ocean. Serious-tempered gentlemen had no resort to divert it in dancing and wine, so they gratified their urge to be fuming in petty quibblings. They said, 'While they didn't serve us with red-bean rice on the day of the commemoration of the late Emperor, it is a shame to give a *sayonara* dinner to the foreigners landing at Colombo the next day'. That's not so bad, but even about the notice in the saloon that they are selling Flanders poppies for the sake of relieving ex-soldiers on Armistice Day, they said, 'It's a shame that they are flattering foreigners like that!' And they advised me not to buy one. When those who were to form the backbone of Japan showed such an attitude in regard to these things, I could not help regretting rather the narrow-mindedness of my compatriots than the right and wrong of the matter. As things were like that, there were only too few among the Japanese who put red poppies in their buttonholes on November 11th. In the evening on that day the notice was published at last that Viscount Shibusawa died at the age of ninety-two. Walking down to the stern of the boat, I threw the artificial flower, which I had put on my breast, into the sea. The red colour turned round and round and was soon swallowed up by the waves.

§ 3

Afterwards

On my return home, my mother also died in two and a half months. She died without hearing my talks about the

journey which she had looked forward to so much. It is not
that in the two and a half months we had no leisure at all,
but when I saw my mother busying herself about the things
which were left after my grandfather's death, I said to myself,
'There is still something for my mother to do. After the
hundredth day she will probably have times when she will
find herself in utter ennui. I had better keep my chats
until then'. But my mother followed my grandfather in
only a little more than eighty days. As she had asked me,
'Draw me a big map and tell me the story, will you?' the
unfinished map, which I had been drawing with all the
countries in different colours, was lonesomely left in my
hands: therefore I began to make a fair copy of my diary
imagining that I was talking to my mother. When, quite
unintentionally, my pen went astray, my mother's image
appeared in my eyes, when she often used to say, 'Oh, now
you are talking too freely'. She loved my frankness, but she
knit her brows anxiously from the thought of other people,
still revealing near her mouth a flickering smile which she
could not hide well, and this image of my mother made me
sometimes cross out one whole page of my writing. Really
I sometimes found my courage of chattering waning when
I thought for whom I was writing all this.

As my mother would have said, 'I don't like that word,
because it smells too Western', I won't write 'dedicate', but
with all reverence I offer these stories of our travels to my
dead mother.